THE BAD SIXTIES

Race, Rhetoric, and Media Series
Davis W. Houck, General Editor

THE BAD SIXTIES

Hollywood Memories of the Counterculture, Antiwar, and Black Power Movements

KRISTEN HOERL

University Press of Mississippi / Jackson

www.upress.state.ms.us

The University Press of Mississippi is a member of
the Association of American University Presses.

Copyright © 2018 by University Press of Mississippi
All rights reserved
Manufactured in the United States of America

First printing 2018

∞

Library of Congress Cataloging-in-Publication Data

Names: Hoerl, Kristen, author.
Title: The bad sixties: Hollywood memories of the counterculture, antiwar, and Black power movements / Kristen Hoerl.
Description: Jackson: University Press of Mississippi, [2018] | Series: Race, rhetoric, and media series | Includes bibliographical references and index. |
Identifiers: LCCN 2017055601 (print) | LCCN 2018000311 (ebook) | ISBN 9781496817242 (epub single) | ISBN 9781496817259 (epub institutional) | ISBN 9781496817266 (pdf single) | ISBN 9781496817273 (pdf institutional) | ISBN 9781496817235 (cloth: alk. paper)
Subjects: LCSH: Motion pictures and history. | Nineteen sixties. | Politics in motion pictures—20th century. | Black power—United States—History—20th century. | Motion pictures—Social aspects—United States.
Classification: LCC PN1995.2 (ebook) | LCC PN1995.2 .H64 2018 (print) | DDC 791.43/658—dc23
LC record available at https://lccn.loc.gov/2017055601

British Library Cataloging-in-Publication Data available

FOR CASEY, WHO MAKES
EVERYTHING BETTER

CONTENTS

	Acknowledgments........................ix
INTRODUCTION	Selective Amnesia in Hollywood's Imagined Sixties 3
CHAPTER ONE	The Sixties in History and Entertainment Memory 27
CHAPTER TWO	Growing Up from the Counterculture in *Family Ties* and *The Wonder Years* 61
CHAPTER THREE	Good Citizens, Ambivalent Activists, and Macho Militants in *Forrest Gump* and *The '60s*............................ 93
CHAPTER FOUR	Traumatic Victimhood or Black Rage? Contrasting Visions of Black Power 123
CHAPTER FIVE	The Criminalization of Late Sixties Militancy in Television Police Procedurals....157
CONCLUSION	Contestation over Sixties Memory in the New Millennium 187

Notes 199

Bibliography 207

Index 219

ACKNOWLEDGMENTS

I am very fortunate for the many friends, colleagues, and family members who offered their feedback, encouragement, and television knowledge that made this book possible. My list of individuals to thank must begin with my parents, Lesley and Donald Hoerl. Anecdotes about their own dissent during the late sixties surely inspired this project, as has their love of television and movies. I am also grateful for my brother Kent Hoerl, whose insightful analysis of the opening credits for the situation comedy *Dharma and Greg* prompted me to think more deeply about television's fascination with the counterculture.

Butler University helped by providing internal funding from the Butler Awards Committee and a sabbatical release from teaching in the fall of 2015. My colleagues in the Department of Critical Communication and Media Studies have encouraged me through every step of my research, and my dean in the College of Communication, Gary Edgerton, gave helpful advice about the publication process. My research assistant Alex Hancock and my editorial assistant Natalie Verhines were both instrumental in the timely completion of this work, and I am thankful for their quick and careful attention to this manuscript.

I dearly appreciate the University Press of Mississippi's support for this project. Davis Houck, the editor for the Race, Rhetoric, and Media series, has warmly shepherded this project and has provided valuable feedback. I am honored to be included among the authors who have contributed to this important book series that has centralized racial justice as a key issue for rhetoric and public-address scholarship. Acquiring editor Vijay Shah has been a delight to work with. Among his many admirable qualities, he has responded to my inquiries and earlier drafts of this book with remarkable speed.

I am also grateful for the constructive criticism of generous colleagues and friends, Leslie Hahner, Bryan McCann, Kristin Swenson, and Jonathan Rossing, who responded thoughtfully to early chapter drafts. Special thanks goes to the incredible Lisa Corrigan, who provided detailed and perceptive advice for revising this manuscript amid her busy schedule fighting the white, heterosexist patriarchy. Numerous others have also contributed to this project through their commentary over conversation including Claire Sisco King, Kendall Phillips, Mary Triece, Susan Owen, Peter Ehrenhaus, Michael Lacy, Darrel Wanzer-Serrano, Katie Feyh, and Audrey Bianco. In addition, Lisa Bianco, Paul Johnson, Dan Berger, Steve Macek, and Deron Overpeck drew my attention to several of the films and television programs that have found their way into the pages that follow. Deborah Bianco also helped me in a moment of panic, in a very early stage of work, when I called on her to record an episode of a television program and mail it to me cross country.

Beyond those who have supported me in recent years, I am indebted to the people who nurtured and challenged me during my years at the University of Texas at Austin. Dana Cloud has been the most supportive and knowledgeable advisor a young radical scholar could hope for, and she continues to be an invaluable mentor and friend. Likewise, Rosa Eberly has prompted me to think more deeply about the rhetorics of citizenship ever since the scream of 1998. I am also grateful for the friendship of Lisa Foster, Angela Aguayo, and Caroline Rankin. Had I not met them, I'm pretty sure I would have graduated all head and no heart. Of course, my head is much better for knowing them as well.

Finally, I thank my spouse, colleague, and coconspirator Casey Ryan Kelly, for his unflagging support and insightful feedback throughout my writing process. In addition to putting plates of food in front of me to make sure I never forgot to eat during my race to book completion, he enthusiastically listened as I read almost every word of this monograph to him over the course of the past three years. The hours he has spent listening to and commenting on my project while he cooked dinner are among the many generous gifts he has given me. I have yet to figure out exactly what I have done in my life to deserve them. Casey is my proof that love and resistance are complimentary and necessary in the ongoing struggle for social and economic justice.

THE BAD SIXTIES

INTRODUCTION

Selective Amnesia in Hollywood's Imagined Sixties

Although the decade of the 1960s has been over for nearly fifty years, the memory of what is commonly referred to as "the sixties" lives on, if only to remind us that the ideals associated with the time period are long gone. One of the earliest and most widely remarked-upon films about the decade's legacy is the 1983 Academy Award–nominated film *The Big Chill*. Set to a nostalgic soundtrack of sixties-era rock and soul music, the movie portrays the relationship among seven baby boomers who became friends during their college years in the late sixties. They reunite over a decade later following the suicide of their friend Alex. Unlike Alex, who never let go of his sixties-era idealism, the group reflects that their lives became more conservative after college. To amplify this theme, the reunion takes place in the large colonial estate owned by married couple Harold and Sarah, whose wealth was earned in part by Harold's successful retail chain store that specializes in running shoes that are popular among yuppies.

Dialogue throughout the film suggests that the economic and social realities of the characters' professional and personal lives required them to realign their priorities and expectations to fit with the growing conservatism of the times. Although they hold Alex dear in their hearts, these hippies-turned-yuppies embrace one another's conservative lifestyles as they rekindle their friendships. By the film's conclusion, characters accept the lesson of the fortune cookie from Chinese takeout that character Michael receives on their second night together, "Friendship is the bread of life but money is the honey." This scene amplifies the predominant message: the antimaterialist values associated with the sixties-era counterculture are no longer salient to the white college-educated generation who found opportunities to prosper during the ensuing decade.

In addition to commenting on the waning influence of the counterculture, *The Big Chill* responds to ongoing contestations over racial justice and women's liberation rooted in sixties-era struggles. The movie suggests that the values of the decade's radical movements failed to provide fulfillment for its supporters. This failure is most vividly illustrated by the character Meg, who expresses some disdain for the radical politics of her college years. A single real estate attorney, Meg entered the legal field with the dream of becoming a public defender to represent the likes of Black Power leader Huey Newton. She explains that she altered her career path because most of her clients turned out to be "real scum bags." Desperate for a child, she spends the weekend propositioning the unattached men in the house to have sex with her with no strings attached. The film's climax includes sentimental scenes of Sarah and Harold's efforts to help Meg conceive. Showing in theaters months after conservatives refused to pass the Equal Rights Amendment in Congress, the film affirms conservative arguments that women's autonomy outside of the traditional spheres of motherhood and the nuclear family offer few satisfactions for even the most educated women.

The Big Chill's brief reference to Huey Newton also conveys a dismissive attitude toward the black freedom struggle. Meg's turn from public defense to real estate law suggests that her commitment to racial justice was a youthful fad. Her description of her presumably poor and nonwhite clients as "scum bags" implies that the black freedom struggle was either a short-lived phenomenon or that radicals' claims for justice were a ruse to legitimate criminal behavior. Either way, the film's glib attention to Black Power aligned with the decade's conservative backlash against civil rights initiatives and tough-on-crime legislation that was driven by a white panic over crime and gangs in urban centers populated by black and Latinx communities. Reflecting on the film shortly after its release, *Washington Monthly* editor Timothy Noah (1984, 40) notes that the film's overarching idea is that "the possibility for social change is a thing of the past." The idealism that motivated young people during the 1960s could not survive the "cruel pragmatism" of the following decades.

The Big Chill's jaundiced view of the counterculture, Black Power, and women's liberation is part of a broad pattern of Hollywood depictions of the late sixties in recent decades. The film's critical acclaim and the commercial success of its soundtrack pointed to an ambivalent nostalgia for media products about sixties-era dissent. While these products have celebrated the music and aesthetics of the late sixties, they have also disarticulated sixties style from the decade's radical politics. Spanning several decades, a myriad of prominent and popular films and television programs have coded the sixties counterculture and protest movements as objects for derision and ridicule. They include the Academy Award–winning movie *Forrest Gump*. In one scene, the title character finds himself caught up in the middle of an anti–Vietnam War protest rally surrounded by caustic activists wearing peace signs who are too caught up in the movement to realize that Forrest Gump is not one of them. They also include the last season of the Emmy-winning period drama *Mad Men*, in which Don Draper's countercultural and very pregnant niece shows up at his doorstep seeking money because her boyfriend has been jailed for selling pot. More niche television programming has also expanded upon Hollywood's penchant for remembering the sixties with a jaundiced eye. In the latest season of the FX television dark-comedy thriller *Fargo*, twenty-something Simone plots to overtake a local crime syndicate with her lover Mike. She pauses to mourn the loss of sixties-era countercultural lifestyles only to have Mike rebuff her, "You know, the 70s were always coming. Like a hangover. You know what happened to Flower Moon Blossom? She's on methadone at Bismark, turning tricks for breakfast meat." Set in 1979, *Fargo* cynically remembers countercultural resistance to mainstream social norms as the prelude to drug rehabilitation and prostitution.

Across these and many additional Hollywood narratives, the lesson is that the values of wealth accumulation and the traditional family have triumphed over sixties-era resistance to corporate culture, trenchant racism, and patriarchy. These messages portray the 1960s in ways that suggest dissent is irrelevant to contemporary young peoples' lives, even as movements such as Occupy Wall Street and Black Lives Matter have drawn public attention to wealth inequality and police violence. The purpose of this book is to analyze how a variety of narratives in mainstream films and television programs have derided and trivialized late sixties activism since the mid-eighties. This book also reflects upon the lessons of these narratives for contemporary society and politics.

In popular and political culture, "the sixties" have become synonymous with the decade's left-of-center activism. It is a condensation symbol of images, ideas, and protest actions that challenged the legitimacy of traditional American values and the United States' relationship to the rest of the world. Activists organized around a variety of causes including civil rights, campus free speech, ending the Vietnam War, women's liberation, gay rights, and decolonization. Because all of these groups repudiated the established norms and values of mainstream society, they are often referred to as "the Movement" (Anderson 1995; Hunt 1999). Glib references to "the Movement" have the potential to obfuscate important distinctions between the decade's many dissident groups and organizations. Many histories and memoirs feature the student New Left as the impetus for the decade's activism. Consequently, these narratives lose sight of how international movements against colonialism and antiracist activism in the United States were the driving force behind the decade's dissent.

References to the sixties have focused on the period between 1968 and 1972, when youthful fashions of long hair, tie-dyed garments, and bell-bottoms signaled the growth of the counterculture.[1] Movements for Chicanx rights, Native American self-determination, women's rights, gay liberation, disability rights, environmentalism, and consumer protections are largely excluded from popular discourses about the sixties. Likewise, labor activism is disregarded in popular memory despite the surge of worker militancy during this time period (Elbaum

2002). The rise of Right-leaning activism is also excluded from popular culture's attention to the decade. Echoing the predominant historical narratives of the time period, Hollywood has foregrounded the male-driven, white student New Left. An unfortunate consequence of this tendency is that much of this book looks at the depictions of the most privileged dissident groups who are the focus of Hollywood's imagined sixties.

The variety of references to the sixties in more contemporary films and television programs contribute to the public memory about the decade. Public memories are rhetorical expressions of cultural knowledge and values about past events that are produced in various forms of officially sanctioned discourse and popular culture. Regardless of whether they are presented by a presidential address, a memorial structure, a Hollywood film, or a television program, public memories are inherently political. During his book tour in 2004, former president Bill Clinton observed that, "If you look back on the Sixties and think there was more good than bad, you're probably a Democrat. If you think there was more harm than good, you're probably a Republican" ("First Night," 2004, para. 9). Inevitably partial and incomplete, public expressions about the past reflect the perspectives and ambitions of those involved in their construction. George Lipsitz (1990, 34) writes that "what we choose to remember about the past, where we begin and end our retrospective accounts, and who we include and exclude from them—these do a lot to determine how we live and what decisions we make in the present." While they offer resources for shared understanding about the past, public memories about defining national events also provide civics lessons about what we should value and how we should enact our roles as citizens.[2]

I am interested in the public memory of the late sixties for a variety of reasons. Events during this time period provide rich case studies in how groups of people raised fundamental questions about the nature and limits of democracy under late capitalism, shifting the tone of political life in the United States from the relative quiescence of previous decades. The counterculture challenged traditional social values regarding marriage, family life, gender norms, and sexuality, fomenting lasting changes in social behavior, style, and openness to nontraditional family structures. A variety of dissident groups strongly and vocally objected to the Vietnam War and reenvisioned political and social life to promote social justice for people of color exploited by legacies of colonialism.

Radical politics surged during the late sixties, especially among young people and communities of color in ways that drew upon yet departed from earlier radical labor activism. Although the majority of protesters opposing the Vietnam War were politically moderate, radical ideals and strategies grew at a rate unseen since the progressive movements of the 1930s. At the end of 1967, *Newsweek* magazine reported "a sharp scent of crisis in the American air . . . a tension in society and a stress among men not known since the 1930s" (Anderson 1995, 182). After the US government invaded Cambodia in 1970, the number of students who self-identified as radicals grew to 11 percent. These changing attitudes were partially a consequence of law enforcement's often brutal response to even nonviolent dissent. Sixty percent of students felt the nation had become a "'highly repressive society, intolerant of dissent" (Anderson 1995, 352). Radicalism grew among communities of color as well. According to *Time* magazine, 9 percent of black people across the country, more than two million black Americans, identified themselves as "revolutionaries" (Foner 1995, xxiv). During the late sixties "the global domination of capital was challenged from within on a more serious scale than ever before" (Sayers et al. 1984, 7). For many activists, the idea of a revolution against imperialist capitalism in the United States was both desirable and possible.

Although the spirit of radicalism that animated the late sixties is not as prominent today, the United States continues to struggle with the social and economic problems that the radical Left highlighted over forty years ago. Divisive issues including racial justice, military actions overseas, women's rights, human sexuality, and traditional family structures remain hotly contested in American politics. Ongoing interest in the turmoil of the late sixties reveals the ways in which social conflicts from that period continue to resound in contemporary politics. In many ways, "the sixties" has become shorthand for current disagreements over the American Dream and who should have access to it. References to

Vietnam alone call up images of dissent, pointing to conflicting values regarding the role of the military and who should serve that continue to polarize the nation (Morris and Ehrenhaus 1990). The events of the late sixties shattered assumptions about national consensus and metanarratives of Western history and progress; since then, public memories about the late sixties and other historic events continue to negotiate and redefine this crisis.[3]

The decade of the sixties is also a reference point for thinking about how ordinary people with little political or economic power sought to expand opportunities for civic engagement and reframe the meaning of social belonging. According to Meta Mendel-Reyes (1995), references to the decade stand in for the idea of participatory democracy in which each person contributes to the life of their community. Simon Hall (2011) observes that the protest strategies of direct actions, street theater, and civil disobedience used by civil rights and antiwar activists provided templates for subsequent progressive and conservative movements to demonstrate for expanding notions of rights and citizenship. Public memories about the sixties are resources for envisioning the future of protest for social change, and the scope and depth of those resources both enable and constrain how we might pursue fundamental transformation of the institutions that shape our lives.

I am particularly interested in Hollywood films and television programs that have provided fictionalized portrayals of late sixties dissent because Hollywood is a central point of access to the late sixties for generations of people born in the following decades. Media scholar and former New Left activist Todd Gitlin (2003, 576) contends that television entertainment is the "most pervasive and (in the living room sense) *familiar* of our cultural sites." Fictionalized film and television depictions are particularly salient resources of shared understanding for audiences born after 1970 because they provide the most accessible visual medium for observing the decade's social movements. They also offer viewers a sense of participation and experience in the decade's defining events.[4] Media content designed to entertain audiences have played a prominent role as the purveyors of common culture in recent decades. Thus, audiences born after the sixties are more likely to glean meaning and shared understanding from entertainment media than the news (Gray 1997).

Although they cannot offer a complete view of late sixties dissent, film and television portrayals provide resources that enable audiences to share understandings about the function of protest and dissent. Popular culture is an important arena of cultural discourse that responds to and participates in the political struggles of the contemporary era. Michael Ryan and Douglas Kellner (1988) argue that popular movies transfer the discourses of politics and society into cinematic narratives that in turn contribute to our social reality. The same could be written about broadcast television over the past several decades. Television portrayals of radicalism have transcoded the debates about the meaning of the sixties, providing implicit messages about which political investments are worth considering and what constitutes legitimate civic engagement. As Bonnie Dow (1996, xv) attests, "television works rhetorically to negotiate social issues: to define them, to represent them, and ultimately, to offer visions of their meanings and implications." Like Dow, I situate mediated depictions of social movements within the contexts in which they are produced and circulated. I explain how fictionalized portrayals of the sixties era of dissent have made particular perspectives about the decade's radicalism more legitimate and attractive than others. These perspectives are not only produced by Hollywood but by the variety of messages about the late sixties provided by politicians and other public figures in the ensuing decades.

Political leaders have continually referenced the sixties over the past several decades. Since the rise of the Moral Majority, conservatives have expressed negative views of the sixties to win votes and pass legislation. As Bernard von Bothmer (2010, 2) puts it, "Republicans have been campaigning against 'the sixties' ever since the 1960s themselves." The decade of the sixties has been a poignant symbol for conservative movements because it has come to stand in for a variety of political ideas and social trends that have challenged traditional ideals of family life and notions of American righteousness and exceptionalism propagated during the fifties. Daniel Marcus (2004, 75) explains that the dissident movements of the sixties were seen by their opponents as "attacking the keystones of American life—God, family, the military, material prosperity, and education—in favor of Eastern religions and atheism, the Sexual Revolution and feminism, antiwar protests and draft dodging, hippie antimaterialism, and campus disruptions and dropping out." Consequently, the memory of these movements was a powerful resource for marshalling conservative support for policies premised on conservative ideals of military authority, the nuclear family, and individual responsibility. Republicans routinely conflated liberalism with the movement, blaming both for the decline in personal responsibility, military strength, and commitments to family values. "The specter of 'the bad sixties'" was a "political weapon to attack Johnson's Great Society, the antiwar movement, and the era's loosening of social restraints on family structure and personal responsibility" (von Bothmer 2010, 2-3). Thus, conservatives envisioned the decade as a "time of urban riots, antiwar protesters, difficulties in fighting the Vietnam War, increased incivility, crime, drug abuse, and social unrest" (2).

Sixties-baiting proved to be a tremendously successful campaign strategy. Republicans won seven out of ten presidential elections between 1968 and 2004 with campaign rhetoric that heavily lambasted the bad sixties. In his 1968 campaign, Nixon appealed to white voters disturbed by the ostensible excesses of sixties movements. In his memorable silent majority speech, Nixon praised the "forgotten Americans, the nonshouters, the nondemonstrators" whose values were under siege by antiwar protesters, urban rioters, criminals, and antipoverty liberals (Lassiter 2011, para. 4). Presidents Reagan, George H. W. Bush, and George W. Bush followed Nixon's lead, drawing further upon negative public attitudes toward antiwar dissent. Reagan waxed nostalgic about a pre-sixties past to which the United States should return; George H. W. Bush's supporters accused Kitty Dukakis (the wife of Democratic presidential candidate Michael Dukakis) of burning an American flag during an anti–Vietnam War protest; and the Swift Boat Veterans for Truth cited democrat John Kerry's involvement in the antiwar movement as evidence for his lack of patriotism. Marcus (2004, 149) concludes that "the negative attitude toward the Sixties ... was a cornerstone of GOP politics." In contrast to the "corporate managers, entrepreneurs, and workers" that Reagan and Bush purported to speak for, "the legatees of the Sixties were accordingly identified as nonproductive, removed from the daily concerns of most Americans, and dismissive of national values."

In addition to helping conservatives win elections, sixties-baiting offered a legitimizing framework for their legislative agenda and public policies. The rhetoric of the bad sixties paired nicely with Reagan's agenda to gut Johnson's Great Society and War on Poverty programs, roll back affirmative action, and take covert military action against leftists in Latin America. Von Bothmer (2010, 6) concludes that the sixties was crucial to the rise of the Right because it enabled conservatives to foment and exploit hostility to the "perceived excesses" of the antiwar movement, the counterculture, and Black Power. "The 1960s rejection of traditional values challenged the established view of American exceptionalism, and in doing so eventually destroyed liberalism and propelled the modern Right to power" (6).

Although they led the charge against the bad sixties, conservatives are not the only ones to have held the decade accountable for the nation's problems. Democrats have tended to speak more favorably upon the civil rights activism of the first half of the decade, but they have also blamed late sixties dissent for the erosion of civility and for national division (Marcus 2004). In 1995, Clinton's (1995b) own rhetoric advanced a negative interpretation of the late sixties as a time in which "more and more people dropped out and became more self-indulgent" (para. 1047). Around this time period, Clinton was seeking support for his agenda that extended Reagan-era efforts to curtail federal welfare support to single women. Journalist David Sirota (2011, 29) concludes that Democrats "largely surrendered the memory of the sixties" because they did not want to re-litigate the decade.

Democrats' reluctance to defend the late sixties has also impaired liberal and progressive politics. Efforts to paint Bill Clinton as a pot-smoking draft-dodger did not dissuade the electorate from putting him in office in 1992 or reelecting him in 1996. However, references to the bad sixties have helped to position an antiwar agenda as outside of the realm of legitimate debate and weakened public support for federal welfare and affirmative action policies. For both centrist-liberals and conservatives, the late sixties was a period of troubling national division and moral decay that has warranted a rightward shift in public policy.

While a negative memory of sixties-era protest has been crafted by political moderates and conservatives, a different version of the bad sixties has been crafted by activists involved in the dissident organization Students for a Democratic Society (SDS), in what John McMillian (2003, 1–8) refers to as the "New Left consensus." In this narrative, the spirit of optimism held by young progressives devoted to social justice and participatory democracy was broken by the intransigence of the Vietnam War and by brutal repression against nonviolent dissent. Thus, radicals resorted to uncivil protests and nihilistic violence while many members of the counterculture retreated into hedonism and drug abuse. Rather than warrant support for conservative and neoliberal policy, the New Left consensus has blamed the bad sixties for the failures of the Left, suggesting that—if only the movement had maintained its commitment to grassroots democratic organizing—progressivism might have held a more prominent place in US politics in the ensuing decades. One of the most prominent adherents of the New Left consensus, Todd Gitlin (2003, 335) explains Nixon's 1968 election as a direct consequence of the New Left's increasingly confrontational antiwar protests toward the end of the decade. He notes that the news broadcast images of student radicals throwing trash cans and yelling obscenities appalled the majority of US citizens. Gitlin laments that, even as the antiwar movement was reaching its peak in the early 1970s, antiwar radicals were hated more than the war itself. More recently, the New Left consensus has been questioned. Countering Gitlin's conclusion that the New Left's incivility led to its downfall, David Barber (2008) argues that the white, male-driven New Left's biggest impediment was its failure to respond meaningfully to the burgeoning movements for racial justice and gender justice. Despite this challenge, the New Left consensus is a predominant myth that has structured public discourse from the left about the meaning of late sixties dissent. The diversity of negative commentary about the sixties has characterized the decade's end as a tragic chapter in US history. Across the political spectrum, this vision of the bad sixties has obscured the political motives underlying the growing radicalism at the end of the decade and has diminished the broad range of movements that advanced diverse goals and strategies for achieving social justice.

In this book I explore how a variety of television programs and Hollywood films have buttressed images of the bad sixties, even as they superficially appear to idealize sixties-era dissent. I argue that a variety of prominent media products in each of the last three decades have contributed to the narrative of the bad sixties through their depictions of the counterculture, New Left, women's liberation, and Black Power movements. Since the mid-eighties, radical activists have been portrayed as immature, caustic, angry, and dangerous.

Admittedly, narratives about the meaning of sixties activism have shifted over time in response to the changing political and social contexts in which they emerged. Not all portrayals of the sixties in recent decades have been negative. As Gil Troy (2007, 121) comments, many elements of eighties-era popular and commercial culture idealized sixties-era politics. Troy suggests that nostalgia for the sixties tended to discount later activist efforts such as environmentalism and the nuclear freeze movement, which brought 700,000 demonstrators to Central Park in New York City in 1982 (136). Protest demonstrations in more recent decades remind us that the spirit of dissent that has come to define the sixties continues to shape US politics. This is precisely why public memories of the sixties matter to contemporary politics.

While images of sixties protest are varied, the figure of the late sixties dissident has been remarkably resilient in light of the political changes over the past thirty years. Over and over again, the narratives of popular media pose late sixties-era dissent and radical protesters as problems that must be overcome to protect the nuclear family, community safety, and national unity. These depictions promulgate *selective amnesia*, a term I use to highlight how popular media render radical Left-wing ideas and political projects illegitimate within contemporary public life. Through selective amnesia, public discourse routinely omits events and issues that defy seamless narratives of national progress and unity. Peter Ehrenhaus (1989, 101) observes that commemorative discourse can be "strategically silent by being mute regarding particular concerns," as was the case when President Ford announced the end to the Vietnam War in 1975 and avoided any mention of the devastating consequences of US intervention for Vietnamese people and returning US soldiers. While I share Ehrenhaus's concern for strategic silence regarding issues of social injustice, my rhetorical approach to selective amnesia involves more than the critique of US culpability for human suffering that has gone unspoken within forms of public remembrance.

Departing from conventional or psychological understandings of amnesia as a loss or gap in memory, I attend to selective amnesia as a discursive structure that does rhetorical and ideological work in public life. All forms of remembrance are inevitably partial and incomplete, thus, forgetting itself is essential to public memory's existence. As Marita Sturken (1997, 3) notes, the culture of amnesia in American politics "involves the generation of memory in new forms." Complementing Sturken's observation, Bradford Vivian (2010) argues that memory is not the antidote to forgetting. Vivian highlights the productive dimensions of public forgetting. While they enable new forms of memory to emerge, deliberate acts of forgetting can help publics respond to current social and political conflicts. As Vivian emphasizes, forgetting is a rhetorical phenomenon insofar as advocates may decide to discontinue or reject customary forms of remembrance (13).

My own approach to analyzing forgetting as a rhetorical phenomenon focuses on the process by which popular media routinely trivialize and negate the contributions of late sixties activists to politics and society. While forgetting is not necessarily problematic, I believe it is imperative that memory scholars highlight how seemingly innocuous forms of remembrance and forgetting function to buttress normative and exclusionary visions of citizenship and national identity. My approach is aligned with Kent Ono's (2009, 11) attention to colonial amnesia, which he defines as "contemporary discourse that masks over images of colonialism that seep through our public memory indirectly and elliptically." Broadening Ono's conceptualization, selective amnesia foregrounds the processes in which media culture obscures the legacy of activism for broader inclusion and justice for historically exploited groups. Popular portrayals of the sixties promulgate amnesia by focusing on the white student New Left, attending to Black Power to a lesser extent, and virtually ignoring the other diverse movements for racial justice, feminism, gay liberation, labor, and Third World activism. Selective amnesia of late sixties dissent also involves narratives that decontextualize the spectacular events and individuals that have defined the late sixties from the motives and context that drove dissidents, flattening their meaning into reductive stereotypes.

The construction of the bad sixties that relies upon selective amnesia has implications for subjectivity and citizenship. Mass cultural narratives about the past provide particular frameworks of national identity and belonging. Barbara Biesecker (2002, 406) writes that "what we remember and how we remember it can tell us something significant about who we are as a people now, about the contemporary social and political issues that divide us and about who we may become." Hollywood's selective amnesia of radical sixties movements aligns with a series of conservative positions that have been articulated at least since the mid-eighties. The issues and concerns facing Hollywood's fictionalized sixties-activists, their friends, and family members speak to ongoing political controversies about the meaning of citizenship, gender roles, sexuality, racial profiling, and the military. Resolution to these narratives provide lessons about the importance of traditional family values, entrepreneurialism, national identity, law and order, and security. Thus, Hollywood routinely remembers the sixties in order to teach us to dismiss the role of dissent in fostering progressive social change. I conclude that the consistently negative depictions of protest function rhetorically as civics lessons by placing radical dissent, including its criticisms of capitalism, colonialism, patriarchy, and two-party politics, as outside of the boundaries of what it means to be a proper citizen in a late-capitalist democracy.

By focusing on the processes by which selective amnesia regarding the late sixties has been constructed in fictionalized film and television portrayals, this book itself is a site of public recollection. Kendall Phillips (2010, 220) argues that traditional rhetoric's longstanding concern over memory has been driven by anxiety over the process of misremembering, or claiming knowledge of the past that is inaccurate or different from previously held memories. Admittedly, this project is concerned that Hollywood's memories of the bad sixties depart sharply from the narratives about the late sixties provided in extant memoirs and academic histories. This book aims to disrupt the ideological common sense of the bad sixties and continues the struggle between the frameworks of remembrance that have calcified the sixties into a reductive caricature and the countermemories that may overturn them. It is my hope that this disruption may contribute to more inclusive and socially just frameworks for remembering radicals' efforts to create social change in recent US history.

Each of the case study chapters of this book address a particular set of themes and messages about sixties radicals that have converged across similar television programs or films since the Reagan revolution. In the following section, I explain how my intertextual approach to analyzing this selection of Hollywood products illuminates the process by which fictionalized films and television programs have given political and ideological meaning to the late sixties for more contemporary audiences. This introduction concludes with a summary of the remaining chapters of this book that explore how Hollywood film and television have contributed to the public memory of the bad sixties.

THE INTERTEXTUAL CONSTRUCTION OF THE BAD SIXTIES IN FILM AND TELEVISION

The emphasis of this book does not and could not reflect the entirety of Hollywood's attention to late sixties dissent. As chapter 1 elaborates, film and television have offered a broad array of messages about this time period. The variety of references to and depictions of late sixties dissent highlight a diversity of attitudes about the meaning and legacy of the late sixties and illustrates how Hollywood is a site of hegemonic struggle. In order to maintain its relevance, the entertainment industry must address the social and political conflicts of its time (Dow 1996; Gitlin 2000, 574–94; Hall 1986, 5–27; Ryan and Kellner 1990). In the process, it routinely contains *and* resists movements for social change. The entertainment industry provided several sympathetic representations of antiwar and countercultural activists during the late sixties in order to attract young people to its programming (Bodroghkozy 2001). Thus, nostalgic reflections on the counterculture and antiwar movements were likely to appeal to the baby-boom generation in more recent decades.

In order to explain how entertainment media have constructed an overarching message about the bad sixties, this book focuses on a subset of the myriad films and television programs that have referenced late sixties activism since the early eighties. My selection is premised on the understanding that the structure of entertainment media consumption and the narrative patterns across prominent films and television programs help to make particular lessons about the sixties more accessible and salient than others. This book features many of the more prominent films and television programs that circulated broadly and, in many cases, garnered critical acclaim. Films produced and distributed by major studios are more likely to have large audiences and strong box office returns than independent films that circulate among smaller audiences. Thus I analyze the depiction of the Black Panther Party in *Forrest Gump* even though they only appear in one brief scene because audiences are more likely to recall this image of the Black Panthers than they are from less commercially successful films, such as Mario Van Peebles's crime-action thriller *Panther*, which was released just a year after *Forrest Gump* appeared in theaters.

Just as major Hollywood films are more prominent resources for public memory than independent and small-budget films, television programs running in prime-time broadcast television networks are more likely to be viewed and remembered than programs that appear on cable. For this reason, I focus on prime-time programs and miniseries including NBC's *Family Ties*, ABC's *The Wonder Years*, NBC's *Law & Order*, and the television miniseries *The '60s*; all of these television depictions received higher ratings and have run in syndication, in contrast with other fictionalized depictions of late sixties protest such as HBO's 2006 made-for-television movie *Walkout*, based on Chicanx student protests in Los Angeles. Although film and television depictions of the late sixties are not monolithic, the smaller set of these depictions that are the focus of this book are particularly prominent resources for remembering and evaluating the legacy of the sixties.

My selection is also informed by my understanding that meaning is constructed intertextually in popular culture. Media studies scholar John Fiske (2011, 16) observes that meanings depend upon a cultural product's "intertextuality with *all* texts that contribute to and draw upon" generalized familiarity with the codes of popular culture. Elaborating upon the work of Roland Barthes (1975), Fiske explains that "codes" provide the links that connect texts, enabling constant interplay between them and providing the basis for viewers' sense of shared reality, which itself is a product of the interrelations of cultural products. For Fiske, a television program can "only be understood by its relationship to other television programs, not by any relationship to the real" (116). (I would add that print, aural, online, and television texts of popular culture all contribute to the codes for social meaning about public issues and controversies.)

One way in which broadcast television has given meaning of late sixties dissent is through the repetition of a variety of visual and aural codes that have come to represent the aesthetics of the counterculture. These codes act as cues that position the television program's or film's narrative within the context of the late sixties. The typology of cues includes archival news footage from the decade, recreated news footage that shares the grainy film quality, editing, and cinematography style of sixties-era news broadcasts, countercultural clothing and hair styles, and sixties-era rock music. Frequently, jargon-laded dialogue among individuals dressed in countercultural fashion cues audiences to the narrative's function as a resource for reflecting on the meaning of the sixties. The recurrence of these cues and their resemblance to one another across Hollywood texts over the past three decades make the sixties decade recognizable for media audiences, particularly for those born after the decade's end.

In some instances, these cues position the narrative within the context of the late sixties. Elsewhere, they indicate that characters' motivations in later years were profoundly shaped by sixties-era radicalism. The opening scenes of two eighties-era television programs, *Family Ties* and *The Wonder Years*, illustrate this distinction. The opening credits and pilot episodes of both programs provide a variety of visual and aural cues that assert these programs' investments in late sixties-era nostalgia. The pilot episode of *The Wonder Years* situates the program in the context of the turbulence of 1968. During the first scene, The Byrd's 1965 song "Turn, Turn, Turn" accompanies a montage sequence of archival news footage of events from that year. The rapid succession of images includes Nixon holding two fingers in the air after winning the presidential election campaign, a large antiwar march within an urban cityscape, Robert F. Kennedy's election campaign, Martin Luther King's funeral, urban riots, and a medium-close-up shot of a man holding an upside-down American flag at a protest rally. *The Wonder Years* also foregrounds the program's meaning as a site for reflection about the late sixties counterculture through its depiction of adolescent Karen, who appears prominently in the series' first five seasons. In the pilot episode, Karen wears a leather vest with long bead-covered fringe, strappy sandals, dangly earrings, and long hair. When her mother complains that Karen didn't come home in time to help her with dinner, Karen tells her that she has "bad karma." Karen's fashion style and hip jargon quickly reveal that Karen is a hippie and that tensions with her mother are rooted, at least in part, by her resistance to traditional feminine roles.

The first episode of *Family Ties* similarly cues audiences to the program's meaning as a site for reflection of the meaning of the counterculture for 1980s culture and politics. The opening credits to the first season feature a series of photographs of the Keaton family leading up to the present. In the first photo, parents Elyse and Stephen are participating in a protest rally; Elyse has a daisy in her hair and Stephen appears in front of a large banner displaying a peace sign. The next photo depicts the couple's outdoor garden wedding in which Stephen wears love beads and Elyse has a garland of purple flowers in her hair. These images indicate that Elyse and Stephen's relationship was cemented in their mutual participation in the counterculture and antiwar movements. The rest of the photographs depict the couple on a camping trip with their then-young children. The shift in emphasis suggests that the Keaton parents' relationship to other characters on the program are connected to how they relate to and draw meaning from the late sixties protest movements. During the first scene, the Keaton family discusses slides from an anti–Vietnam War protest that parents Elyse and Stephen attended during college. The slides depict a throng of protesters surrounding a large but not fully decipherable banner and a group of young people wearing tie-dyed tunics, painted faces, long hair, and bandanas. Stephen is holding a poster that reads, "Shut it down." Behind him is a peace sign poster. The last slide is a medium close-up of Elyse and Stephen. Stephen wears love beads and a fringed suede leather jacket, and Elyse wears Indian jewelry. These images contextualize the relationship between the Keaton parents and their children as a commentary on the legacy of the sixties for contemporary family life. As I explain in chapter 2, the children are comically annoyed by their parents' nostalgia for the sixties.

The first episodes of *Family Ties* and *The Wonder Years* are early examples of television's recreated depictions of countercultural protest that appear across a wide variety of the television programs and films that I discuss throughout this book. Images of people holding protests signs and wearing peace symbols, tie-dyed shirts, bandanas, beaded and fringed leather vests, strappy leather sandals, round glasses, and other hippie-styled fashions cue audiences to the importance of particular media texts for understanding and giving meaning to the sixties. These particular fashions are ubiquitous as signifiers of the decade. Even those of us born after the sixties understand the decade principally as a set of images of the counterculture. In the context of the films' and television programs' narratives discussed in this book, these cues evoke humor, dismissal, or revulsion toward radical characters and their circumstances. These cues suggest that the films and television programs are not only reflections on the relationships among characters but commentaries about Left-leaning politics during the Age of Aquarius.

In addition to repeated visual cues that reference the decade, selective amnesia of the late sixties is constructed intertextually through the narrative patterns that run across different television programs and films about the era. This observation is the central organizing framework for this book. Rather than focus on one particular film or television program that features late sixties dissent, each chapter highlights how different television programs and/or films share similar generic conventions, plot devices, character types, and narrative structure to cultivate and reinforce a particular perspective about the legacy of radical sixties-era protest. Patterns across several of these more prominent films and television programs construct a structured symbolic environment that circumscribes our shared resources for interpreting the meaning of the sixties (Condit 1989). As Kenneth Burke (1969, 25–26) observed, rhetoric is comprised of a "general *body of identifications* that owe their convincingness much more to trivial repetition and dull daily reinforcement than to exceptional rhetorical skill." Lesser-known sympathetic portrayals of late sixties dissent are drowned out by a sea of depictions that trivialize dissent or characterize activists pejoratively.

My attention to the patterns across fictionalized film and television depictions of sixties-era dissent is grounded in the assumption that agreed-upon meanings may be gleaned from media texts when they are analyzed within the particular historical and political context in which they are consumed. Other analytical approaches might focus on the viewer as the site of meaning. Many media scholars have embraced John Fiske's (2011) concept of polysemy, which suggests that different audiences may draw different meanings from the same cultural product based on their own subject positions and experiences. Just as viewers bring their unique experiences to any text, they might also attend to discrete moments in particular texts and draw specific conclusions from them. For instance, a scene depicting a mass antiwar protest with a soundtrack of popular sixties-era rock music may be read as a nostalgic celebration of sixties-era dissent. Certainly, my own reading does not preclude alternative interpretations of the texts I have selected for analysis.

Although no one interpretation can make universalizing claims about the meaning of any film or television program, I also believe that media implicitly invite audiences to develop shared associations and understandings about past events when these events are routinely presented via similar narrative devices and character constructions. As the following chapters elaborate, character types including the hippie-turned-yuppie, the good citizen, the ambivalent activist, the macho militant, the angry black man, and the dangerous fugitive appear in a variety of fictionalized television programs and films across multiple decades. These reductive character types form the basis for selective amnesia as they discourage audiences from identifying with people who have questioned the legitimacy of mainstream society and politics.

A central insight of this book is that Hollywood is particularly concerned with the legacy of the sixties for gender relations and family life. Spanning multiple decades, the recurring character type of the ambivalent activist across a variety of films and television programs depicts a former countercultural or radical woman who abandons or denounces her politics to pursue heteronormative romance and childrearing. As I argue throughout the book, Hollywood's portrayals of radical women reinforce the gendered constructs of citizenship and the nation in which masculine subjects strive to preserve and protect a feminine nation from radical challenges to traditional family values and capitalist imperialism. Through an analysis of the ambivalent activist and related character and narrative patterns, this book highlights how a diversity of films and television programs encourage audiences to dismiss or deride the contributions of late sixties dissent on behalf of historically exploited and marginalized women, GLBTQ+ groups, and people of color worldwide.

PREVIEW OF THE BOOK

The first chapter provides a broad historical review of late sixties dissent and Hollywood's efforts to capitalize on the decade's activism. I provide a brief historical account of late sixties activism to orient readers to the organizations and events that are routinely featured in Hollywood's imagined sixties. I also discuss the movements that are largely excluded from this vision including Chicanx activism, radical women's liberation, and gay liberation. The second half of the chapter reviews a wide variety of Hollywood films and television programs that responded to late sixties radicalism, both at the time dissident movements were active and in the proceeding decades. The diversity of portrayals of late sixties radicalism demonstrates that film and television portrayals have given cinematic and televisual form to a variety of perspectives about the late sixties and ongoing controversies about the social and political changes that emerged from the time period. However, the narrative patterns across multiple media texts also illustrate how mainstream media avoided sustained attention to the political beliefs that motivated activists.

Chapter 2 analyzes portrayals of late sixties activism in two popular family television programs that aired during the eighties: *Family Ties* and *The Wonder Years*. Although these programs offer halting nostalgia for moderate sixties-era dissent, their narratives are grounded in the neoconservative politics of the eighties. The programs' central characters, Alex Keaton of *Family Ties* and Kevin Arnold of *The Wonder Years*, reject or are confused by sixties-era activist causes. Supporting characters, the Keaton parents of *Family Ties* and Karen Arnold of *The Wonder Years*, are more reductive characters who evince the stereotype of the hippie-turned-yuppie. They are profoundly influenced by their participation in the counterculture and antiwar movement; however, these characters eventually abandon their countercultural ideals to pursue lucrative careers and participate in nuclear family life. This chapter also discusses similar themes in the critically acclaimed television drama *thirtysomething* in which hippie-turned-yuppie couples exchange their countercultural politics for economic stability and stay-at-home motherhood. One lesson to draw from the narratives of hippies-turned-yuppies in these media texts is that left-of-center politics is childish. It is activism, not age, which characters learn to outgrow. By recentering the family as the site of individual agency and moral action, they give televisual and cinematic form to the assumptions of neoliberalism and postfeminism undergirding the Reagan revolution.

The third chapter looks at how the motion picture *Forrest Gump* and the NBC miniseries *The '60s* contributed to heteronormative and gendered meanings about the late sixties counterculture and anti–Vietnam War movements during the mid- to late nineties. The central narratives revolve around good citizens, male characters who strive to win the hearts of women they love amid the turmoil of the late sixties. While these male protagonists embrace mainstream values, their love interests are divided between the affections of these good citizens and macho militants who embrace radicalism. I argue that the interpersonal conflicts portrayed in *Forrest Gump* and *The '60s* stand in metaphorically for the divided nation, torn asunder by sixties conflicts over the Vietnam War and gender roles. While macho militant characters stand in symbolically for the imagined threats to mainstream American values, women radicals are objects of masculine desire and the stakes of ideological conflict. Ultimately, *Forrest Gump* and *The '60s* are narratives of national reconciliation and white masculine redemption. These gendered portrayals of activism delimit cultural resources for imagining women's political agency and contribute to the backlash against feminism.

Chapter 4 explores Hollywood's ambivalent response to the legacy of the Black Power movement and to the civil rights subject since the mid-nineties. The first half of this chapter interprets the motion pictures *Malcolm X* and *Panther* as sources of traumatic countermemory that consign black dissent to the memory of a traumatic past even as they celebrate radical black political agency. The second half of this chapter looks at more simplistic and reductive depictions of the Black Panthers that run across the films *Forrest Gump*, *Barbershop 2*, *The Butler*, the television miniseries *The '60s*, and an episode of *Law & Order*. Targeting wider—and whiter—audiences, these Hollywood products provided brief caricatures of the Black Panther Party as comically ineffectual or as menacing threats to white society. These reductive portrayals foreground black rage, not racial injustice or economic disparity, as the primary threat to civil society and black achievement. The proliferation of negative portrayals of the Black Panthers participate in the backlash against civil rights and Great Society legislation and contribute to an environment in which political figures and the press can offer dismissive commentary about black activism at present.

The last case study chapter analyzes several television police procedural programs inspired by the publicity surrounding the Weather Underground, the Black Liberation Army (BLA), the Symbionese Liberation Army (SLA), and other militant organizations from the late sixties and early seventies. Since 1984, a myriad of Hollywood texts has featured clandestine activities of these underground radical groups. Focusing on episodes of *Law & Order*, *Life on Mars*, and *The Chicago Code*, I explain how these programs integrate political and journalistic discourse about militant Left dissidents with the generic conventions of the television police procedural. Although these episodes grapple more or less with the political circumstances surrounding militant actions to determine suspects' guilt or innocence, conclusions of each of these episodes depict late sixties militants as violent criminals who deserve punishment via arrest, legal prosecution, and—in the case of one program—police brutality. These episodes' demonization of the radical Left cultivates norms of democratic citizenship that call for uncritical assent to law enforcement and suspicion toward dissidents. Hence, they discourage audiences from questioning government programs and policies that have suppressed activism since 9/11.

The concluding chapter discusses the implications of selective amnesia of late sixties dissent for contemporary activism after 9/11. The memory of the bad sixties continues to reverberate in popular culture, yet several independent films have recently celebrated late sixties radicalism and critiqued law enforcement's repression of dissent. These varied portrayals of radical dissent highlight how the memory of late sixties activism remains a powerful resource for imagining how we might work collectively to transform the conditions that perpetuate social injustice and inequality.

CHAPTER ONE

The Sixties in History and Entertainment Memory

To appreciate how popular film and television have constructed selective amnesia of late sixties-era protest movements, it is important to review the broader history of dissent that Hollywood has largely forgotten or dismissed. The dissident movements that have come to stand in for the entirety of the sixties were part of a second wave of protest that followed on the heels of earlier civil rights, free speech, and antiwar activism. Whereas the first wave of activists sought to reform the corruption within American institutions, the second wave viewed injustice as embedded in the nation's fabric. While Black Power activists, the student antiwar Left, and the counterculture differed in important respects, they all repudiated mainstream or "establishment" norms and values. These groups at times overlapped as they often shared mutual critiques of racism, sexism, and the Vietnam War. The escalation of the Vietnam War drove much of the decade's radical dissent. In 1967, Martin Luther King concluded that Vietnam was a symptom that showed that the United States was deeply ill and described the country as the "greatest purveyor of violence in the world" (para. 11).

Anticolonial struggles in Africa, Asia, and the Caribbean Islands also propelled revolutionary activism in the United States. Drawing connections between the struggles of people of color in the United States and the Global South, many activists recognized Western imperialism as the common source of poverty, discrimination, and brutality facing nonwhite peoples worldwide. Armed struggles for national independence in Africa and the revolutions in China and Cuba affirmed that revolutionary change was possible. Furthermore, the writings of Mao Zedong, Franz Fanon, and Régis Debray offered resources for radicals in the United States to theorize and strategize their own resistance (Young 2006).

Brutal repression against civil rights and antiwar protesters fueled activists' growing alienation from mainstream politics and society.[1] The Democratic Party's refusal to seat the Mississippi Freedom Democratic Party delegation during the 1964 national convention was seen as a betrayal of justice from the perspective of students who witnessed the violent repression of voting rights activists in the state. The confluence of these events demonstrated that the United States had not lived up to its promise of democracy. Thus, sixties-era radicalism refers to those activists who believed that US capitalism, party politics, and traditional social values were fundamentally flawed and must be transformed.

BLACK POWER AND THIRD WORLD ACTIVISM

The Black Power movement developed in response to black freedom activists' disenchantment with national politics. Disillusionment among organizations including the Student Nonviolent Coordinating Committee (SNCC) and the Congress on Racial Equality (CORE) was kindled by ongoing racial violence and harassment of civil rights workers after President Johnson signed the Civil Rights Act into law, making it illegal for states to compel formal racial segregation. A few weeks after the law was passed, civil rights activists James Chaney, Michael Schwerner, and Andrew Goodman were murdered in Neshoba County, Mississippi, by local Klan members.[2] Numerous arrests of activists and the racist abuses within the criminal justice system also fueled growing radicalism within the black freedom movement. As rhetorical scholar Lisa Corrigan (2016) argues, the experience of imprisonment was critical to Black Power's development because it presented resources for incarcerated dissidents to invent new forms of black identification that resisted hegemonic constructions of whiteness and civil rights discourses.

Stark economic disparities, housing discrimination, and police harassment of black people in northern cities also exposed racial injustice as a national issue that existed well beyond the southern states and fueled race rebellions in cities across the country including Los Angeles, Detroit, Harlem, and Chicago. In a series of speeches delivered to northern black audiences throughout the country in 1964, former Nation of Islam minister Malcolm X pointedly argued that the entire political system was responsible for the exploitation and political repression of black people in the United States. Influenced by Franz Fanon's anticolonial philosophy, Malcolm X asserted that they had a right to defend themselves "by any means necessary" (X 1992). After Malcolm X's assassination on February 21, 1965, his rhetoric continued to inspire black and white radicals throughout the remainder of the decade. By the late sixties, Martin Luther King had also expressed more radical views about capitalism as the source of racial and class inequality. During the last year of his life, he helped organize the Poor People's Campaign in Washington, DC, which was a multiracial effort to put economic justice on the national political agenda. Public officials in the White House including President Johnson dismissed King due to his growing concerns about the inherent injustices impeded within the US economy.

In contrast to the more moderate civil rights movement, Black Power activists advocated for self-determination, self-defense, and solidarity among black people worldwide. Black Nationalist strands of the movement called for the political and economic liberation of black people independent from whites. Overall, the movement signaled a new political consciousness among African Americans. SNCC members first introduced the slogan, "Black Power," during the 1966 March Against Fear that traversed the state of Mississippi. The march picked up where civil rights activist James Meredith's own march ended when he was shot by a sniper. SNCC leader Stokely Carmichael announced the organization's departure from civil rights' strategies by declaring, "The only way we gonna stop them white men from whuppin' us is to take over. What we gonna start saying now is Black Power" (Joseph 2006, 2).

The Black Panther Party (BPP) was the decade's most prominent Black Power organization.[3] Huey Newton and Bobby Seale founded the Black Panther Party for Self-Defense in Oakland, California, in 1966 with a broad-ranging community empowerment agenda, including an end to police violence against black people. The group garnered news media attention by carrying arms with them as they monitored police officers and marched on the California state capitol in Sacramento in 1967 to advocate for their rights to armed self-defense. In response, the California state legislature passed the Mulford Act that repealed the law allowing citizens to carry loaded firearms. The BPP dropped "Self-Defense" from their name the next year as their political ideology shifted to embrace what they referred to as intercommunal socialism, which asserted international solidarity with people who were exploited by capitalist imperialism. The Panthers' bravado attracted young members, and the organization grew rapidly during the late sixties. By 1970, the BPP had thirty chapters and ten community centers across the country. However, disagreements over strategy created conflict within and outside of the organization. Huey Newton emphasized survival programs that might recruit new members to the organization and soften its image, including free breakfast programs for children, sickle-cell anemia testing, and meetings to raise awareness about racism in the United States. By contrast, Eldridge Cleaver emphasized police confrontations. Violent encounters with police led to casualties on both sides, including the shooting death of party treasurer Bobby Hutton.[4]

In addition to internal weaknesses, Black Panther Party members were targets of extraordinary political repression. In 1967, Federal Bureau of Investigation (FBI) director J. Edgar Hoover instructed field agents to engage in a covert and illegal operation to "expose, disrupt, misdirect, or otherwise neutralize the activities" of civil rights and Black Power organizations.[5] That year, Huey Newton was arrested on charges of murdering a policeman, charges that were dismissed after two trials ended in hung juries. The Panthers' nationwide campaign to have Newton released drew large multiracial audiences that attested to growing enthusiasm for black radicalism. As radicals' support for the Panthers swelled, so did Hoover's commitment to disabling the organization. The FBI launched 295 operations against the Panthers between 1967 and 1971 (Self 2006, 45). On December 4, 1969, Chicago police used information provided by the FBI to raid Chicago Panther headquarters and kill leaders Fred Hampton and Mark Clark. As a consequence of intense repression and internal strife within the organizations, the Panthers' national presence dwindled.

Although the Panthers are the most widely remembered, a variety of radical black political organizations sought liberation and justice for people of color. In 1968, the Republic of New Africa sought to form an independent state for African Americans in the United States, and in 1969, the League of Revolutionary Black Workers organized in Detroit against the inhumane working conditions for blacks laboring in the automotive industry. Other Third World radical organizations challenged Western exploitation of communities of color including Chicanx groups (the Brown Berets and Movimiento Estudiantil Chicano de Aztlán, or MEChA), Puerto Ricans (the Young Lords), Asian Americans (I Wor Kuen), and Native Americans (the Indians of All Tribes).

The late sixties and early seventies also witnessed coalitional efforts to resist US colonialism and empower communities of color worldwide. Amiri Baraka led the Congress of African People to advocate for African liberation, national independence, and NGO status in the United Nations (Woodard 2006, 75). With multiple chapters nationwide, the African Liberation Support Committee (ALSC) mobilized 100,000 demonstrators across thirty cities for African Liberation Day on May 26, 1973 (Elbaum 2002, 84). Black Power organizations also formed coalitions with other radical anticolonial groups. Before his death, Fred Hampton organized the Rainbow Coalition with members of the Brown Berets, the Young Lords, I Wor Kuen, and the Young Patriots (a white radical organization).

Activism for the rights of Chicanx groups flourished in the American southwest. In 1968, twenty thousand high school students participated in organized walkouts of East Los Angeles high schools to protest academic prejudice and substandard facilities. The Brown

Berets took direct action against police brutality and for Chicanx self-determination. The group also organized the Chicano Moratorium against the Vietnam War in 1970, drawing together thirty thousand demonstrators to East Los Angeles. In Texas, La Raza Unida challenged the predominantly white two-party political system in an effort to foster greater political autonomy to Mexican Americans in the state. Activism for the rights of Mexican American and Filipino farmworkers also gained the national spotlight during the late sixties when Cesar Chavez and the United Farm Workers led a strike and boycott movement to protest low wages and poor working conditions. The strike ended in 1970 when farm growers signed contracts with the workers' union.

THE STUDENT NEW LEFT AND ANTIWAR MOVEMENT

The brutal treatment of civil rights activists and growing consciousness about the interconnections between colonial wars abroad and racism at home also spurred white student activism. After 1965, the white movement expanded as the government continued to commit troops to the seemingly endless war in Vietnam. The New Left, and its most recognizable organization, the Students for a Democratic Society, is a routine feature of most Hollywood depictions of antiwar dissent. In actuality, the New Left had a broader agenda including the promotion of participatory democracy, civil rights, and various university reforms. After 1966, the movement turned much of its focus toward ending the war. Certainly, the New Left did not comprise the entirety or even the majority of the antiwar movement; however, their confrontational demonstrations and the violent responses by law enforcement attracted considerable media attention that overshadowed larger and tamer protest gatherings.

Violent repression of antiwar activists in 1967 and 1968 propelled student radicalism. Police beat students and protesters during the October 16–20 Stop the Draft Week protests in Oakland, California, after some protesters threw rocks at police. During that week, between fifty thousand and one hundred thousand protesters including middle-class liberals, student radicals, and civil rights workers gathered in Washington, DC. In a protest tactic that has become an iconic image of pacifist, countercultural dissent, several protesters who had gathered at the Pentagon placed flowers in the troops' rifle barrels. Later that day, paratroopers and US marshals kicked and clubbed the seated crowd.

Events in 1968 amplified tensions between the state and dissidents. The Vietcong's assault during the Vietnamese New Year, Tet, signaled that the US military was not close to winning the war, prompting many activists to campaign for war critic and senator, Eugene McCarthy. When Martin Luther King was assassinated on April 4, black communities in one hundred cities revolted by looting stores and setting downtown areas on fire. Later that month, student activists occupied multiple buildings at Columbia University to protest the school's expansion that removed nearby apartments occupied by lower-income minority tenants. After several days, the police ended the sit-ins by attacking the student protesters and arresting seven hundred of them.

Demonstrations during the Democratic National Convention in Chicago put the tensions between dissidents and law enforcement in sharp relief. Ten thousand activists gathered in the city despite Major Daley's adamant refusal to issue parade permits for them to march. Instead, Daley sent his police force of twelve thousand officers and six thousand Illinois National Guardsmen to control the crowd. The Chicago activists were a coalition of pacifists and radicals, including the irreverent Yippies led by Abbie Hoffman and Jerry Rubin. City officials did not appreciate that the Yippies' threats to lace the city's water supply with LSD during the convention was merely a "put on," and police intervened when the Yippies performed their own election of a pig for president by confiscating the pig. Police responded to activists' defiance by launching tear gas indiscriminately into the crowds and clubbing both protesters and news reporters covering the event. Although most people who witnessed the events at home sided with Mayor Daley, the crackdown on activism in Chicago further radicalized many young people alienated by mainstream politics.

Popular sentiment continued to turn against the war. Members of the Resistance, an antidraft organization, publicly declared their willingness to go to jail rather than fight in Vietnam. In October 1969, millions of people participated in local demonstrations across the country, and in November, the Mobilization Against the War, or MOBE, brought over 500,000 protesters to Washington, DC, to comprise the single largest march in US history up to that point (Anderson 1995). After President Nixon announced that the United States had expanded the war to Cambodia in the spring of 1970, student strikes and protests shut down campuses nationwide. That May, over 100,000 people rallied in Washington, DC, and thirty ROTC buildings were burned or bombed (Gitlin 1996). Kent State University became shorthand for tragedy caused by antiwar dissent after National Guardsmen fired their rifles into a crowd of rowdy protesters and killed four students. Antiwar organizations such as the Vietnam Veterans Against the War (VVAW) grew in membership during the early seventies. The VVAW's 1971 demonstrations in Washington, known as Operation Dewey Canyon III, drew public attention to returning veterans' horrific experiences. Lieutenant John F. Kerry spoke out against the war before a televised national audience and a thousand veterans publicly tossed their Vietnam combat medals out. That week, half a million people visited Washington to protest the war (Zaroulis and Sullivan 1985).

Although outspoken radicals made headlines by calling for revolutionary violence, the New Left's revolution was mostly symbolic. As historian Terry Anderson (1995) notes, very few segments of the antiwar movement resorted to physical violence. However, most citizens, journalists, and public officials did not acknowledge the distinction. Mainstream press attention to revolutionary violence was aided by a visible minority of militant activists, several of whom engaged in deliberate destruction of property and street fighting with police. Between September 1969 and May 1970, hundreds of bombings and bomb attempts were linked to the white Left. (The proliferation of campus bomb threats gave fodder to numerous comedic Hollywood depictions of bomb threats on high schools and college campuses designed to salvage the reputations and GPAs of many fictional underachieving students.)[6] The real-life repercussions of such political violence were not humorous. To protest the deaths at Kent State, a group calling themselves the New Year's Gang bombed the Army Mathematics Research Center at the University of Wisconsin in Madison, accidentally killing a graduate student.

The Weathermen, a splinter group that emerged after the SDS disbanded, are the most widely recognized militant New Left organization. As the antiwar movement burgeoned, SDS fractured and isolated themselves from the mass movement. The Weathermen organization led the sparsely attended Days of Rage protests in Chicago to protest the city's devastating response to the Democratic National Convention demonstrations during the previous year. In 1970, the group made headlines after a failed bomb-making attempt exploded a Greenwich Village townhouse, killing members Ted Gold, Diana Oughton, and Terry Robbins. Weeks earlier, the group had firebombed the New York City home of John Murtagh, the judge presiding over a case against Black Panther Party members who were eventually acquitted. After the townhouse explosion, the entire organization went underground and pledged to solely target inanimate structures. Over the next seven years, the renamed group, Weather Underground, bombed over twenty additional government and corporate structures including the New York City police headquarters, the US Capitol, and the Pentagon (Berger 2006). Weather Underground members saw themselves as freedom fighters within the United States and argued that their actions were far less damaging than the consequences of the war and Western imperialism; however, their actions also alienated the mainstream public and the moderate antiwar movement (Anderson 1995, 2007; Berger 2006; Dohrn, Ayers, and Jones 2006; Jacobs 1970; Jacobs 1997; Varon 2004). During the early seventies, other radical Left organizations, including the Symbionese Liberation Army and the Black Liberation Army, also made headlines by engaging in various crimes including armed robbery, kidnapping, and killing civilians, purportedly to further revolutionary aims. Armed attacks by these and other clandestine groups during the seventies provided plenty of fodder for the mainstream media to frame the meaning of sixties-inspired activism in terms of violence.

THE COUNTERCULTURE

While the New Left organized protests to change government and university policies, the counterculture expressed its rejection of mainstream culture by practicing alternative lifestyles. References to the counterculture do not point to a unified social movement, but to a set of attitudes and behaviors that the mainstream press pointed to as an indication of the changing youth culture between 1967 and 1970. The economic growth of the white middle class created conditions for many young white people to imagine a society in which human activities were freed from the drudgery of labor (Braunstein and Doyle 2002). Flower power blossomed during the Summer of Love in 1967 when journalists drew attention to the 100,000 hippies who gathered in Golden Gate Park in San Francisco. In the following years, the number of people who identified themselves as hippies surged. One influential attendee at the Haight-Ashbury gathering was Timothy Leary, a Harvard professor who was dismissed from the university for touting the therapeutic uses of LSD. Leary famously urged young people to "turn on, tune in and drop out," by embracing cultural changes through the use of hallucinogenic drugs.

Many young people flouted tradition by wearing alternative fashions, smoking pot, experimenting with psychedelic drugs, promoting environmental conservation, and living communally. Rejecting the ideas that premarital sex was immoral and that nudity was shameful, they embraced free love. Men who advocated free love often used sexual liberation to their own advantage by dismissing women's claims of chauvinism and discrimination; alternatively, challenges to normative sexual relationships also included greater acceptance of gay liberation and women's pursuit of sexual pleasure (Echols 1989).

Most young people were not part of the counterculture during the late sixties; however, the image of the pot-smoking hippie is often synonymous with the baby-boom generation. Likewise, Hollywood has collapsed the differences between countercultural hippies or "freaks" and the New Left "politicos" by circulating images of hippies with long hair, round classes, tie-dyed clothing, and peace signs hanging from their necks. The counterculture was distinct in many ways from the antiwar movement; however, the two groups intersected and overlapped near the end of the decade. Thus, the growing radicalism of the movement coincided with proliferation of the hippie subculture as both increasingly distanced themselves from mainstream politics and society.

Many countercultural groups formed communal living arrangements that radically broke from mainstream, bourgeois family structures. By 1970, there were two thousand rural and five thousand urban communes or collectives that embraced countercultural lifestyles (Anderson 2007, 139). Hog Farm, a still-operating commune located in New Mexico, is one of the most familiar countercultural communities, owing in part to its notorious founder Wavy Gravy, an antiwar activist-clown and performer whose name inspired a Ben & Jerry's ice cream flavor that appeared on supermarket shelves until 2001.[7] Wavy Gravy also helped organize the most frequently discussed countercultural event of the late sixties: the Woodstock music festival. In August 1969, four hundred thousand people gathered for the three-day event on farmland in the Catskill Mountains in New York. Despite bad weather, insufficient food, water, and sanitation facilities, it is routinely remembered as an expression of countercultural cooperation and style.

Other events in 1969 have been remembered as the death-knell of the counterculture. The Rolling Stone's free music concert at Altamont, California, in December was intended to represent the West Coast's version of Woodstock, but ended tragically when members of the Hell's Angels biker gang murdered a concertgoer who was supposedly armed with a gun. Months earlier, Charles Manson convinced several of his followers to murder seven people in California including actress Sharon Tate. Manson's long hair and cult-like devotees prompted journalists to describe the events as the consequence of murderous hippies "devoid of true compassion" (Anderson 2007, 143).

The events following the creation of People's Park in Berkeley, California, earlier that year illustrated the counterculture's inability to restructure dominant institutions. After volunteers built the communitarian park on property owned by the University of California at Berkeley, police officers were ordered to retake the property. Clashes between two thousand to three thousand demonstrators and over seven hundred police officers led police to open fire indiscriminately into the crowd, resulting in the hospitalization of thirty-two gunshot victims and nineteen police officers, as well as the death of James Rector, who was only observing the melee. To restore order, then-governor Ronald Reagan brought in twenty-seven hundred National Guardsmen and ordered that tear gas be dropped over the entire city. Rather than allow university officials to compromise with park supporters, Reagan insisted that they find another use for the space. Anticipating Joni Mitchell's well-known lyrics to the song "Big Yellow Taxi," the university paved the countercultural paradise to put up a parking lot (Cash 2010, 8–29).

WOMEN'S LIBERATION AND GLBT RADICALISM

While popular culture has routinely reimagined the events surrounding the Black Panthers, anti–Vietnam War movement, and counterculture, radicalism during the late sixties and early seventies included a broader diversity of groups and organizations. The scope and dynamism of women radicals' leadership and feminist organizing is obscured or ignored in Hollywood's imagined sixties. Although the Black Panther's gender politics were marred by sexist and misogynist practices, women comprised over 50 percent of the organization's rank-and-file membership during its later years. Kathleen Cleaver was the party's communication secretary and Elaine Brown served as minister of information and chaired the party after Huey Newton fled to Cuba in 1974.[8]

Frustrated by rampant sexism within the New Left, many white movement women became actively involved in second-wave feminist organizing and put the issue of sexism equality in radical terms. The New York Radical Women disavowed the male-dominated New Left in pursuit of a genuine feminist revolution and garnered national attention when they protested the 1968 Miss America Pageant by crowning a sheep as the winner of their alternative demonstration. When the group disbanded in 1969, it split into the Women's International Terrorist Conspiracy from Hell (WITCH) and the Redstockings. The organizations engaged in direct-action protests to challenge patriarchal capitalism and regressive abortion laws, respectively. The broader women's liberation movement held its first nationwide conference in 1968 and hundreds of consciousness-raising groups emerged to discuss women's experiences with patriarchy by 1972 (Echols 1989).

Other activist organizations focused on the multiple forms of oppression facing women of color. Organizers of the National Welfare Rights Organization, who were primarily poor, black mothers, drew attention to the racial and class biases inherent in national welfare policies (Triece 2013). In 1970, the Black Women's Alliance foregrounded the significance of black feminism for anti-imperialist projects; that summer, the group expanded to form the Third World Women's Alliance to focus their struggle on the racial, gendered, and economic exploitation of people of color worldwide (Ward 2006, 119–44).

Radical feminist organizing coincided with moderate liberal feminist achievements including the formation of the National Organization for Women and the passage of the Equal Rights Amendment in the Senate in 1972, which would have banned discrimination based on sex. The states never ratified the ERA, but its success in the Senate put feminist issues in the foreground of national politics. Although liberal and radical feminist groups disagreed over their assessment of the causes and solutions to women's oppression, conservative opposition to the ERA decried all women's rights advocates, labeling them as radicals who threatened the sanctity of the home and the nuclear family.

Radical strands within the rising gay and lesbian movements were also influenced by Black Power, the student New Left, and the counterculture. Queer resistance to homophobia and transphobia in the mid-sixties led to the emergence of radical GLBTQ rights activism in the late sixties. In 1966, picketers protesting the police arrests of transgender patrons of Compton's Cafeteria in San Francisco led to violent clashes between police and transgender activists. Three years later, the riots outside of New York City's Stonewall Inn following a police raid prompted the formation of Gay Liberation Front (GLF) groups across the country. Departing from the homophile movement of the previous decades, GLFs sought to promote justice and freedom for gays and lesbians through marches, sit-ins, and zap demonstrations that challenged discrimination against the community. GLFs also formed coalitions with other leftist organizations including the Black Panthers, the Puerto Rican Young Lords, and the United Farm Workers. Radical lesbian feminism organizations also grew during the early 1970s. The Radicalesbians objected to second-wave feminists' dismissal of lesbian rights and called upon women's liberationists to reject heterosexism and prioritize their relationships with women as a central means of resisting patriarchy (Stein 2012).

Although radical activism continued throughout the seventies, it did not flourish at the same rate as it had during the late sixties. The pace of dissent declined for a variety of reasons, including internal divisions within activist organizations and political repression by local authorities and the FBI. The end of the Vietnam War removed a primary issue that had united and motivated different leftist organizations. Furthermore, white, male, and straight-dominated groups like the Students for a Democratic Society failed to adapt their agendas and organizing practices to incorporate the demands of black radicals, women's liberation advocates, and gay liberation supporters.[9] Lackluster media attention to activism that continued into the seventies and eighties also contributed to the public perception that the sixties was a decade of protest unlike any other. Despite the mainstream press's construction of dissent as a unique phenomenon of the sixties, the culture of protest that thrived during the decade has continued and evolved, as evidenced by more recent protest movements against US foreign policies in Latin America and the Middle East, environmental devastation, neoliberal globalization, wealth inequality, and police violence against black people, among other causes. Ongoing activism and dissent highlights how movements have expanded beyond the image provided by Hollywood's imagined sixties.

IMAGES OF RADICALS IN HOLLYWOOD DURING THE LATE SIXTIES AND EARLY SEVENTIES

Hollywood studios produced a variety of countercultural films between 1966 and 1971 in an effort to attract white, college-aged audiences drawn to the movement's resistance to mainstream cultural values. Although many films were not explicitly political, they carried markers of countercultural resistance including illicit drug use, rock music, overt sex, and rebellion against authority. Some of the earliest countercultural films were the products of the low-budget film studio American International Pictures (AIP), who shifted its youth-oriented exploitation films away from its focus on beach parties toward what the studio's president James Nicholson referred to as "protest films" (Heffernan 2015, 3). They include the trilogy of films directed by exploitation film luminary Roger Corman: *The Wild Angels* (1966), *The Trip* (1967), and *Gas-s-s-s* (1970). *The Wild Angels* and *The Trip* depict the transgressive lifestyles of California's motorcycle gangs and psychedelic drug culture, respectively. *Gas-s-s-s* is the most openly political (and least commercially successful) of the three, portraying young radicals with different political agendas who establish a peaceful utopian commune at an American Indian pueblo in New Mexico (Heffernan 2015, 3).

The myriad of cheaply made films featuring hippies' lifestyles and drugs highlights Hollywood's desire to capitalize from public fascination with the counterculture. Several of these movies reflected the mainstream public's apprehension about countercultural lifestyles and values. While *The Trip* offers a somewhat positive portrayal of psychedelic drug use, other films warn audiences about the perils of youth drug culture. Drug panic films such as *Hallucination Generation* (1967), *Riot on the Sunset Strip* (1967), and *The Big Cube* (1969) highlight the dangers that LSD and the counterculture pose to decent people. Similarly, *Wild in the Streets* (1968) depicts hedonistic hippies who take control of the US government by dosing adults over thirty-five with the drug.

Major studios responded to AIP's success with *The Wild Angels* by creating a series of their own protest films that sought to evoke the turbulence of late sixties dissent. Films featuring campus activism and protest among white youths include Paramount's *Medium Cool* (1969); Columbia's *Getting Straight* (1970) and *RPM* (1970), an acronym for "revolutions per minute"; and MGM's *Zabriskie Point* (1970) and *The Strawberry Statement* (1970). In 1970, Universal bought the rights to an independently produced film, *The Activist*, which was loosely based on events during the student takeover at Columbia University two years earlier. Film studios strove to realistically depict campus radicalism and political agitation in these movies. *The Activist*, *Zabriskie Point*, and *The Strawberry Statement* feature appearances by nonactors involved in radical campus organizing, and *Medium Cool* includes actual footage from the Chicago Democratic Convention protests and the ensuing police assault on activists. As Aniko Bodroghkozy (2002, 38–58) notes, each of these films used the codes and conventions of cinéma vérité in their scenes of campus uprisings to establish their authenticity. Like much of the Hollywood fare about the decade, these student protest films depict late sixties activism as a series of explosive events rather than as an organized effort for structural change. At the time the films appeared on screen, mainstream news coverage provided a variety of "deprecatory themes" about the New Left, including an emphasis on violence during demonstrations (Gitlin 2003, 27–28). Hollywood expanded upon the cultural resources provided by nonfiction media that solidified particularly pejorative meanings to late sixties dissent in public culture.

The landmark counterculture film of the late sixties is Dennis Hopper's *Easy Rider* (1969), a road movie about long-haired motorcyclists Billy and Wyatt who travel cross country together. The characters encounter a series of people and events that mark the turmoil of the late sixties: a hippie commune in the desert, menacing law enforcement officers, deadly vigilantes, and psychedelic drugs. Popular rock-and-roll music by artists including Bob Dylan, Steppenwolf, and Jimi Hendrix provide the soundtrack to their adventure. The film concludes when an anonymous rural southerner shoots both Billy and Wyatt from his pickup truck, killing Wyatt. *Easy Rider*'s bucolic imagery and celebration of the road expresses the fantasies of alienated youth and the counterculture's search for personal freedom and authenticity, yet its conclusion evokes the feelings of disillusionment and despair at the end of the decade (Farber 1970; Herring 1983; Lev 2000).

Easy Rider was the most notable among several films that projected images of violence against hippies. In the biker movie *Angel Unchained* (1970), a hippie commune falls victim to a violent biker gang. The action drama *Billy Jack* (1971) portrays a part-American

Navajo Indian and Vietnam War veteran who defends a hippie-run freedom school from menacing townspeople and a violent sheriff's deputy. Complementing television news broadcast images of repressive violence against dissidents toward the end of the decade, these Hollywood movies reinforce the message that the counterculture had little legitimacy or sympathy from mainstream society.

In addition to inspiring movie themes, Hollywood's film aesthetics were also influenced by the counterculture. By the late sixties, the filmmaking process often evoked a psychedelic experience on screen through experimental techniques including canted camera angles, wild colors, and fast edits. The emergence of "New Hollywood" during this period was marked by depictions of rebellion against authority and social deviance that evoked the alternative cultures of late sixties-era social movements. The use of disjunctive editing techniques in films such as *Bonnie and Clyde* (1967), *They Shoot Horses Don't They* (1969), and *The Graduate* (1967) facilitated discontinuity in narrative structure and ruptured traditional film narratives about American patriotism, heroism, and capitalist success (Ryan and Kellner 1990, 18–19).

Although the legacy of the counterculture can be observed in New Hollywood narratives about alienated and rebellious youth, most countercultural films privileged the spectacle of dissent and countercultural lifestyles over nuanced attention to radicals' politics. Bodroghkozy (2002) explains that campus protest films' visual strategies evoke the political turbulence of the times, but they also obscure the motives underlying protesters' actions. Likewise, Peter Lev (2000) argues that the films *Easy Rider* and *Alice's Restaurant* (another film released in 1969) were surprisingly apolitical. While visual imagery and music suggest the counterculture, the two films do not explicitly address antiwar resistance as a part of the lifestyle. These movies prefigured Hollywood's shallow interest in countercultural dissent and mirrored the mainstream press coverage of the counterculture and the New Left. News media routinely featured the most flamboyant leaders of the antiwar movement and circulated spectacular images of protest demonstrations, yet they routinely ignored or delegitimized countercultural ideals and beliefs (Gitlin 2003).

In addition to fictional counterculture films, the documentaries *Monterey Pop* (1968), *Woodstock* (1970), and *Gimme Shelter* (1970) provide a visual spectacle of countercultural music festivals. The movies' imagery helped to establish the radical sixties' aesthetic identity, which was largely devoid of political meaning beyond hedonistic pleasure and rock-and-roll music. *Gimme Shelter* concludes with footage of the disastrous events during the 1969 rock festival at Altamont, California, where concert organizers hired the Hell's Angels biker gang to work security. Footage of the Hell's Angels' brutal murder of a black concertgoer projected real-life images of tragic violence against the counterculture (Kitts 2009).

Entertainment television also sought to maintain its relevance to the baby-boomer generation by incorporating social conflicts and dissident themes into its programming. Lynn Spigel and Michael Curtin (1997, 8–11) note that prime-time programs "were centrally involved in sustaining, interrogating, and even transforming social relations" during the sixties; however, the extent to which television incorporated social movements into their programming was limited. Many programs included shallow references to late sixties' countercultural rebellion and protest. The *Monkees*, *Laugh-In*, and *The Smothers Brothers Comedy Hour* regularly included images of hippies for comic effect. Some fictionalized television narratives about late sixties rebellion paralleled the story lines from the Hollywood movies of the period. Scenes of violent clashes between demonstrators and police were frequently featured in prime time (Bodroghkozy 2001, 4). A variety of television programs including *Ironside*, *The Name of the Game*, and *Hawaii Five-O* contributed to the media drug panic by depicting subversive, uncontrollable adolescents driven mad by the hallucinatory effects of LSD and STP (76–86). The pilot episode of *Dragnet '67* entitled, "The Big LSD," chronicled the efforts of police detectives who attempt to break up an acid party after they encounter a young man with a face painted blue and gold and chewing the bark off a tree (75–87). Episodes of *Star Trek* and *Bonanza* depicted hippies more favorably as idealistic young people who challenged main characters to envision an alternative society. However, their efforts to create new communities based on countercultural values end in tragedy, reinforcing the lesson from films like *Easy Rider* that the counterculture was destined to fail (87–89).

Other television shows point to the industry's lukewarm and ambivalent interest in conveying dissident messages in its entertainment programming. CBS launched *The Smothers Brothers Comedy Hour* to appeal to younger audiences with comedic performances that vaguely alluded to moderate dissent, but the network canceled the variety show after the program's stars expressed explicit antiwar protest sentiments on the air. ABC's successful cop drama *The Mod Squad* made subtle nods to the Black Power movement and the counterculture in its depiction of the program's three main characters as young people compelled to work as undercover police officers to avoid jail time for their past criminal behavior. *The Mod Squad* had more longevity than *The Smothers Brothers* because the program balanced its sympathetic depictions of sixties radicalism with halting respect for law and order, thus reaching both baby boomers and their parents (Bodroghkozy 2001).

By the early 1970s, television dramas such as *Bracken's World*, *Marcus Welby, M.D.*, and *The Bold Ones* incorporated radical politics into the narratives of discrete episodes. An episode of *Bracken's World* modeled its character Jenny on Diana Oughton, a member of the militant Weathermen who was killed earlier that year by the Greenwich Village townhouse explosion. Remarkably, the episode offered a moderately sympathetic depiction of Jenny even though it never clearly explained her motives. In an episode of *Marcus Welby, M.D.*, a pregnant young hippie woman is found wandering San Francisco's Haight Ashbury district after her lover, another hippie drifter, has abandoned her. (The pregnant hippie drifter character reappears on the television miniseries *The '60s* and in the 2014–2015 season of AMC's *Mad Men*. The absence of reliable fathers in the hippie subculture is a central feature of these television narratives about young countercultural women. As I explain in subsequent chapters, countercultural women's despair and eventual return to the nuclear family celebrate a pre-sixties vision of family and nation and reveal how public memories of the sixties are bound up in ongoing contestation regarding gender roles and feminism.)

These aforementioned programs illustrate how late sixties radicalism influenced entertainment television. While television has included images of well-intentioned protesters, they rarely offered a nuanced explanation of radicals' beliefs. Most of these shows foregrounded the perspectives of older, more mainstream adults and failed to draw a younger audience (Bodroghkozy 2001, 226). By contrast, the situation comedies *All in the Family* and *M*A*S*H* reached large audiences with satiric depictions of family life and the military, respectively, that resonated with many aspects of the counterculture and antiwar movement.

Hollywood also sought to commercialize images of Black Power, although not nearly to the same extent as the white counterculture and the New Left. *Uptight* (1968) updated John Ford's classic *The Informer* (1935) by replacing Irish Republican Army members with black revolutionaries who murder a comrade for informing on their leader to the police. Fitting the conventions of the gangster film, *Uptight* foregrounded black militants' criminal behavior. Although the film provided a brief discussion of Black Power activists' critique of nonviolent dissent, it reduced the racial justice struggle to issues of interpersonal violence.

Later films provided more revolutionary messages about racial justice struggles. Melvin Van Peebles's comedy-drama *Watermelon Man* (1970) portrayed a white man who wakes up one day to find he is black. After experiencing the same racial prejudice that he once espoused, he becomes a radical militant. The next year, Van Peebles's independent film *Sweet Sweetback's Baadasssss Song* incorporated themes of black radicalism by depicting a black man's escape from police after witnessing police brutality against a black revolutionary.

Eager to capitalize on black film audiences' enthusiasm for images of empowered black characters, Hollywood produced a series of action-crime films featuring black actors. Themes of black machismo and sexually explicit content helped to shape the blaxploitation film genre. Although the genre appropriated several themes of black independent cinema, the most commercially successful movies of the genre excluded revolutionary messages that animated the Panthers and Van Peebles's film. The title character of *Shaft* (1971) solicits help from black radicals but advises them to embrace political moderation, and a brief scene in Gordon Parks's 1972 film *Super Fly* depicts black militants as unable to help their community resist exploitation by a local drug dealer (Lyne 2000).

A couple of films from the seventies provided more sympathetic depictions of black radicalism. The protagonist of Ivan Dixon's *The Spook Who Sat by the Door* (1973) advocates for radical structural change. This character uses his skills as a former CIA agent to teach Chicago gang members to commit revolutionary actions throughout the city. According to the filmmakers, United Artist distributors pulled the film from theaters after FBI officers expressed concerns about the film's potential to radicalize audiences (Acham and Ward 2011). Given the variety of Hollywood studio films about revolutionary white student activism that circulated in theaters in the preceding years, the suppression of *The Spook Who Sat by the Door* illuminates mainstream white culture and law enforcement's racist fears about Black Power.

Four years later, the film *Brothers* recalled George Jackson's radical activism through its depiction of the fictional character David Thomas. Inspired by Jackson's friendship with Angela Davis, the film depicts Thomas's relationship with a female college professor after he is imprisoned for a crime he didn't commit. Similar to many films about radical black dissent in the late eighties and nineties, *Brothers* couches the memory of the prison justice movement in terms of trauma and loss. As Michael Ryan and Douglas Kellner (1990, 23) observe, the film's refrain "strikes a note of hopeless caution: 'Any time a black leader appears on the horizon with any kind of charisma, he's cut down.'" The same conclusion might be made from the off-beat comedy *Car Wash* (1976), which includes a sympathetic depiction of a radical Nation of Islam member Abdullah, an employee who is fired for missing two days of work. In a concluding scene, Abdullah weeps over the fate of black militancy. Although *Car Wash* provides a satirical portrayal of black participation in American entrepreneurial capitalism, it offers no resolution to conditions of racial exploitation and wealth inequality.

Within prime-time television, positive portrayals of black characters routinely featured images of racial uplift in which characters strive to succeed within the confines of mainstream, white institutions. Programs such as *Soul Train* provided expressions of self-affirmation and pride central to Black Power; however, few programs overtly portrayed the movement's agenda or rhetoric. A couple of episodes of *Mod Squad* included oblique references to Black Power ideology via character Linc Hayes, who joined the police unit after participating in the 1965 Watts riots in Los Angeles (Bodroghkozy 2001, 193–97). Likewise, several episodes of the situation comedy *Sanford and Son* expressed the ideology of the urban black underclass and ridiculed white police officers. Another sitcom, *Good Times*, provided contradictory political messages about Black Power. Revolving around the conflicts experienced by a black family living in Chicago, the program articulated Black Power's criticisms of institutional racism through the character of Michael. However, Michael is the youngest member of the family; consequently, his militancy seems childish (Acham 2004).

Contrasting depictions of the counterculture and Black Power movements in seventies-era Hollywood and television highlight ongoing political and social divisions over the meaning of activism and dissent as the decade progressed. Some movies affirmed the ideological commitments of late sixties radicals. In *Dog Day Afternoon* (1975), bank robbers become local celebrities and earn sympathy with the bank tellers. Bank robber Sonny, played by Al Pacino, riles a crowd of cheering onlookers with the rallying cry of "Attica," a reference to the brutal police shooting at the Attica State Prison of New York that killed thirty-three prisoners and ten guardspersons. The Attica shootings ended a prison standoff between police and inmates who took guards hostage in protest for political rights and better living conditions. The 1979 musical *Hair*, based on the successful Broadway musical of the same name, attested to ongoing nostalgia for the flower children of the late sixties. Other films such as *One Flew Over the Cuckoo's Nest* (1975) and *All the President's Men* (1976) obliquely acknowledge radical sixties perspectives by offering dark or critical portrayals of American political, social, and cultural institutions; however, the themes of injustice and corruption in these movies could easily be read as appeals for institutional reform rather than as radical statements for change.

Other Hollywood films of the seventies drew upon mainstream culture's disdain for sixties-era dissent by depicting dangerous criminals as affiliated with the counterculture and radical Left. In 1976, two films loosely drew from news coverage of the Symbionese Liberation Army. *Network* (1976) parodies the radical organization's activities in its depiction of the fictional Ecumenical Liberation Army (ELA), an ultra-left militant organization that robs banks and kidnaps a wealthy heiress to propel the revolution. In the film, cynical television programming executives create a reality show following the group in order to boost the network's ratings. Later, the television executives pay members of the ELA to assassinate the lead protagonist who is threatening the network's profits. The third movie of the *Dirty Harry* series starring Clint Eastwood, *The Enforcer*, also references the radical terrorist group in its depiction of the Revolutionary Strike Force. The film's radicals claim that they are stealing firearms and murdering police detectives "for the people," but Harry Callahan's informant confides that they are really "in it for the bread." In these darkly cynical movies, leftist militants are as self-interested and dishonest as the local politicians and journalists. Five years earlier, the first *Dirty Harry* film indirectly references the counterculture in its depiction of the psychotic serial killer Scorpio. Although the killer's name alludes to the Zodiac killer who murdered several victims in California during the late sixties and early seventies, Scorpio's long hair and crooked peace sign belt buckle associate him with the movement. Likewise, the murderous gangs in *Death Wish* (1974) wear bandanas, leather jackets, and hats reminiscent of the counterculture. These menacing countercultural criminals are cinematic counterparts to the real-life cultural villain Charles Manson, who convinced his hippie-adorned followers to commit a series of grisly murders in 1969.

The contrasting and varied depictions of the counterculture, antiwar, and Black Power movements illustrate how Hollywood responded and contributed to public discourse about radical dissent. Reflecting ongoing political disagreements and social tensions, the films reflected disdain, enthusiasm, and ambivalence toward the counterculture and activism. Of course, not all of these media products reached a broad audience. Aside from *Easy Rider*, few of these countercultural films are familiar to audiences younger than the baby-boomer generation; television programs such as *Bracken's World* are equally unfamiliar. Thus, the memory of the sixties is not established through ongoing memory of these films and television programs per se. Instead, these texts' narratives, character constructions, imagery, and music provided the textual resources for filmmakers and television writers to expand upon in the following decades.

HOLLYWOOD MEMORIES OF THE RADICAL SIXTIES DURING THE REAGAN ERA AND BEYOND

After the mid-seventies, Hollywood's depictions of the late sixties responded to shifting political and social currents. George Lipsitz (2012) describes the eighties as a period of activist ferment in which artists and writers turned toward music, film, and the arts to express dissident ideas that had previously been voiced by social movements. Increasingly conglomerated media industries shared with conservative political leaders an interest in valorizing individual consumption and private enterprise but could not alienate segments of the viewing audience moved on some level by aspects of sixties protests and the counterculture. References to the sixties at this time responded to the emergence of the baby-boom generation as an important market for higher-end consumer items. Unsurprisingly, mainstream television and film navigated this tension in ways that commodified and depoliticized the decade's activism.

Hollywood films and television provided a variety of images and references to the late sixties radicalism and dissent in the eighties. Films such as *1969* (1988), *'68* (1988), *More American Graffiti* (1979), *Daniel* (1982), and *The World According to Garp* (1982) set narratives about interpersonal drama in the context of the political turbulence of the late sixties. In most of these films, characters' participation in activist causes and political demonstrations is a source of conflict between family members and friends. Oliver Stone's *Born on the Fourth of July* (1989) depicts real-life activist Ron Kovic's decision to enlist in the military as the product of his close relationship with his patriotic mother. Toward the end of the film, his dissent against the Vietnam War marks the development of his own political identity.

Disagreements between baby-boomer characters and their more conservative parents in a variety of films drew and expanded upon the construction of the "generation gap" promulgated by sociologists such as Theodore Roszak (1969), who argued that class struggle had been supplanted by generational conflict during the late sixties. The television comedy-drama *The Wonder Years* (1988–1993) drew upon the concept of the generation gap for comic effect. Set in the late sixties, adolescent main character Kevin Arnold is mystified by the ongoing arguments between his World War II–era father and older countercultural sister Karen. To some extent, the program parallels the generation conflicts depicted in *All in the Family*, although Kevin's dad is calmer than the loud-mouthed Archie from the earlier sit-com. The situation comedy *Family Ties* (1982–1989) reverses the dynamic by depicting the struggles of former hippies who have raised a son who idolizes conservative author William F. Buckley. Another situation comedy, *Dharma and Greg* (1997–2002), featured contemporary family disagreements as rooted in sixties-era conflicts. In this program, generational struggle becomes class struggle once again as married couple Dharma and Greg work to reconcile Dharma's countercultural upbringing with Greg's wealthier, more traditional background. Dharma's hippie parents frequently clash with Greg's Republican family. By transcoding the political conflicts of the sixties as interpersonal conflicts, these films and television programs avoided sustained attention to the underlying political and social context that motivated activists.

While programs like *Family Ties* and *Dharma and Greg* depicted former sixties activists struggling to come to terms with the conservatism of later decades, several films set in more recent decades featured characters who were profoundly influenced by sixties-era counterculture and protest movements. Many of these movies featured countercultural styles and drug use to convey characters' attitudes and motives. The stoner hippie is a staple Hollywood character type. The comedy duo Richard "Cheech" Marin and Tommy Chong created a series of stoner movies in the early eighties that revolved around their personae as pot-smoking hippies.[10] The main character of the Cohen brothers' cult film *The Big Lebowski* (1998) spends his days smoking pot and drinking white Russian cocktails in his bathrobe until a case of mistaken identity forces him to assist a wealthier, conservative man with the same name. Early in the film, Lebowski asserts that he was one of the original authors of the Port Huron Statement (the founding document of the Students for a Democratic Society), and that he was one of the Seattle Seven. Audiences familiar with sixties history might recognize the reference to members of a radical antiwar organization who were charged with conspiracy to start a riot following violent incidents during a protest rally. Ostensibly, Lebowski's radical past explains his lackadaisical attitude and offers a humorous counterpoint to the stodgier Lebowski, who needs his help. Lebowski somewhat resembles the main character in the more recent crime-comedy film *Inherent Vice* (2014) in which a stoner detective caters to countercultural clients in Venice Beach, California, in 1970.

Caricatures of pot-smoking hippies are also presented via supporting characters in movies and television whose countercultural perspective provides comic relief. In *The Abyss* (1989), a character who goes by the name of "Hippie" thinks everything is a conspiracy. Similarly, Dharma's pot-smoking father Larry is comically distrustful of government agencies. During the first season of *Dharma and Greg*, Larry plans to go underground when he learns that the entire family's background will be reviewed by the FBI in order for his son-in-law to receive security clearance. Larry is devastated to learn that he has a clean record.

Another recurring character type is the "sell-out" or "hippie-turned-yuppie," a former member of the counterculture or antiwar movement who reversed course to embrace materialism and capitalism. Sell-outs appear in lesser-known movies such as the *The Big Fix* (1978) and *Rude Awakenings* (1989), and in the Academy Award–nominated film *The Big Chill* (1983). The television drama *thirtysomething* (1987–1991) echoes several of the themes presented by *The Big Chill* as main characters Hope and Michael Steadman realize, with some discomfort, that they aspire to live more conventional lives than they had anticipated during their more radical college years.

In *The Big Chill*, *thirtysomething*, and other eighties-era movies, baby-boomer characters who came of age during the sixties have grown out of the counterculture and radical Left movements. Characters' decisions to abandon social justice causes to pursue more conventional careers and family life is portrayed as an inevitable process of maturation into adulthood. Characters in *The Big Chill* agree that their friend Alex could not function after the sixties because he continued to embrace radical values. Alex dies tragically as a consequence, as do similar characters Georgia in *Four Friends* and Susan in *Daniel*. Other films depict the post-sixties grown-up obliquely. In the action comedy *Bird on a Wire* (1990), a scene reveals that corporate attorney Marianne Graves was once a hippie chick when her ex-boyfriend chances to look up her dress and asks, "Since when did you start wearing underpants?" To remind audiences of the main characters' sixties-era background, the film's title is named after a Leonard Cohen song released in 1969 (Metcalf 1996).

A variation on the depiction of the former activist-turned-political-moderate is the portrayal of more conservative children of former sixties-era radicals. In the movie *Flashback* (1990), hijinks ensue when FBI agent John Buckner is assigned to escort a former sixties-era radical to stand trial for a crime that he did not commit. The film's plot twist is that Buckner himself was raised by hippies on a commune. In *Running on Empty* (1988), the adolescent son of two fugitives who bombed a napalm factory in 1970 shows more interest in music than in politics. His parents are in anguish when he decides to leave them to pursue a career as a concert pianist. One of the most well-known conservative characters of eighties-era television is Alex Keaton of *Family Ties*. While his parents attend nuclear proliferation protests and sing folk songs, Alex aspires to become a banker and work on Wall Street. By repeatedly depicting former activists who have outgrown their zeal for dissent and contemporary young people alienated by their parents' radical politics, these films and television programs contribute to the ideological common sense that radical dissent is a phenomenon that belongs in the past.

Certainly, my attention to these recurring character portrayals does not tell the whole story about how Hollywood has given meaning to the sixties for more contemporary audiences. Eighties- and nineties-era Hollywood has offered a variety of perspectives about the legacy of sixties dissent. While many movies portrayed baby boomers' youthful idealism as a perspective that dissipated as they entered middle-age, some films offered sympathetic treatments of characters' sixties-era values. John Sayles's *Return of the Secaucus 7* (1980) bears striking similarity to *The Big Chill* as it depicts the reunion of seven college friends during a weekend at a summer house in New Hampshire. However, unlike the baby boomers of *The Big Chill*, Secaucus's former radicals appear to have held onto their countercultural values even if they seem uncertain about how to enact these values a decade later. In *Field of Dreams* (1989), former hippies Ray and Annie Kinsella graduate from Berkeley and move to Ray's family home in rural Iowa. They are dismayed to find that most of the more conservative members of the community never "experienced even a little bit of the Sixties." Ray's desire to build a baseball diamond in the middle of a corn field is influenced by his sixties-era idealism. It is not clear that Ray ever learns to grow out of the sixties or that he should.

While *Return of the Secaucus 7* and *Field of Dreams* counter the image of the hippie-turned-yuppie, other movies depict adult children who develop newfound appreciation for their parents' sixties-era activism. A final scene of *Flashback* depicts Buckner on a motorcycle, headed out west to visit his parents. These movies suggest that the ideals of the late sixties continued to shape life in the eighties and are reflected in efforts of baby boomers and their children who question authority, seek alternative family structures, and defy convention. Likewise, films depicting the callousness of US military officials during the Vietnam War including *Full Metal Jacket* (1987) and *Born on the Fourth of July* (1989) convey lingering antiwar sentiment during the late eighties. The presence of positive depictions of characters who were influenced by late sixties activism illustrates how popular culture retains "oppositional potential" so long as audiences believe that governing institutions have ignored their interests (Lipsitz 1990, 12–13).

The diversity of films and television programs that portrayed late sixties counterculture, antiwar, and racial justice movements after the eighties attests to the ongoing relevance of sixties memory for contemporary culture and politics. Films *Forrest Gump* (1994) and *Across the Universe* (2007) and the miniseries *The '60s* (1999) portrayed fictionalized characters caught up in the tumultuous events of the decade. Their rock-and-roll soundtracks evince nostalgia for sixties-era music even as their narrative and character development advance conservative messages about the damaging consequences of late sixties dissent for families and national identity. In these three texts, women who are ambivalent about their radical commitments are bullied by macho militants; resisting the allure of militancy, these women return to the security of mainstream society and the nuclear family. More recent sixties-music-nostalgia-films *Taking Woodstock* (2009) and *The Music Never Stopped* (2011) illustrate ongoing efforts to capitalize off of the popularity of sixties-era rock music while avoiding serious attention to the decade's politics.

Post-seventies Hollywood and television have paid far less attention to the Black Power movement than it has to white radical movements of the late sixties. As Herman Gray (1997, 353–56) argues, prime-time television is invested in deploying the image of "the civil rights subject" that embodies neoliberal values of success, mobility, hard work, and individualism. As benefactors of the civil rights movement, this figure displaces and contains memories of black radicalism that highlight the failures of civil rights discourses for black communities plagued by persistent conditions of poverty and institutionalized racism. The relative dearth of images of Black Power activism highlights Hollywood's investment in whiteness and white audiences. Nonetheless, some movies have signaled ongoing public interest in late sixties-era claims for racial justice and self-determination for people of color in the United States. Spike Lee's biopic *Malcolm X* (1992) and Mario Van Peebles's crime thriller *Panther* (1995) positively portray Black Power activists' critique of the criminal justice system. More recently, the 2007 film *Talk to Me* depicts the career success and decline of charismatic disc jockey Ralph "Petey" Greene, who frequently expressed Black Power activists' critique of structural racism in the United States.

Other Hollywood films and television programs offset the sympathetic portrayals of Black Power by presenting limited one-dimensional portrayals of the Black Panthers. In a brief scene of *Forrest Gump*, the title character is confronted by a couple of Panthers who are too busy ranting about their ten-point program to notice that their white radical associate has smacked his girlfriend a few feet away from them. The Panthers object to Forrest's violence after Forrest punches the white radical. This scene contributes to a dominant memory of the Panthers that obscures and trivializes their claims for racial justice and structural change. In other movies and television programs including the movie *Barbershop 2: Back in Business* and episodes of television programs *Big Brother* and *Law & Order*, racial tensions and national division are attributed to radical black activists' rage, not to racial injustice, economic disparity, or racial profiling by law enforcement.

More recent films including the independent motion picture *Night Catches Us* and the major studio release *The Butler* have also portrayed Black Panthers as murderous thugs. In *The Butler*, tensions between main character Cecil and his activist son Louis mount when Louis joins the Black Panther Party. Their conflict is resolved after Louis concludes that the Panthers' agenda revolves around their willingness to kill white people and he leaves the organization. *Night Catches Us* provides a more developed depiction of the Panthers. In this film, former Panther Marcus struggles to move on with his life after he is accused of informing on a fellow Panther who murdered a police officer four years earlier. The film foregrounds police violence and harassment against the black community, but the conflict ultimately revolves around Marcus's efforts to protect loved ones from Jimmy, the only character who remains committed to Panther militancy. The film concludes when Jimmy fatally shoots a police officer and is shot to death by a squadron of police officers in return. Negative portrayals of the Black Panthers legitimate the political backlash against civil rights and Great Society legislation by molding the Panthers' image to symbolize the excesses of black activism.

While Hollywood's depictions of black radicalism are limited, its attention to other racial justice movement organizations including the Puerto Rican Young Lords and La Raza are virtually nonexistent. The film *Cesar Chavez* (2014) and the HBO movie *Walkout* (2006) are rare exceptions to Hollywood's amnesia regarding sixties-era Chicanx activism. A few movies sympathetically recalled the FBI's repression of the American Indian Movement (AIM). Michael Apted's 1992 movie *Thunderheart* portrays fictional FBI agent Ray Lavoi as he reconnects with his Sioux heritage during his investigation of a murder supposedly at the hands of the "Aboriginal Rights Movement," a thinly veiled reference to AIM. The agent realizes that his corrupt supervisor has framed the activists in order to prevent them from exposing a government land deal with a local mining company whose practices poisoned the reservation's water supply. The same year that *Thunderheart* appeared in theaters, Apted's documentary *Incident at Oglala* explored the events surrounding the shoot-out on the Pine Ridge reservation in South Dakota that resulted in the questionable conviction of AIM activist Leonard Peltier. Two years later, the TNT docudrama *Lakota Woman: Siege at Wounded Knee* drew from the autobiography of activist Mary Crow Dog to tell the story of AIM's activism and standoff with law enforcement during their 1973 occupation of the village of Wounded Knee, South Dakota (Reed 2005). The 2014 French film *The Activist* revisits the standoff in a melodramatic depiction of two AIM activists who are arrested during the occupation. These films provided cinematic countermemories of Native American dissent that challenged other nostalgic Hollywood images of the "noble savage."

White militant radicals who went underground after engaging in criminal activity have received ongoing attention in Hollywood. Groups including the Weather Underground and the Symbionese Liberation Army are routinely referenced. The animated half-hour comedy *The Simpsons* modeled the character of Homer Simpson's mother, Mona, after Weathermen activist Bernardine Dohrn (Oakley 2005). Most frequently, radical fugitives are depicted as wanted criminals suspected of murdering civilians or police officers. The murder rate by Leftist radicals is much higher in Hollywood's version of the sixties than it is in real life. In the movies *Running on Empty* (1988), *Sneakers* (1992), and *The Company You Keep* (2012), main characters are depicted sympathetically as they struggle with the consequences of their earlier activism; however, their less-sympathetic former associates feel little remorse for the deaths of bystanders and civilians. These portrayals complement television and film depictions in which radical sixties-era militants are caustic and cold, unconcerned with how their violent actions affect those around them.[11] Radical fugitives have been the focus of individual episodes of television police procedurals including *Hill Street Blues* (which ran from 1981 to 1987), *Law & Order* (1990–2010), *The Practice* (1997–2004), *Cold Case* (2003–2010), *Bones* (2005–present), *Life on Mars* (2009), and *The Chicago Code* (2011). In these programs, former radicals invariably deserve punishment for their radical antiwar activities and are often driven by selfish desires. These portrayals of radical fugitives teach viewers to be distrustful and suspicious of dissidents' motives.

Although Hollywood has provided an abundance of narratives about the perils of late sixties activism, the last fifteen years have shown renewed interest in cinematic countermemories of dissent. The biopic *Steal This Movie* (2000) and the animated docudrama *Chicago 10* (2007) are sympathetic depictions of Abbie Hoffman's spectacular antiwar activism. Likewise, an array of documentaries has favorably recalled the contributions of the counterculture, antiwar, and Black Power movements to social justice and collective empowerment. These films explore how people with little political or economic power have organized to create meaningful change and provide damning portrayals of FBI and police repression of nonviolent dissent.[12] Their radical nostalgia and condemnation of extralegal actions by law enforcement disrupt mainstream discourses that have characterized radicals as threats to national security and the public welfare.

Certainly, Hollywood film and television attention to late sixties dissent is not monolithic. Both independent and mainstream media have given fictionalized cinematic and televisual form to a variety of perspectives about the late sixties and to ongoing controversies about the social and political changes that emerged from the time period. However, the narrative patterns and character portrayals across multiple media texts illustrate how mainstream media have established the meaning of the late sixties around a variety of caricatures of activists: the hippie-turned-yuppie, the macho militant, the ambivalent activist, the angry black radical, and the deadly fugitive.

The following chapters in this book take up each of these caricatures to explain how their portrayals position dissent itself as a practice that should be consigned to public memory.

CHAPTER TWO

Growing Up from the Counterculture in *Family Ties* and *The Wonder Years*

For many of us who grew up during the eighties, the meaning of the sixties is comprised primarily of popular cultural images of antiwar dissent and free love. Popular family television programs including *Family Ties*, *thirtysomething*, and *The Wonder Years* featured countercultural characters whose lives were transformed by their participation in the anti–Vietnam War and free love movements. These family television programs are important resources of public memory because they are a source of commentary about contemporary politics and society. According to Lynn Spigel (1992, 154), the situation comedy has been "one of television's preferred modes for addressing the nation's families since the 1950s." As they depict family members' efforts to negotiate and resolve conflicts, these television programs responded to the social controversies that animated public life and politics.

On their surfaces, each of these programs might seem to provide a counterpoint to the broader political trends of the mid-eighties, a period many political pundits have lauded as the "Reagan Revolution." During his first term of office, President Ronald Reagan spearheaded the dismantling of several New Deal programs, the deregulation of the economy, and a policy of staunch anticommunism. Reagan's agenda was grounded in a policy of undoing the sixties (Marcus 2004; von

Bothmer 2010). Collapsing Johnson's Great Society programs with countercultural movements later in the decade, conservatives agreed that "the Sixties had been disastrous for the nation" (Marcus 2004, 39). For these conservatives, the sexual revolution, feminism, antiwar protests, hippies, and campus disruptions severely weakened America's character. Reagan's adherents deployed negative memories of the sixties counterculture as the basis for a new coalition united around values of Western Christianity, the nuclear family, military prosperity, and materialist ambition (Grossberg 1997, 232–43). Daniel Marcus (2004) argues that "Reagan was seen by supporters as embodying, or at least performing, the virtues of the pre-Sixties past, to which the United States should return" (61).

In contrast to political discourse that decried sixties-era values, *Family Ties*, *thirtysomething*, and *The Wonder Years* position relationships among family members within the context of characters' nostalgia for the late sixties. This chapter explains how the generational conflicts of several fictional families give meaning to the late sixties for eighties-era television and film audiences. These popular and critically acclaimed programs foregrounded characters' involvement in the New Left, feminism, and the counterculture to explain their motivations and conflicts with others. However, they reframed the meaning of these movements in ways that affirmed eighties-era neoconservatism. Over the course of multiple seasons, characters renegotiate their ideals to accommodate to the new political climate. This process of renegotiation rearticulated the memory of the sixties in the terms of the traditional values central to fifties nostalgia: the nuclear family, private life, and wealth consumption. Ultimately, these programs give televisual form to the assumptions of neoliberalism and postfeminism undergirding the Reagan revolution. Although the families of *Family Ties*, *thirtysomething*, and *The Wonder Years* gave expression to feminists and critics of neoliberalism who challenged breadwinner conservatism, they ultimately establish neoliberalism as a common-sense inevitability.

While Reagan's administration justified its neoconservative agenda as a reaction against the sixties, the popular situation comedy program

Family Ties gave audiences a narrative portrayal of a sixties-influenced family grappling with the decade's rightward political and social shifts. Airing from 1982 to 1989 on NBC, *Family Ties* featured the relational dynamics of the Keaton family, comprised of two former sixties-era activists and their more conservative adolescent children. While parents Elyse and Stephen reminisce about their radical college years, their children Alex, Mallory, and Jennifer wish their parents would just "grow up." A central point of humor is built around Elyse and Stephen's relationship with Alex, an avowed neoconservative who idolizes William F. Buckley. Although the show's creators initially intended to foreground the Keaton parents, Alex became the program's focus after the first season. Perhaps not surprisingly, Ronald Reagan claimed it as his favorite show on television (Blumenthal 1988, 275).

In 1988, the same year that Reagan's former vice president George H. W. Bush took over the Oval Office, the half-hour family comedy-drama *The Wonder Years* began its first of six seasons on ABC. Diverging from earlier programming in which characters living in the eighties look back nostalgically at the sixties counterculture, *The Wonder Years* is set in the context of the political and social turbulence of the late sixties and early seventies. The program foregrounds the perspective of adolescent Kevin Arnold, who lives in a middle-class suburb with his parents and two older siblings, Wayne and Karen. Most of the plots revolve around interpersonal conflicts between Kevin's friends and family members. Story lines in each episode are narrated through voiceovers of Kevin's reflections as an adult. Much of the program's attention to the decade's social and political conflicts is articulated via its depiction of Kevin's older sister Karen, who embraces countercultural values and wears hippie-style clothing. Just as *Family Ties*'s comedy revolves around the tensions caused by intergenerational conflicts between the Keaton parents and their more conservative children, Karen's frequent clashes with her World War II–generation parents is a frequent point of comedy and tension.

Featuring young adult male characters, *Family Ties*'s and *The Wonder Years*'s portrayals of white male adolescence corresponded to the shifting political currents during the Reagan revolution. In opposition to previous constructions of adolescent resistance to authority, these programs depict conservative or apolitical concerns as a rebellious break from previous generations. Thus, the programs periodize the eighties as a decade in which youthful individual self-interest and enterprise superseded concerns for the collective good or social justice.

In addition to discussing *Family Ties* and *The Wonder Years*, this chapter also considers the plot and character development of the television drama *thirtysomething*. This program ran on ABC from 1987 to 1991. Like *Family Ties*, *thirtysomething* is set in the context of the eighties. *Thirtysomething* depicts a group of baby boomers who befriended one another in college through their involvement in the counterculture and antiwar movements. The program revolves around the daily activities of married couple Michael Steadman and Hope Murdoch as they adjust to their suburban middle-class lives. Michael sacrifices his goal of becoming a novelist to work for an advertising agency, while Hope leaves her job as a consumer advocacy journalist to raise her daughter from home. Michael and Hope share the Keaton parents' gnawing anxiety that they have sold out their sixties-era ideals to embrace bourgeois family values.

The narratives of each of these programs negotiate liberal and conservative values through the conflicts between the characters who fondly reflect on radical sixties-era activism and those who disparage late sixties-era idealism and dissent. Although they provide sympathetic portrayals of characters profoundly influenced by the New Left and the counterculture, the narrative and character development of each program provides a welcoming environment for the decade's political and economic shifts. Across many seasons, multiple episodes in each program suggest that political ideals of pacifism, feminism, and anarchism are concomitant with the sixties decade itself, and is thus passé in the eighties. Characters portraying former activists realize that the practical values of wealth accumulation and participation in the nuclear family trump impractical ideals of social justice and equality. By suturing radical politics and activism to the sixties decade, these programs encourage audiences to temper or dismiss enthusiasm for progressive movements and causes.

THE POLITICS AND RHETORIC OF AMERICA'S TELEVISION FAMILIES

There is some paradox in situation comedies that take the sixties counterculture as a central point of its humor. One of the counterculture's main points of departure from mainstream culture was its rejection of middle-class conventions of nuclear family life. For hippies and freaks, free love was an expression of one's authenticity and individualism. Sexual relationships unrestricted by expectations of monogamy, marriage, and procreation freed them from the repressive conformism of mainstream society. Yet, these conventions have defined the sitcom genre. Programs such as *Father Knows Best* and *Leave It to Beaver* typically included "a suburban home, character relationships based on family ties, a setting filled with middle-class luxuries, a story that emphasizes everyday complications, and a narrative structure based on conflicts that resolve in thirty minutes" (Spigel 1992, 136). The family situation comedy genre was influenced by shifts in public consciousness embraced by the sixties-era counterculture. As Ella Taylor (1991) explains, social conflicts from the sixties and the collapse of the World War II consensus were expressed in seventies-era programs in the "troubled family" of the Bunkers of *All in the Family*. However, this influence was blunted by new challenges to countercultural ideals in the ensuing decades.

During the eighties, social conservatives objected that the family sitcoms of the 1970s tarnished the image of the traditional family that had been constructed by earlier television programs. Conservative commentator Allan Carson (1980, 74) lamented that programs such as *One Day at a Time* and *Three's Company* represented the "decline of the nuclear family and the rise of 'nontraditional' family forms and single life." Political leaders also lambasted the influence of popular culture in shaping public attitudes toward the family and the nation. In his 1989 farewell address, Reagan opined that people older than thirty-five years "grew up in a different America" in which a variety of institutions including family, neighborhood, school, and popular culture taught them "what it means to be an American." Reagan elaborated that "the movies celebrated democratic values and implicitly reinforced the idea that America was special. TV was like that, too, through the mid-Sixties.... But now we're about to enter the Nineties, and some things have changed.... [F]or those who create the popular culture, well-grounded patriotism is no longer the style" (Reagan 1989). Carson's and Reagan's criticisms put television on the front lines of the cultural war over the meaning and structure of family life in the United States.

Amid conservative calls for a cultural revival of "traditional" American values, the nuclear family was "rediscovered as a premise for broadcast television programming" (Dow 1996, 96). *Family Ties* and *The Wonder Years* negotiated the trends of prime-time family situation comedies of the fifties and sixties and the "troubled families" of the seventies. The resurgence of the nuclear family on television occurred in tandem with neoconservative political movements that touted "family values" as central to national stability. Robert Self (2012) argues that the neoconservative movement's emphasis on "family values" helped to legitimate neoliberal policy. Sixties social movements provoked the rise of breadwinner conservatism that was premised on the position that the policies arising from feminism and the Great Society had "cast the nuclear family as in crisis" (5-6). The Reagan and Bush administrations regularly appealed to family values to warrant the dismantling of Johnson's Great Society programs. Reagan set the pace for the neoliberal practices during the Clinton and Bush era through his emphasis on budget cuts and deregulation, the reversal of policies favorable to labor, and revisions of the tax code to allow many corporations to avoid paying taxes. Such policies were justified by the premise that personal satisfaction could ultimately be found in the private sphere of consumption and family life.[1]

Given the nuclear family's centrality to the rhetoric of the Reagan revolution, television programming centered on the nuclear family became an important resource for debating the merits of neoliberal politics. While Reagan reported that *Family Ties* was his favorite television program, it was popular among other audiences as well. Between 1984 and 1988 the program consistently rated among the top three in the Nielsen ratings. In 1987, the *New York Times* reported that it was one of the most watched programs in the history of television, taking second place to the *The Cosby Show* (Greely 1987, 1).

Michael J. Fox won three Emmys for his performance as Alex Keaton between 1986 and 1988. The *Wonder Years* did not reach the same audience as *Family Ties* but also received solid ratings and critical acclaim during the span of its six-year run, receiving the Emmy for Outstanding Comedy Series in 1988.[2] That same year, *thirtysomething* won the Emmy for best drama series. *Thirtysomething* would go on to win twelve more Emmys during its four-year run. These programs' popularity and critical acclaim suggest that their messages and themes resonated with television audiences. Through references to the sixties counterculture, these programs interpreted and participated in the broader political and cultural controversies about the family and government responsibility to support particular idealized visions of family life. As these television programs responded to changing expectations of family life articulated by the counterculture and the ensuing conservative backlash, they also offered instruction about how we might think about these expectations as well.

THE NEOLIBERAL ANTIPOLITICS OF ALEX KEATON AND KEVIN ARNOLD

The most significant characters who facilitated selective amnesia about sixties social movements in *Family Ties* and *The Wonder Years* are the programs' central protagonists Alex Keaton and Kevin Arnold. Neither of these main characters seemed particularly troubled by the political events occurring around them. Although secondary characters of both programs evolved over the course of multiple seasons as they negotiated between mainstream and countercultural value systems, Alex and Kevin's political orientations remained relatively stable. Alex never questioned his political commitments, and Kevin did not seem to have any political commitments at all. By featuring characters disengaged from the politics that animates their family members and friends, these programs consigned the radical Left to the margins of public memory.

Family Ties's Alex is a caricature of the neoliberal citizen. This is also a basis for much of the program's humor. Alex is adorably befuddled as he applies market logics to his family members' aspirations. He continually attempts to maximize the profitability of friends and family members' achievements. This character presents a vivid illustration of Wendy Brown's characterization of the neoliberal subject as an entrepreneurial actor in every sphere of life. In contrast to the model of the citizen seeking to create social change through public engagement and protest, the model neoliberal citizen is one who "strategizes for her/ himself among various social, political and economic options" (Brown 2003, para. 15). The prominence of neoliberal characters such as Alex Keaton in popular film and television contributes to a climate in which the notion of public life itself loses its meaning; subjectivity becomes constituted through practices of profit-seeking, consumption, and the imperatives of instrumental rationality.

Although Alex embraces entrepreneurship, things never go quite as well as planned. His friends and family members articulate strong resistance to Alex's neoliberal logics. Frequently, his efforts to maximize profits result in failed projects and hurt feelings. The lessons highlighted at the conclusions to most of these episodes are almost always framed in terms of the family's well-being; Alex learns that he needs to respect the wishes and values of his siblings, friends, and parents. However, this lesson never carriers over to the next episode. Alex is never deterred from pursuing his ambitions of wealth, an obvious and intrinsic good. He pursues business school at a prestigious university, takes a series of internships at regional banks, and continues to berate his friends and family members for pursuing interests that are not directly marketable. At the series' concluding episode, the Keaton family wishes Alex farewell as he makes plans to pursue a business career on Wall Street.

While Alex Keaton is a neoliberal subject, Kevin Arnold is what Lauren Berlant (1997) might refer to as an infantile citizen. Kevin's political subjectivity is "based on the suppression of critical knowledge and a resulting contraction of citizenship to something smaller than agency: patriotic inclination, default social membership, or the simple possession of a normal national character" (27). The opening monologue of the pilot episode of *The Wonder Years* cues audiences toward a depoliticized understanding of the decade. The opening voiceover from Kevin as the adult narrator explains what was most important to him at the time of the events depicted on the nightly news: graduating from elementary school and growing up in the suburbs. As images cut from news footage to kids playing in the front driveway of his suburban neighborhood, Kevin-as-narrator refers to the early to mid-sixties as "the golden age for kids" and describes the summer before the start of junior high school as his "last summer of pure unadulterated childhood." The monologue encourages audiences to understand the end of the decade from the pre-political perspective of adolescent Kevin, who is aware of but largely removed from the year's political upheavals. Although several episodes open with stock images of contentious and traumatic events from the decade, the narrator routinely admits none of these events actually mattered to him at the time, nor does he suggest that they matter to him now.

The program's focus on the intimate space of the home is the real scene of agency for the program's characters. Throughout the series, the politics of the sixties, including the war in Vietnam, is positioned as ambient noise in the background that Kevin tunes out in order to focus on the issues that really mattered to him: pursuing relationships with girls and finishing school. While Kevin is aware that antiwar exists, such dissent is largely invisible. Instead, the relationship among friends and family members within Kevin's suburban neighborhood is the site of political intrigue and significance. This theme is acute in the first episode of the final season in which Kevin's concerns about war revolve around the "war between the sexes" and a rival high school. From the vantage point of Kevin, suburban American life during the sixties is invested in the same concerns that animated people during the fifties. *The Wonder Years* were *Happy Days* after all. By framing the decade's political turmoil as virtually irrelevant to Kevin and his friends, the program is a rebuke of the commemorative retrospectives and journalism coverage of sixties social movements that constructed the meaning of the sixties as a harbinger of social change. Rather than extend the memory of social justice dissent, *The Wonder Years* gives televisual form to the imagined communities that Nixon articulated in his references to the great "silent majority." The program cues audiences to remember the style and political turmoil of the decade as it dismisses activists' calls for social justice, civil rights, women's liberation, the end of Western imperialism, and participatory democracy. Thus, *The Wonder Years* remembers sixties-era politics in order to teach audiences to forgo political commitments.

HALTING NOSTALGIA FOR ANTIWAR AND FREE SPEECH DISSENT

Although characters Alex and Kevin are unconcerned about the issues that animated the New Left, neither *Family Ties* nor *The Wonder Years* entirely dismiss characters' admiration for sixties-era protest movements. In some ways, these programs appeared to offer a politically balanced depiction of the late sixties counterculture and antiwar movements. Edward Morgan (2010, 271) remarks that *Family Ties* "provided ideological balance in which viewers could laugh at whichever character was the greater butt of the joke in their own ideological frame." Conflicts between the Keaton parents and their children articulated liberal and conservative attitudes toward the decade, thus appealing to a wide audience. While the program appealed to conservative audiences through the depiction of Alex, it appealed to liberals through its positive portrayal of antiwar dissent and free speech activism. Similarly, conflicts between Kevin's parents and his sister offered conservative and liberal perspectives on the political and social conflicts of the late sixties. Main characters of *Family Ties* and *The Wonder Years* voiced support for sixties-era protest movements as an important form of civic engagement in a democracy. However, these characters' participation in protest events were purely episodic and framed as fanciful attachments to ideals that had little meaningful consequences for politics or society. Characters wistful but distant attachment to the sixties offered halting nostalgia for protest movements that looked favorably upon participation in moderate dissent via marches and sit-ins, but positioned more confrontational methods of protest and appeals for fundamental social and economic change as illegitimate and dangerous.

Two episodes during the first season of *Family Ties* illustrate how halting nostalgia for late sixties dissent was written into the program's narratives. Episode 7 of season 1 revolved around Elyse and Stephen's participation in an antinuclear-arms protest rally and subsequent arrest on Thanksgiving Day. Several cues suggest that the Elyse and Stephen's antinuclear-arms stance was rooted in their experiences protesting the Vietnam War. Before the protest rally, Elyse explains to Jennifer that the meaning of "flower power" "was another way of telling people to put down their weapons and give each other flowers and love instead." In jail, Elyse and Stephen remember when they were arrested in Washington, DC, for protesting "the war." Their nostalgia for antiwar dissent is not shared by the judge presiding over their case who tells Elyse and Stephen that they will be released if they pledge to never participate in a nuclear-arms protest again. The Keaton parents refuse. The episode concludes as Alex, Mallory, and Jennifer decide that they should support their parents for standing up for their beliefs and bring dinner to their jail cell. This early episode of *Family Ties* provides the series' most overtly sympathetic depiction of progressive, albeit moderate, activism.

Later episodes offer more ambivalent portrayals of dissent. In episode 21, Jennifer embraces her parents' enthusiasm for protest and insists on delivering a report about Huckleberry Finn despite her school board's ban of the book. When Jennifer is suspended from school, Elyse and Stephen hire a former Berkeley college friend, now attorney, Susan "Raindrop" White, to represent Jennifer at the school board hearing. Both Raindrop's name and her relationship with Jennifer's parents are a focus of the episode's humor; a laugh track follows Elyse and Stephen's revelation that Raindrop was born on a commune that they had lived on before they settled into suburban family life. The episode concludes when Jennifer learns that her dissent motivated a faculty-wide walkout until her suspension was revoked.

Although Jennifer is more engaged in liberal-oriented politics than her older siblings, a generational divide still separates her from her parents. Jennifer is a reluctant dissident throughout the episode. When her father remarks that she is "off to a great start as an activist," Jennifer responds, "No, I think I'm going to retire, Dad.... I had no idea it would be so hard." Later, a local high school newspaper calls her for an interview, and she tells Alex to tell the paper she isn't at home. And when her grandmother calls, she gruffly tells her that she is sick of talking about the issue. One of the lessons of this episode is that, for adolescents coming of age during the eighties, protest is exhausting and unrewarding.

The Wonder Years similarly offers halting nostalgia for antiwar protest and free speech activism. The first season introduces limited sympathy for the antiwar movement through its portrayal of Louis, who is dating Kevin's sister Karen. During episode 4, Karen introduces Louis to her family. Louis is among a variety of nonrecurring radical characters who appear in particular episodes of eighties-era television programs. Unrelatable and often caustic, these throwaway characters facilitate other characters' distance from and distaste toward the radical Left. As the program provides only a limited explanation of Louis's politics, he functions to humanize and explain more moderate main characters' motivations.

In the episode's beginning voiceover, Kevin tells viewers that Louis is a "college radical." Multiple visual cues highlight Louis's membership in the counterculture, as the screen image below indicates. Louis drives a psychedelic painted Volkswagen bus with peace symbols painted on the back and wears torn blue jeans with the American flag patched on the left cheek, long hair, round glasses, a leather vest, and a loosely buttoned shirt. He organizes marches against the war on his college campus and has an open relationship with Karen and another girl named Marisa. Louis doesn't eat meat and implies that Norma's work as a housewife is unfulfilling. (Louis's concern here problematically conflates antiwar and feminist movements. Given that the male New Left was notorious for assigning domestic duties to movement women, Louis's feminist perspective contradicts historical accounts of campus antiwar organizing in 1968.)

During dinner, Louis and Jack fight about the purpose of Vietnam and American values. Louis suggests that the supporters of intervention in Korea and Vietnam are brainwashed. He is a somewhat empathetic character during this scene as he explains to Jack that his motivation is to prevent the deaths of himself and other young men like Jack's sons Kevin and Wayne. This scene negotiates between prowar and antiwar sentiments; opposition to the war is given a hearing as one among multiple acceptable perspectives. However, Louis's

Karen and her countercultural boyfriend Louis reject monogamy, patriarchy, and the Vietnam War. "Angel," *The Wonder Years*, April 5, 1988, ABC.

perspective is backgrounded to Jack's because Louis's antiwar sentiments are only aired during this episode. Further, Louis's credibility is tarnished by his cavalier attitude toward Karen, as I elaborate in a further section of this chapter.

Although the episode lends legitimacy to the anti–Vietnam War movement on the basis of its threat to American soldiers' lives, it positions Kevin's doubt and political moderation as the most relatable response. As the program's narrator, Kevin is the "voice of reason" who is perplexed by Louis's arguments. Speaking as the adult narrator, Kevin explains that he remembers being confounded by the interaction between Jack and Louis. "Who was right and who was wrong? Well, I'm supposed to be an adult now and I still can't completely figure that one out."

Later episodes of *The Wonder Years* also provide halting nostalgia for antiwar activism on the basis of the war's toll on American lives. In season 5, Kevin's older brother Wayne enlists in the army in order to win his parents' respect. The episode's opening scenes feature video news footage of bomb missiles falling from the sky and an aerial view of trees bursting into flames. Adult Kevin's monologue reminds audiences that in 1972 "the war was still raging... people kept dying and no one seemed to know why." One might wonder how even an adult Kevin has remained unaware that US officials believed that fighting communism in Southeast Asia was in the United States' political and economic interests. That Kevin still remembers that no one seemed to understand the war indicates that no one, including his parents, ever discussed it with him. Even as an adult, Kevin has remained an infantile citizen. Although they never discuss the war with the family, Jack and Norma are devastated to think that their son might be sent to combat in Vietnam. Fortunately, Wayne fails his physical examination, and his parents are relieved. This conclusion amplifies the program's efforts to avoid serious reflection on the political turbulence of the sixties; by making Wayne ineligible to serve, the Arnold family is not forced to confront the disastrous consequences of US foreign policy.

In contrast to their sympathetic treatment of moderate opposition to the Vietnam War, *Family Ties* and *The Wonder Years* depict radical activists' objections to imperialism and outrage over the deaths of Vietnamese people with derision. During episode 10 of season 2, Kevin's junior high school student council supports a student body walkout in opposition to the war. The walkout is initiated by an older and more radical student, Mark, who decries "the immoral, imperialistic colonialist oppression of the People's Republic of Vietnam by the running dog lackeys of the fascist US government." Mark is a reductive stereotype of the radical sixties protester, even more alienating than Karen's boyfriend Louis from season 1. Given that the program never provides an explanation for his remarks, Mark's jargon seems trite, clichéd, and bizarre, which distances him from more moderate and relatable characters. When Mark continues to critique imperialism during a planning meeting, his faculty advisor tells him that he is going into "a coma." The advisor asks the students to explain their decision to walk out "in their own words." Mark is at a loss for what to say. Presumably, his rhetoric is just empty sloganeering. Finally, Kevin replies, "A lot of people were getting hurt and it didn't seem to be doing anybody any good." Kevin's reasoning is rather childlike for his early adolescence. As was the case in earlier episodes of the program, this episode eschews developed criticisms of the war. The lack of attention to the political commitments of antiwar activists throughout the episode obscures the antiwar movement's commitment to social justice. While Jennifer of *Family Ties* is a reluctant activist in one episode, Kevin in *The Wonder Years* is an accidental one. Although Kevin is excited about the prospect of the walkout, he does not want it to appear "on his permanent record." When the time comes to walk out, Kevin darts into the bathroom instead. To his surprise, his classmates mistakenly believe that he has left the building in protest, and everyone marches outside. By framing the impetus of the walkout as a case of mistaken intentions, the episode disavows the political agency of student protesters.

The episode's halting nostalgia for antiwar dissent is reinforced in the final scene in which Kevin wistfully recalls the campus walkout as a moment of camaraderie with his classmates. Despite the principal's warning that any student who walks out would be penalized, the entire student body participates. The last scene provides an aerial shot of hundreds of students on the football field, many of them linked arm in arm, singing, "All we are saying is give peace a chance." The episode concludes as adult Kevin explains what the memory of walkout means to him now. "I suppose the war would have gone pretty much the same if we had stayed in our homerooms but one thing would be different. We wouldn't have had the memory to carry with us today of 800 children on a football field singing." The episode's closing monologue articulates nostalgia for student protests in terms of the camaraderie it established among members of Kevin's junior high school class. The nostalgic closing monologue suggests Kevin's experiences with collective organizing and protest ended in early adolescence. By emphasizing that the student walkout was personally meaningful for students but politically inconsequential, the closing monologue frames the antiwar movement in largely privatized terms that were a hallmark of eighties political culture.

Echoing themes in *Family Ties*, the monologues by adult Kevin highlight the virtues of political tolerance as it reveals that Kevin grew up to be politically open-minded, even though he has never quite formed any clear political investments. Politically tolerant but lacking any real commitments, Kevin Arnold provided a model of citizenship that was ideally suited to neoconservative politics. For conservatives seeking broad-based support for their legislative agenda, the image of the tolerant moderate helped to position political liberalism as the source of intolerance and as a threat to civil society.

FORMER HIPPIES EMBRACE YUPPIE VALUES

A central theme across *Family Ties*, *thirtysomething*, and *The Wonder Years* is that left-of-center politics and activism was part of an adolescent stage of development peculiar to people who came of age during the sixties. It is politics, not age, which characters learn to outgrow. Conflicts between characters reveal that radical Left ideals are incompatible with nuclear family life. As characters abandon their political ideals to marry and raise children, the programs craft a privatized vision of adulthood. *Family Ties* and *The Wonder Years* address the legacy of the sixties counterculture for family life by featuring profound social differences between parents and their adolescent children. Disagreements between children and parents over politics and social values are designed to produce laughter and act as the driving force for each episode's narrative arc. The idea of the generation gap illustrated in the programs has its history in sociological literature about the late sixties counterculture itself. Commenting on the social divisions arising as a consequence of the youth counterculture, Theodore Roszak (1969, 34) concluded in 1969 that "technocratic America produces a potentially revolutionary element among its own youth. The bourgeoisie, instead of discovering the class enemy in its factories, finds it across the breakfast table in the person of its own pampered children." Family sit-coms that foregrounded the generation gap supported oft-articulated assumptions in public culture during the eighties that dissent itself is a stage of adolescent development rather than an expression of one's political commitments.

The comedy surrounding *Family Ties* revolves around its transmutation of Roszak's formulation, for the children are now adherents of the Reagan revolution, much to their parents' chagrin. Elyse and Stephen represent the counterculture's crisis during the eighties. A recurring joke on *Family Ties* is that Elyse and Stephen need to grow up; their idealism is as adolescent as their teenage children. The point of humor across multiple episodes foregrounds the Keaton parents' hapless attempts to inspire their children with the same spirit that animated them when they were young adults. The parents cannot bridge the generational divide. The first episode revolves around the conflict that emerges when Alex wants to attend an event at a country club that does not allow black members. Although Elyse and Stephen forbid it, Alex attends the event. Stephen disrupts the country club dinner and embarrasses both himself and his son. Later that evening, Stephen tries to explain himself and admits that he is struggling to recognize Alex as capable of making his own decisions. Alex reproaches his father: "I'm not you, Dad. We're two different and separate people." Then, Alex asks, "Think this kind of thing is going to happen again?" The screen capture below depicts the heartfelt moment that follows after Stephen comes to terms with his son. Stephen sighs and reaches out to shake Alex's hand, "I don't know. We're both getting older. One of us is bound to grow up sooner or later."

The lesson of the series' first season is that the sixties have lost their relevance to the generation of young adults coming of age under the Reagan administration; former activists must reconcile their enthusiasm for the counterculture with this reality if they are to maintain a connection to their children. Indeed, *Family Ties* is not about the coming of age of Alex or his sisters Mallory and Jennifer, for these characters' attitudes and behaviors never really change. Over the course of the program's seven seasons, it is Elyse and Stephen who seem to "grow up." They begin thinking critically about their commitments to the New Left and observe that their increasingly moderate political stance is a reflection of their own process of maturing and their commitment to family. Changes to the opening credits in the program's second season announce the characters' shifting political mindset. As I elaborate in the first chapter, the opening credits to *Family Ties* signal the program's attention to the legacy of the sixties counterculture by displaying a series of faux photographs depicting

Stephen comes to terms with his son Alex's decidedly conservative values. "Pilot," *Family Ties*, September 22, 1982, NBC.

Elyse and Stephen at protest events and getting married in an informal outdoor ceremony. Throughout the photographs, Elyse wears love beads and flowers in her hair. In place of these images, season 2's opening credits feature clips of the family from season 1 crosscut with an image of their family portrait above the fireplace. In the portrait, Elyse's love beads are replaced by a string of pearls. As the seasons of *Family Ties* progress, the program offers the lesson that dissent is a form of youthful indiscretion that must be transcended.

By season 5, Elyse and Stephen come to terms with the way that their children have moderated their own political outlooks. In episode 4, Stephen discovers that his values have become more centrist than he had realized after an old college-era friend Matt invites him to restart the newspaper they began in Berkeley. Even before Matt arrives to visit them, Alex reminds his parents that their activist days were juvenile. Observing their old "Ban the Bomb" banner that they hung above the fireplace in anticipation of Matt's arrival, Alex quips, "Every time one of those ex-hippies comes prancing in from yesteryear, we've got to get out the love beads, pretend we care about people. I'm just a little too old for that." Stephen embraces his new role as editor of the revamped newspaper, but is dismayed by Matt's advocacy of anarchism as an alternative to bipartisan politics. He complains to Matt that the article preaches "stale rhetoric" and that "times have changed." Stephen is adamant, "Things aren't as black and white as they used to be!" In response, Matt and the other members of the newspaper fire Stephen. Matt is a reductive stereotype of the sixties radical. His insistence that the paper be committed to revolutionary politics is a foil for Stephen's more moderate and relatable political stance. Presumably, Matt is unable to grow up. The program never elaborates on Matt's position, and he does not appear again on the program. Thus, while Matt appears to be out of touch with contemporary politics (and is generally unpleasant), Stephen is the program's moral center. Matt is a throwaway character who prompts the maturation process of the Keaton parents.

Dejected after being fired, Stephen returns home and asks Elyse if she still respects him. Elyse responds, "You make a statement by the way you live your life, by the way you raise your children, by choosing a job that doesn't compromise your principles. Those are political acts, as strong as anything you did back in Berkeley." By foregrounding Stephen's role as a father and worker, Elyse articulates a neoliberal concept of choice that relegates all worthwhile activity to the private spheres of work and family. The individualized actions of raising children and choosing a career are the only politics that matter. After Stephen's talk with Elyse, Alex comforts his father by telling him, "Even though we haven't agreed on anything yet, I respect your ideals and the fact that you respect mine." The program offers paradoxical lessons for audience members sympathetic to the Keaton parents. On the one hand, the program advocates political open-mindedness. Just as Elyse and Stephen must accept their son's political choices, the political Left must respect the decade's rightward political shifts. Tolerance for difference is an imperative for both home and politics committed to the democratic pluralism. On the other hand, such tolerance need only be extended to groups committed to mainstream politics. Matt's anarchism, his rejection of the two-party system, is an outmoded relic of the sixties. The depiction of Stephen as more open-minded than Matt helps to render radical critiques of mainstream politics outside of the sphere of legitimate consideration. The Keaton parents' acceptance of Reaganism and the paradoxical construction of political tolerance extols an anemic model of progressivism. The imperative to be open to Reaganism suggests a pathway for former critics to accept neoliberalism. By constructing radicalism as outside of the bounds of political tolerance, the program advocates a rightward shift to the political spectrum's center. Further, as the program celebrates political tolerance, it invites audiences sympathetic to Elyse and Stephen to get over their own nostalgia for radical social change. Ostensibly, peace and stability requires us to "let go" of old orthodoxies.

Learning to accept neoliberal values of free-market capitalism is a recurring theme in eighties popular culture. In *thirtysomething*, characters express anxiety over pursuing private goals of material wealth and nuclear family life. The television drama was loosely inspired by the 1984 motion picture *The Big Chill*, a movie that focuses on the internal conflicts among baby boomers who worry that they have "sold out" to embrace yuppie values.[3] As Jane Feuer (1995, 60–81) explains, characters of *thirtysomething* routinely expressed "yuppie guilt" for sacrificing their sixties-era political consciousness in favor of financial success. Across multiple episodes, main characters Hope Murdoch and Michael Steadman fret about their decisions to live a conventional nuclear family lifestyle despite their earlier participation in the counterculture. Michael laments that he has "sold out" by choosing a career in advertising. Radical sixties jargon is briefly used to give levity to a scene in the program's first season. In episode 3, Michael dreams that he is on trial for being a "profit mongering capitalist" with an "insatiable quest for corporate hegemony." The costume and set design of the dream scene announce that Michael's anxiety is rooted in his nostalgia for the sixties. In this scene, Michael's jury wears long hair, headbands, and bandanas. A poster of a raised fist appears in the background. Michael's friends testify that he has become "ideologically corrupt." His business partner Elliott declares that Michael is "merely a dupe of the yuppie imperialist elite." This scene pays homage to Roger Corman's hippie exploitation film *The Trip*. In this earlier movie, main character Paul, played by Peter Fonda, becomes high on LSD and develops anxiety about his career as a director of television commercials. Paul watches himself standing trial as his countercultural friend Max declares him guilty of spreading lies. Nick Hefferman (2015, 9) observes that "the annihilation that Paul fears is not literal but symbolic, that of his bourgeois self, threatened with disintegration as a result of the insight generalized by the psychedelic experience." In *thirtysomething*, Michael's anxiety is the reverse of Paul's; he fears losing his countercultural identity for the trappings of a bourgeois lifestyle. During the rest of the episode, Michael's concerns are subsumed by efforts to host a housewarming party with Hope. Although his yuppie guilt is never entirely resolved, Michael puts his misgivings aside and focuses his time and attention on his advertising business and family life throughout the program's four seasons.

Yuppie guilt and the image of the yuppie itself are rooted in selective amnesia of the sixties. Central to the narratives surrounding yuppie culture is the image of a former activist who has abandoned leftist political commitments in pursuit of material wealth. This caricature draws from news coverage surrounding Jerry Rubin's new career as a stockbroker in 1980. In an op-ed page of the *New York Times*, the former cofounder of the Yippies called upon readers to "make millions of dollars together" and "make capitalism work for everyone" (Rubin 1980, A21). Four years later, *Newsweek* magazine declared 1984 "the year of the Yuppie" (Adler 1984, 14). The magazine's extended article on the subject reinforced the image of the yuppie as a former sixties radical who has embraced the individualism and materialism of the eighties. Its opening paragraph speculated that "the banker who was horrified in 1968 when Columbia students occupied the president's office will not necessarily be reassured to discover that one of those students now has an M.B.A. and an office down the hall from him, and is full of plans for streamlining the headquarters staff" (14). The article imagines the hippie-turned-yuppie as a leader in neoliberal economic policy with visions of making businesses more profitable by eliminating jobs for workers. A quote from "onetime Columbia radical James Kunen" supports *Newsweek*'s assertion that former sixties activists have turned their energies "inward, on lives, careers, apartments and dinners" (14). Kunen explains that yuppies like himself "were upper-middle-class white kids who were used to getting what we wanted ... I really felt strongly about the strength of our will—that if we wanted the bombing stopped it would stop" (14).

The hippie-turned-yuppie articulates cultural anxieties over fundamentally opposed value systems embodied by the sixties activist and the eighties entrepreneur; however, the yuppie is a social construction more than an actual demographic category. Feuer (1995, 67) notices that characters depicted in programming including *thirtysomething* were too young to have taken part in late sixties-era social movements. Further, the image of the upwardly mobile urban professional belied the downward economic mobility of the baby-boom generation of the mid-1980s (Adler 1984, 14). Feuer (1995) argues that the yuppie was a social construct mobilized for political and economic purposes. During the Reagan years, the major networks were not so much interested in "pure" yuppie demographics as they were in constructing *yuppie* spectators for advertising (58). Thus, the hippie-turned-yuppie facilitated new modes of advertising directed toward middle-class consumers who came of age during the sixties. Early use of the term "yuppie" in the mainstream press emphasized "the continuity of the baby boom generation from a period of social protest to a period of concentration on corporate upward mobility in the 1980s" (43).

In *thirtysomething*, Michael's yuppie guilt is exacerbated by his left-leaning college-era friend Gary, who chides Michael for prioritizing his family and his business over his friendships and political concerns. Sneering at Michael's more lucrative career in advertising, Gary chooses a career as an English professor at a local university. Gary is the idealistic (and sexist) counterpart to the mature and responsible Michael. The contrast between the two characters is marked by a variety of aesthetic and narrative cues. In contrast to Michael's short hair, Gary's hair is long, blond, and wavy. While Michael typically wears a crisp white shirt and suspenders, Gary's favorite item of clothing resembles a letterman's jacket. The program marks Gary's countercultural values and style as a sign of his own emotional immaturity and inability to get over the sixties (Feuer 1995, 78). Throughout season 1, he appears unable to maintain committed romantic relationships with the women he sleeps with. This creates conflict between Michael and Gary because he routinely seduces and then abruptly distances himself from Michael's younger sister Melissa.

As the program's narrative revolves around Michael and Hope's daily lives, Gary is positioned as the well-intended but misguided bachelor who needs to grow up. Near the end of season 1, Gary is denied tenure because he could not navigate the politics of the academy. Here, Gary's failure illustrates the financial costs of maintaining sixties-era commitments in the eighties. Unlike Stephen's unwavering anarchist friend Matt in *Family Ties*, Gary follows a path to maturity in the following seasons, culminating in his marriage to Susannah and the birth of their daughter in season 3. Perhaps not surprisingly, Gary's political investments appear to decline as he develops stronger commitments to his family.

Through their portrayal of characters who learn to let go of sixties' idealism for the sake of bourgeois family life, *Family Ties* and *thirtysomething* promulgate the popular misconception of the rightward shift of the baby-boom generation as its members reached middle age. The idea that former activists turned to the right during the eighties is an ideological construction that periodizes the eighties in terms of its neoconservative politics. However, the image of the hippie-turned-yuppie draws upon unrepresentative stereotypes of the baby-boom generation and leftist dissent. While most members of the baby-boom generation did not participate in the New Left or the counterculture, sixties-era activists maintained left-of-center political commitments, even though they tempered their expectations for revolutionary social change after the mid-1970s (DeMartini 1983; Jennings and Neimi 1981; Whalen and Flacks 1989). The hippie-turned-yuppie naturalizes new modes of consumption and neoliberal policies during the eighties despite declining economic fortunes of people who came of age during the sixties.

RADICAL FEMINISTS INVEST IN THE NUCLEAR FAMILY

Television programming in the eighties also suggested that baby-boomer women needed to outgrow their involvements with second-wave feminism. In *The Wonder Years*, Kevin's older sister Karen learns to outgrow her participation in the sixties counterculture and radical feminist movements. In the pilot episode, Karen wears a leather vest with long bead-covered fringe, strappy sandals, dangly earrings, and long hair. When their mother complains that Karen didn't come home in time to help her with dinner, Karen tells her that she has "bad karma." Later that evening, Karen fights with her parents. As footage of the war appears on the television behind the dinner table, Karen announces her plan to purchase birth control pills, and her father Jack is enraged. Conflicts over dinner between Karen and her parents give televisual narrative form to Roszak's observations about the social divisions that arose during the late 1960s as a consequence of the youth counterculture. The program literalizes Karen's alienation from her family; speaking as the adult narrator, Kevin comments in episode 4 of the first season that Karen had turned into "something stranger than an alien from space." Her embrace of countercultural values destabilizes the family's home life and is a constant source of tension between family members. Fights between Karen and her parents articulate the tensions over sexuality and authority that were a hallmark of countercultural resistance to the nuclear family. However, over the course of the series' first five seasons, Karen's life transforms to closely resemble her parents.

An early glimpse into Karen's impending political and social transformation is provided during episode 4 of season 1. Although she had advocated for an open relationship with her boyfriend Louis during the first half of the episode, Karen expresses her discomfort with it in the episode's final scene. She wails, "I knew you were in love with her, but I didn't know you two were sleeping together!" Heartbroken, she breaks up with Louis. The scene's humor draws from the contradiction between Karen's behavior and her dissident rhetoric; she cannot embrace free love because she ultimately wants to be monogamous.

Contradictions between Karen's political philosophy and her personal desires drive the humor of subsequent episodes. In season 2, Karen cannot dissent against a corporate development despite her objections to it because it conflicts with her dating life. In a memorable scene, Kevin and his friends seek Karen's guidance in order to prevent the woods near their house from being torn down. At first, Karen is indignant. "This is a democracy, isn't it? Exercise your rights. ... There's a planning board meeting every Sunday night downtown. Julie's dad is a member. You should go there and state your case! You should demand to be heard. You should fight for what's important." Visual and aural cues suggest that Karen's rhetoric belies her real commitments. While she is speaking, Karen searches for articles of clothing in her closet and on the floor. At one point, she bends over and tosses articles of clothing in the air. Then, Karen's voice rises as she looks directly at the camera, "You have to take action. Kevin, we are the people." Kevin responds enthusiastically, "Great! Let's go! Can you give us a ride?" Karen stops abruptly with furrowed brows. "Not me! I got a date." Although Kevin and his friends manage to attend the planning board meeting in spite of Karen's refusal to help them, they are unable to prevent the demolition. During the episode's conclusion, the program flashes forward to people shopping in the mall constructed on the woods' grounds later that year. Adult Kevin narrates the scene, informing audiences that he and his family spent many days shopping in that strip mall in the following years. Unsupported by his idealist sister, Kevin exchanges his enthusiasm for green space for the comforts of consumption.

Karen's ambivalence toward countercultural values is most pronounced toward the end of season 5. In this season, Karen has moved out of her parents' house and is cohabitating with her latest boyfriend Michael, much to her father's chagrin. In episode 21, Karen breaks up with Michael because he has asked her to marry him. She explains to her parents, "Marriage is an antiquated, male-centered institution AND I don't believe in it." When her parents look at her quizzically, she adds, "Look, it's very simple. I don't want to spend the rest of my life making meatloaf and mashed potatoes." Karen's statement is an indictment of her mother, who had just finished putting that exact meal on the table. The narrator Kevin comments to the audience. "You'd think a marriage proposal would bring a family together, but this was 1972. Things had gotten very complicated."

Karen's initial hesitation evokes radical second-wave feminist concerns about patriarchy within the nuclear family. However, the program's acknowledgment of feminism is quickly undercut by Karen's decision to propose to Michael at the end of the episode, which illustrates the program's efforts to negotiate between liberal and conservative family values. When Karen insists that she does not want to get married and make meatloaf, her parents do not argue with her; ostensibly this is her choice that must be honored. Karen's decision to make the proposal signals her own autonomy and agency, and it poses some challenge to conventional gender roles. However, Karen's feminist persona never materializes in any meaningful way. The program provides insight into Karen's character only through her relationship with the men in her life. Although we learn that she does not want to cook meatloaf, we do not learn what her goals and aspirations are exactly. Thus, Karen never fully adopts the counterculture ideals that the program associates with her because she is primarily invested in the pursuit of heteronormative romance. Ultimately, participation in the nuclear family structure is where Karen's comfort and satisfaction really lies.

The Wonder Years's treatment of Karen illustrates Elspeth Probyn's (1990) description of new traditionalism as the alternative to feminism in the 1980s. While affirming women's rights to employment and career advancement, the new traditionalism "naturalizes the home into a fundamental and unchanging site of love and fulfillment" (Probyn 1990, 152). It presumes that given the available options, women would clearly choose to invest time in the home. The new traditionalism marks an early iteration of postfeminist messages in popular culture that inverted the meaning of choice to cast women's decisions to reclaim traditional gender roles as a feminist expression of agency (Coppock 1995; D'Acci 1994; Dow 1996; Tasker and Negra 2007; Vavrus 2007). Such postfeminist appeals are rooted in a simultaneous acknowledgment and dismissal of second-wave feminism. As Bonnie Dow (1996) notes, eighties television disavows the implications of feminism even after it implicitly acknowledges feminism's influence on family life. By depicting Karen's decision to embrace the nuclear family as a process of maturation, *The Wonder Years* frames second-wave feminism as a stage of female adolescence. Yet, it also positions Karen's decision as beyond question; presumably, she could choose otherwise. The portrayal of Karen illustrates how practices of selective amnesia are embedded within postfeminist discourse. While they co-opt the rhetorics of women's choice, such discourse distracts attention from and delegitimizes radical feminists' critique of patriarchy in the home.

According to *The Wonder Years*, even countercultural women find ultimate fulfillment in their roles as girlfriends, wives, and mothers. This lesson is amplified in the season 5 episode that positions Karen's choices within the context of a "hippie-style" wedding. Karen is a countercultural bride. She doesn't want the priest to say "man and wife" and prefers "man and woman." Instead of holding the ceremony in a church, she and Michael decide to have an Eastern-inspired wedding in their backyard. The Arnolds arrive at the rehearsal dinner at Karen's house to find sitar music playing in the background. Two attendees at the wedding are named Rainbow and Wind. They both have long hair, and Norma has trouble determining whether Rainbow is a woman's or a man's name. Rainbow wears a tie-dyed button-down shirt over a tie-dyed t-shirt and small framed glasses. Wind wears a garland of baby's breath in her hair. The sitar music punctuates or signals the comedic situation. On the surface, this episode seems to celebrate countercultural values of peace, love, and community. Kevin as narrator reflects that "Little by little we were drawn into Karen's world. For the first time in a long time I saw Mom and Dad smile."

Although the scene elicits nostalgia for free love and women's autonomy, the episode is ultimately about how traditional values subsume countercultural ideals. Norma's uncertainty about the couple's gender identity is designed for comic effect, but it also trivializes feminism's critique of gender norms as oppressive to women and taps into conservative anxieties about feminism's threat to traditional gender roles. Both the counterculture and mainstream culture find common ground in celebrating Michael and Karen's wedding. Michael trades his motorcycle for a Volkswagen van. (Viewers paying close attention to the program might have recognized it as the same van that her boyfriend Louis drove in the first season, marked by its psychedelic paint job and peace symbol painted on the back. Just as Elyse Keaton trades her love beads in for a string of pearls in the second season of

Family Ties, Michael paints over the van's peace symbol with a dark shade of green.) Karen's father Jack is now enthusiastic about Karen and Michael's relationship because the two are legally married. The point of conflict of the episode revolves around Karen's decision to move with Michael to Alaska to pursue work in construction, but no attention is drawn to the consequences of this decision for Karen's life.

Karen's membership within the counterculture is central to the postfeminist narrative about her marriage and move to Alaska. As Karen leaves the program to follow her husband's career, feminism and the counterculture exit the program as well. She does not appear again on the program until the last five minutes of the series finale that features her pregnant with her first child. Karen's resistant values and feminist ideals appear as temporary as her fringe leather vests, tie-dyed t-shirts, and strappy sandals. Clearly, Karen has disregarded both the counterculture's and second-wave feminism's critique of the nuclear family. One lesson is that the counterculture and feminism were temporary hallmarks of the decade, akin to fashion that has since gone out of style. By linking Karen's countercultural styles to her stance against marriage, radical second-wave feminism's critique of patriarchy within the nuclear family itself is periodized, framed as passé and irrelevant.

Thirtysomething's main character Hope Murdoch also exchanges her countercultural ideals for the new traditionalism. A former flower child, Hope leaves her career as a consumer advocacy journalist to raise her infant daughter. Initially, Hope expresses ambivalence over her decision to leave her career. She frequently reminds friends and family members that raising baby Jane is the most enriching aspect of her life, but it seems as though Hope may be trying to convince herself of this as well. In the middle of the first season, she attempts to return to her job as an investigative journalist for a consumer protection magazine. She struggles to juggle competing demands on her time and receives a poor performance review from her employer. Despite her enthusiasm for exposing environmental hazards, she decides to quit her job to commit herself to her family. After the end of a particular grueling day at the office, Hope tells Michael she would rather stay at home. Michael admits that is his wish as well. In the episode's final scene, Hope cradles her daughter and appears blissful. The scene illustrates Probyn's (1990, 149–52) observation that women's career pursuits in *thirtysomething* are framed as viable options, but women's ultimate satisfaction derives from their roles as nurturers and caretakers.

None of the other female characters in *thirtysomething* presents a compelling counterpoint to Hope's embrace of neotraditionalism. Hope's best friend Ellyn is unsatisfied with her life despite her professional success. After she receives a promotion in the series' pilot episode, Ellyn admits to feeling jealous of Hope. Likewise, Hope's sister-in-law Melissa obsesses over her desire to have a baby despite her exciting career as a freelance journalist and hip urban loft apartment. Since both Ellyn and Melissa seem to idolize Hope's marriage and daughter, the program implicitly suggests that women who decide to pursue careers over family life are likely to deeply regret their decisions.

Thirtysomething's embrace of new traditionalism gave televisual form to print media discussions about "cocooning," or the trend of women who left the paid workforce to stay at home to raise their children. Much like the concept of the yuppie, "cocooning" is a cultural construct more than a sociological phenomenon. According to Susan Faludi (1991, 84), women's participation in the workforce rose steadily for women in the eighties, particularly among mothers. Faludi's interview with one of the show's creators Edward Zwick indicates that the program's celebration of new traditionalism was rooted in his disdain for the influence of second-wave feminism on family life and women's aspirations. Zwick explained that "[t]his is a generation of women who, upon their adolescence, suddenly encountered Germaine Greer and Betty Friedan and they were told, 'No, no, wrong, wrong. This way. Take a *left* turn'" (my emphasis). Zwick concluded, "what they are discovering upon having the kid itself is there are some extraordinarily strong biological, and not just biological, attachments or bonding that superseded politics and rhetoric" (Faludi 1991, 163). Although Zwick asserts that the depiction of Hope reflects a natural state of female experience that is beyond politics, Zwick's critique of the second-wave's left-leaning politics is grounded in the politics of the eighties. Indeed, Zwick's own rhetoric and embrace of new traditionalism puts neoconservative fantasies on the small screen.

Both *The Wonder Years* and *thirtysomething* encourage audiences to develop sentimental attachments to characters like Hope Murdoch and Karen Arnold precisely because these women learn to put the counterculture and feminism behind them.

THE NEOCONSERVATIVE TEMPLATE FOR SIXTIES-ERA NOSTALGIA TELEVISION

The resolution of tensions between family members and friends with divergent attitudes toward the counterculture in *Family Ties*, *thirtysomething*, and *The Wonder Years* instructs audiences that countercultural challenges to traditional ideas about the nation and the nuclear family must be abandoned. The programs also suggest that such challenges might be overcome as characters resolve their personal and relationship conflicts through their embrace of domestic, private life. As they foreground the virtues of private wealth and the nuclear family, these programs depict social justice struggles as relics of the past. One implicit lesson across each of these programs is that political organizations rooted outside of the electoral system have no legitimacy in a democracy, rendering feminist and pacifist concerns moot.

The family values constructed across these programs naturalize the neoconservative politics of the Reagan and Bush years by teaching viewers that the counterculture and feminism were youthful indiscretions and that political moderation is a central component of reaching adulthood and raising children. Even if it is for a worthy cause, dissent offers limited personal rewards. By positioning these lessons within narratives about the legacies of the counterculture and protest, sixties iconicity is leveraged to negate the value of dissent in the eighties.

During the same years that *Family Ties* and *The Wonder Years* aired, one of the most successful family situation comedy programs of all times, *The Cosby Show*, also reinforced the values of political moderation and relative quiescence. While the former programs offered halting nostalgia for the white antiwar Left and counterculture, the latter provides few memorable images or cues pointing to the surge of radical black activism that occurred during the late sixties. As I explain in chapter 4, *The Cosby Show* contributes to the selective amnesia of the black freedom struggle that is crafted through the valorization of what Herman Gray (1997) refers to as the "civil rights subject" (353). Across each of these programs, tensions within the nuclear family are the primary obstacles to personal satisfaction, and individual fulfillment is found through an embrace of middle-class lifestyles, personal responsibility, and career achievement.

These programs established narrative and stylistic conventions that are repeated in the following decades in fictional programming and film featuring sixties radicalism. Hollywood's fascination with the bad sixties is not isolated to the Reagan and Bush Sr. years; its dismissive portrayal of sixties protest movements continues into the following decades and under both Democratic and Republican administrations. During Clinton's second administration, the sit-com *Dharma and Greg* revolved around a seemingly mismatched couple who get married despite markedly different family backgrounds. Rather than feature generational disputes, conflict between characters are driven by class and ideological differences. While Dharma's parents still embrace the counterculture, Greg's parents embrace neoconservativism. Reductive stereotypes of the Right and the Left are played against each other to draw laughs; nonetheless, the program extends the selective amnesia of the radical sixties. Dharma's countercultural beliefs are continually proven wrong while Greg's decisions reflect good common sense. Family television in the eighties thus provided a starting point for Hollywood's ongoing selective amnesia of the sixties counterculture. As the next three chapters explain, this fascination took on a variety of forms in the nineties and into the next millennium in several films, a television miniseries, and television crime dramas.

CHAPTER THREE

Good Citizens, Ambivalent Activists, and Macho Militants in *Forrest Gump* and *The '60s*

Hollywood film and television memories of the sixties were important sites of ideological struggle during the cultural wars of the nineties. In 1991, Oliver Stone promoted his film retrospective of Jim Morrison, *The Doors*, by announcing, "the Sixties are back." Stone's remark prompted conservative pundit George Will (1991, 66) to respond. In his regular *Newsweek* column, Will retorted, "the Sixties are dead." For Will, the sixties was just "nostalgia kitsch junk among the clutter in the nation's mental attic." He concluded that the decade should be remembered for "the narcissism it engendered among young people" who were captivated by the "juvenocracy of rock" (66).

Will was not alone in his condemnation of pop culture's promotion of liberalism and sixties-era dissent. Dan Quayle (1992) garnered extensive press attention after he famously excoriated fictional television character Murphy Brown for having a baby out of wedlock. Quayle connected the program's image of Brown's single motherhood to the rise in black families headed by single mothers, even though the sit-com's title character was a career-driven, upper-middle-class white woman. Here too, Quayle focused blame on the sixties and the "Baby Boomers" who "declare[d] war against traditional values," "glamorized casual sex and drug use," and "evaded responsibility and trashed authority" (2). Quayle concluded that while the middle class had the resources to survive the sixties, many of the poor did not. His solution? Cut taxes and "empower" the poor by attaching work requirements for welfare benefits. As Quayle's remarks highlight, conservatives' fight to roll back New Deal and Great Society legislation hinged on advancing a negative interpretation of the sixties and on attacking media portrayals for shining a favorable image on feminism, nontraditional families, and rebellion against authority.

Popular culture portrayals of the sixties and sixties-era liberalism was a prime target of criticism for religious conservatives who blamed the sixties for the breakdown of the traditional family structure. Collapsing the liberal politics of the Johnson administration with the radicalism of the counterculture, feminism, antiwar movement, and gay liberation, the religious right vowed to protect family values against the immorality of the sixties. In 1994, Newt Gingrich promoted his *Contract with America* by appealing to conservative disdain for the "Great Society, counterculture, and McGovernick" legacy (Dowd 1994; Gingrich et al. 1994). Describing President Bill Clinton as a "card carrying member of the '60s counterculture," Gingrich called for a new model of "moral leadership" modeled after a pre-sixties American past. He explained, "until the mid-1960s, there was an explicit long-term commitment to creating character.... It was the work ethic. It was honesty, right and wrong. It was not harming others. It was being vigilant in the defense of liberty." Since then, he noted, society had become "extraordinarily tolerant of violence" and people had let their own personal concerns override their commitments to others (Dowd 1994; Fineman 1994, 24).

References to the bad sixties advanced dubious connections between Johnson's Great Society programs and the counterculture and antiwar movements. Even moderately liberal policies were tarred with the brush of sixties-era excess. Promising a return to the earlier values of the pre-sixties past, the religious right proposed an agenda aimed at rolling back or obstructing liberal domestic programs including government-supported child care, reproductive rights, antipoverty measures, and workplace rights for people of color, women, and lesbians and gay men.

Given conservatives' ongoing disdain for Hollywood, it is perhaps surprising that the Academy Award for Best Picture in 1994, *Forrest Gump*, did not come under fire. Instead, House Speaker Newt Gingrich and presidential hopeful Patrick Buchanan hailed *Forrest Gump* as a cinematic condemnation of liberal sixties-era values. Gingrich described it as a "reaffirmation that the counterculture destroys human beings and basic values" (Barnes 1995, 4–5). Gingrich's praise positioned the movie as an important weapon in the culture war. *Forrest Gump* is perhaps one of the most recognizable fictionalized depictions of the sixties of the past three decades. It received strong critical acclaim and commercial success. In addition to its Oscar for Best Picture, it won Academy Awards for Best Actor for Tom Hanks, Best Director for Robert Zemeckis, Best Adapted Screenplay for Eric Roth, Best Visual Effects, and Best Film Editing. The Golden Globes also gave the film the Best Motion Picture award and awarded Hanks and Director Robert Zemeckis for their work. Earning $317 million in box office sales, *Forrest Gump* was ranked in 1995 as one of the top-ten most commercially successful films of all time and was the first film among that list to win an Academy Award ("Oscar" 1995, 1A). The film's popular success propelled the nostalgia market for sixties memory products.

Six years later, a three-hour NBC television movie, simply titled *The '60s*, explicitly capitalized on nostalgia for the decade. Like its predecessor, the movie depicted defining events of the decade through the perspectives of several fictional participants. The CD music industry influenced the development of both *Forrest Gump* and *The '60s*, as their cross-promotion with soundtracks featuring sixties-era rock music contributed to their sales and profitability. *Forrest Gump*'s soundtrack went platinum and was listed as one of the top-100 CD sales of the nineties. Taking a cue from the success of earlier sixties-oriented film soundtracks, NBC executives' decision to create the *The '60s* was influenced by its potential for revenue from the soundtrack (Carter 1999a, C10; *St. Petersburg Times* 1999, B2; Levin 1991, D3; Schneider 1999, C1). The TV movie originally aired on NBC in 1999, receiving the highest ratings for a miniseries during that television season (Carter 1999b). NBC sold the cable rights to VH1 before it reran the series for a second time that summer (Hontz 1990; *St. Petersburg Times* 1999, 2B).[1] It has reappeared on cable television since then and ran as recently as 2010 on MTV's "Movies that Rock" series. Although cultural conservatives like George Will were surely appalled by the popularity of these soundtracks, they might have found something valuable in *The '60s*'s portrayal of countercultural dissent. Like *Forrest Gump*, the miniseries blamed the sixties for the breakdown of the traditional family.

This chapter explains how *Forrest Gump* and *The '60s* transcoded the public controversies over family values through narratives about characters caught up in the late sixties-era counterculture, antiwar, and Black Power movements. Both the movie and the miniseries foregrounded interpersonal conflicts between recurring character types: the good citizen, the ambivalent activist, and the macho militant. Viewers are prompted to sympathize with the good citizen, whose political moderation evinces an idealized model of citizenship suited to the political climate of the nineties. The good citizen runs into conflict with the macho militant, a reductive stereotype of a radical dissident that is less nuanced and complicated than the good citizen. Both characters vie for the affections of the ambivalent activist, a young woman torn between the earnest good citizen and the passionate macho militant. As these characters express divergent perspectives about radical dissent, what happens to them entails judgments about their politics and activism.

Beyond obvious connotations attributed to the good citizen and the macho militant, the conflict between these characters is an allegory for contestation regarding masculine national identity in the wake of sixties-era challenges posed by women, GLBTQ+ communities, and people of color. Tension between the good citizen and the macho militant over the affection of the ambivalent activist parallels broader ideological conflicts that animate the debate about the viability of the heteronormative nuclear family. The good citizen represents an idealized vision of mainstream political and social institutions that were challenged by sixties-era claims on behalf of marginalized and exploited groups, and the macho militant stands in for radical threats to those institutions.

The ambivalent activist symbolizes the imagined nation itself. Lacking political agency of her own, she is the object of masculine desire. By extension, she is the stakes of ideological conflict over national identity in the wake of challenges to the post–World War II consensus. The ambivalent activist also reveals how women's bodily autonomy was the focus of debate and political struggle during the nineties-era culture wars.

Through my analysis of the narratives and character development in *Forrest Gump* and *The '60s*, I explain how Hollywood has provided symbolic resolution to conflicts regarding the meaning of sixties dissent and to ongoing debates over the traditional nuclear family and women's roles. I argue that both the movie and the miniseries depict the trajectory of the sixties as a quest for national reconciliation and the return of white masculine authority rather than one of political change and newfound political agency among women, people of color, and GLBTQ+ communities. The film and miniseries reinforce the conservative anxiety that traditional womanhood was degraded by radical organizers and countercultural values. I conclude that the lessons of *Forrest Gump* and *The '60s* hinge on selective amnesia of black radicalism, second-wave feminism, and gay liberation activism that challenged the quiescent vision of the nuclear family that these motion pictures ultimately restore.

THE CONSERVATIVE VISION OF THE BAD SIXTIES IN *FORREST GUMP*

Forrest Gump depicts several decades in the life of the film's namesake, a naïve but well-intended man who witnesses many of the defining events of US history between 1954 and 1982. Despite his below-average intelligence, Forrest Gump thrives as a star college athlete, soldier, and business owner. In the process, he improbably comes into direct contact with several cultural icons including Elvis Presley, John Lennon, and Abbie Hoffman; he also meets Presidents Kennedy, Johnson, and Nixon. Humorously, Gump's offhand remarks and actions influence the course of US history. For instance, Gump's claim that people in China "never go to church" inspires Lennon's lyrics to the popular song "Imagine."

A variety of cues signal the narrative's relevance to public memory of the sixties. Filmmakers' visual effects incorporated Gump's character into iconic scenes of political and social significance including George Wallace's 1963 stand against racial integration of the University of Alabama and the 1968 anti–Vietnam War protest at the US Capitol. In several scenes, Tom Hanks's body is digitally included into archival news footage; elsewhere, recreated scenes such as the march on the Pentagon replicate events that have been extensively covered by the national press. These digital techniques and other cues cultivated baby boomers' nostalgia for the decade through the eyes of the title character who observed the decade's turbulence from a distance, thus inviting a bipartisan audience into the film's narrative.

The film's aesthetic nostalgia for the sixties should not imply its affirmation of the decade's protest movements. Robert Burgoyne (2003, 220–37) notes that the film's use of digital effects enabled the film to reprocess history in ways that dovetailed with nineties-era conservative and reactionary movements. For instance, it reconstituted John Lennon's appearance on the *Dick Cavett Show* from the 1960s by integrating Forrest into the scene. The effect transformed the meaning of Lennon's song, originally a critique of materialism, nationalism, and religion, into an affirmation of American values. This scene is a representative example of the broader processes of selective amnesia in nineties-era Hollywood. Popular culture has routinely disarticulated baby-boomer nostalgia for countercultural music and the rock icons who created them from the celebration of free love and pacifism and articulated this nostalgia to the celebration of capitalism and traditional family structures.

Forrest Gump vividly illustrates Hollywood's penchant for constructing images of the past that are absent of or transcend political conflicts. As Thomas Byers (1996, 421) observes, the movie empties out the histories of national division on one hand and rewrites on the other. The film's depoliticized vision of contemporary US history is constructed through its use of first-person narration by the film's title character. Forrest Gump never articulates any political investments, nor does he seem particularly impressed by his experiences. His only emotional investment is in pursuing a romantic relationship with his childhood friend Jenny Curran. Jenny routinely resists Gump's affections and disappears from his life for years at a time to pursue a career in folk music, peace activism, and single life detached from long-term romantic commitments. Toward the last third of the film, Jenny inexplicably decides to live with Forrest in his secluded family home in Greenbough, Alabama. One evening, the two make love before Jenny slips out of his life again. In response, Forrest decides to start running across the country for three years. After he has tired of running, Forrest comes home to learn that he and Jenny have a son together. The two marry a few months before Jenny dies of an unspecified illness that we are led to presume is AIDS.

Although he never expresses a political position, *Forrest Gump*'s title character provides the film's most obvious rejection of the radical sixties. Gump is a unique protagonist of a narrative propelled by the public memory of national traumas and social unrest. Unlike other programs that feature main characters' ambivalence regarding late sixties politics, Gump is incapable of having broad conceptual thought or political consciousness. Early in the film, we learn that Forrest has a far lower than average IQ that disqualifies him for public school. It is only after his mother agrees to have sex with the school principal that he is allowed to attend. Ostensibly, Forrest does not have the mental acuity to reflect upon the implications of the dramatic events unfolding around him.

Sharing several characteristics with the adolescent Kevin Arnold of television's *The Wonder Years*, Gump is also an infantile citizen; his virtues draw from his inability to consider his subjectivity outside of the private spheres of family and the home (Berlant 1997, 181). Lauren Berlant (1997) explains that the infantile citizen is a political subjectivity that is at once simple and complex. It reduces citizenship to patriotic sentiment and yet speaks to an idealized belief in the state's commitment to serving the best interests of the polity. The infantile citizen may elicit derision from those who recognize that faith in the state is naïve, but it may also elicit admiration and nostalgia from those very critics who recall an earlier moment in which they themselves may have held a utopian image of the nation. Hollywood's vision of the bad sixties is buttressed by nostalgia for the infantile citizen; whereas the former elicits memories of national trauma and violence, the latter provides a soothing alternative in which political investments are ancillary and even antithetical to national belonging. As the bad sixties emerged as an image of unacceptable civic engagement during the eighties and nineties, the infantile citizen developed as a norm of national citizenship.

Gump inhabits the virtues of an infantile citizen who expresses naïve faith in the nation and enacts his citizenship by taking personal responsibility for himself and his family. He protects and cares for his friends and his mother, and he honors his promises. A variety of cues including Tom Hanks's performance, the musical score, the soundtrack, and the bucolic imagery of Gump's family plantation all elicit sentimental attachment to Gump's life story and celebrates his naïve response to public affairs. In the absence of political motivation, Gump follows rules and orders literally. In doing so, he unwittingly participates in a variety of political and social movements. During the integration of the University of Alabama, Gump notices that one of the new students has dropped her school book, so he picks it up and hands it to her, unaware of the implications of his action. Later, Gump wins a Congressional Medal of Honor for unflinchingly rescuing several soldiers in his platoon. Afterward, he is accidentally involved in an antiwar rally because a rally organizer mistook him for a participant. Gump complies with the organizer's request that he tell the throng of protesters about his experience in Vietnam. The viewing audience cannot hear what Gump has said, but the main speaker, a caricature of Abbie Hoffman, is deeply moved. As a good—yet infantile—citizen, Forrest Gump is a likable and loyal friend and family member.

Gump's lack of political interest is highlighted during his cross-country run. News reporters run alongside him with microphones in hand, eager for a sound-bite that explains his behavior. Different reporters ask him if he is running for "world peace," "the homeless," "women's rights," "the environment," or "animals." Forrest insists that he was running "for no particular reason." Clearly, Forrest has no interest in the liberal activist causes inspired by the sixties counterculture.

The film's sentimental depiction of a character who consistently denies having political motives and is solely committed to his friends and family members enacts a privatized model of citizenship suited to the neoliberal politics of the mid-nineties. Indeed, much of the political fervor against welfare recipients that anticipated the cutbacks in government assistance to poor families in 1997 focused on the scourge of absentee fathers. The father who failed to provide child support was routinely brought up as a key explanation for poverty in black urban communities. During his stump speeches in 1992, then presidential candidate Bill Clinton exhorted fathers to take responsibility for their children, noting that "governments don't raise children, parents do" (Cloud 1998b, 404). As Dana Cloud (1998b, 404) observes, the rhetoric of family values that foregrounded parents' responsibilities to their children absolved the government's role in ensuring the welfare of its citizens. Gump's dedication to his son, even though he is introduced to him only when Jenny is near death, is a model of paternal authority and commitment. Furthermore, his loyalty to his friends and family provides him with the resources to raise his son comfortably. He inherits his mother's Georgia plantation home and earns a fortune after his good friend and fellow Vietnam War veteran invests money from their shrimp boating business in Apple computer stocks. Gump is the image of success that conservatives have trumpeted: he thrives financially because he knows people who will do anything for him and he achieves greatness without government support or intervention. It never even occurs to him that any such support might be warranted.

The movie's sentimental portrait of Forrest Gump contrasts with its more severe depiction of Jenny, Forrest's romantic interest and ideological foil. While Gump is satisfied to live in his small hometown, Jenny moves to Berkeley, California, after a brief time in college. She pursues a career as a folk singer, engages in antiwar activism, and experiments with a variety of illegal drugs. Further, she expresses no interest in having a traditional nuclear family. She proposes marriage to Gump only after she has become terminally ill. Clearly, Jenny has embraced countercultural values of drug use, free love, and women's liberation from traditional family roles. In addition to her support for the social movements of the New Left and the counterculture, Jenny appears to lack Forrest's discipline and loyalty. She pursues a career as a folk singer after she is kicked out of college for appearing in *Playboy* magazine. Her aspirations only lead her to a job as a stripper; her shtick is that she plays folk music in the nude. Years later, she works as a waitress at a diner. She has numerous short-lived romances with a variety of men. Clearly, she cannot commit to a job or to another person. Jenny also disregards Forrest, the one person who consistently treats her with dignity and respect.

While Forrest is the ideal citizen, Jenny is an ambivalent activist. Her story characterizes conservative messages about moral degradation that follows from embracing sixties-era values. During his infamous speech excoriating fictional television character Murphy Brown for having a child out of wedlock, Dan Quayle lamented the "poverty of values" of the sixties generation for whom "indulgence and self-gratification seemed to have no consequences" (Quayle 1992, 2). Amplifying the image of the counterculture's self-indulgence and irresponsibility, Jenny's actions appear selfish and nihilistic. After a night of partying at a disco club, Jenny contemplates suicide. Wearing gold platform heels, she climbs onto the handrail of a balcony of a high-rise building. Moments later she pulls herself down and collapses into tears. In his editorial for the *Pittsburgh Post-Gazette*, conservative politician and news commentator Pat Buchanan described the film's depiction of Jenny as a commentary about the moral turpitude of the late sixties counterculture and antiwar movements. Comparing her life of "sadness and sorrow" to Forrest Gump's "fidelity and faith," Buchanan concluded that "the way of life this film holds up to be squalid and ruinous is the way of Woodstock" (Buchanan 1994, B3). Jenny's nontraditional lifestyle does not appear to offer her any joy or fulfillment. By focusing on Jenny's involvement in the counterculture as the first among a series of life events that led her to despair, Jenny is the imagistic icon of conservative anxiety about the decline of traditional family values.

As Jenny's history of sexual experimentation is juxtaposed with the tumultuous events of the decade, the film suggests that the country itself has deteriorated alongside the decline of traditional womanhood. Jennifer Wang observes that Forrest is an "eternal representative of the 1950s," and "Jenny represents the 1960s." For Wang, the film's message is that "when a country loses control of its white women . . .

all hell breaks loose" (Wang 2000, 97). Although I largely agree with Wang, I would slightly revise this formulation to note that Jenny is less an image of the sixties than the site of struggle over American values itself.

Jenny's status as an image of the sixties is undercut in part by her own lack of political agency. As soon as she is old enough, Jenny leaves Alabama to overcome the childhood memory of her sexual abuse by her alcoholic father. Her antiwar dissent is one among several of her efforts to overcome her childhood trauma, and she never expresses any political beliefs. The lack of dialogue about antiwar politics or the free love movement helps to position Jenny's activism as a pathological response to personal trauma, not as a political stance.

One scene midway through the film punctuates Jenny's apolitical and pathological involvement in the movement. In this scene, Jenny and Forrest reunite after Jenny spots him at an antiwar rally. Jenny brings Forrest to the Washington, DC, chapter headquarters for the Black Panther Party and introduces Forrest to her boyfriend Wesley as the leader of Berkeley's chapter of the SDS. The screen image below reveals the tense relationship among the three. Although Forrest is clearly more interested in speaking with Jenny, one Panther member confronts Forrest and lectures him about the "racial onslaught of the pig who has brutalized our black leaders, raped our black women, and destroyed our black communities."[2] Little additional information is offered to explain the Panthers' position, and Forrest is clearly only interested in what is happening to Jenny.

As this scene illustrates, *Forrest Gump*'s conservative political memory of the late sixties is achieved, in part, through a narrative that evacuates all political motivations from its depiction of the antiwar and Black Power movements. The film provides shallow context to understand Wesley's and the Panthers' criticisms of the war and police brutality. Wesley is a condensation symbol of a variety of historical figures known for their militant activism against the Vietnam War. His clearest historical referent is Jerry Rubin, leader of several antiwar actions in Oakland and Berkeley, California, before founding the Youth International Party, or Yippies, with Abbie Hoffman in 1967. Rather than elaborate on Wesley's political commitments,

Forrest Gump confronts Jenny's abusive boyfriend while the Panthers observe from a distance. *Forrest Gump.* DVD. Directed by Robert Zemeckis. Hollywood, CA: Paramount Pictures.

the film highlights Wesley's abusive behavior toward Jenny. Shortly after meeting Gump, Wesley forcefully smacks Jenny across her head. Enraged, Forrest throws Wesley to the ground and punches him until Jenny intervenes. In one of the more memorable quotes from the film, Forrest then faces a group of stern-faced Panthers and apologizes to them, "Sorry I had a fight in the middle of your Black Panther Party." Seen through the eyes of Forrest Gump, who is incapable of political consciousness, the Black Panthers are unintelligible; thus, their presence in the film exists solely to serve as a humorous quip to interrupt the horrors of Wesley's callous violence toward Jenny. Of course, the joke only works if audience members recognize that the Black Panthers were a political organization. However, the film never suggests that the Panthers' cause merits consideration.

In addition to making them appear politically alienating, the film suggests that the SDS and the Black Panthers threaten white women's safety by articulating domestic violence to militant antiwar dissent. Wesley apologizes to Jenny the next day for hitting her and blames his act of violence on his anxiety about the war and "that lying son of a bitch Johnson." Audiences are positioned to see through Wesley's feeble excuse. Forrest reminds Jenny that he should not have hit her. The film reinforces Jenny's lack of agency in the scene when she leaves Washington, DC, with Wesley despite his abusive and demeaning behavior. Given Jenny's background as a survivor of childhood assault, Wesley's violence is part of a broader pattern of abusive male relationships in her life.

By articulating Jenny's abuse to countercultural values, the film reverses and thus negates the significance of second-wave feminism for women's lives and the nuclear family. The film's depiction of a male radical as violent toward women obscures the conditions of domestic violence such as patriarchy within interpersonal relationships and the family that gave rise to second-wave feminism's attention to patriarchy within the home. The second-wave slogan, "the personal is political," drew attention to the ways in which issues affecting women's lives inside the nuclear family were political problems that required feminist organizing and collective action. *Forrest Gump* reverses the second-wave's politicization of personal life by depicting Jenny's own political investments as personal. Despite her enthusiasm for the counterculture and antiwar movements, the feminist movement seems to have escaped her. The solution to her traumatic life story has nothing to do with securing rights for survivors of abuse or creating policies to protect vulnerable children. Jenny is redeemed only by her reproductive sex with Forrest. Ultimately, Jenny finds security and protection for herself by having Forrest's son and marrying him.

By denying Jenny's political agency, *Forrest Gump* affirms the political agency and superiority of white heteronormative masculinity. In a psychoanalytic reading of the film, Thomas Byers (1996, 421) concludes that the movie is "an act of repression" that restores hegemonic white masculinity by putting sixties-era challenges to its authority to rest. The film's focus on Gump as the subject of history overcomes threats to the paternalist principle posed by women and other groups who have challenged the authority of white, middle-class, heteronormative masculinity. Given that Gump has no historical understanding of his own dominant subject position, the movie's sentimental portrayal of his life story suppresses countercultural demands that those who share Gump's position of privilege surrender or share power. For Byers, the film's erasure of feminism is central to its restoration of patriarchal authority because feminism emphatically denies the myth of white masculine superiority and belies the film's romantic vision of the heteronormative nuclear family.

While feminism is excised from the film, the broader New Left movement is also demonized to justify the film's celebration of Gump's naïve and nonpolitical worldview. Jenny's demoralized status is a warning about the degradation of traditional womanhood that follows when countercultural ideals are allowed to flourish. As her character development reflects conservative anxiety about the status of the nuclear family, it is not Jenny who represents the sixties but the men she surrounds herself with: Wesley and the unnamed Black Panthers who passively observe when Wesley dares to smack her. Wesley, the macho militant, appears momentarily but crucially in *Forrest Gump* in order to punctuate the threat that radicalism poses to traditional family values. In his commentary about the film, Pat Buchanan (1994) approvingly concludes that "the white trash are in Berkeley and the peace movement; the best of black and white are to be found in little towns in the South, and in the Army of the United States." As his quote suggests, *Forrest Gump* gives cinematic form to Buchanan's image of the sixties-era counterculture as the boogeyman that affirms the desirability of neoconservative politics. It is up to good conservative citizens to regain control of America's white women from the clutches of the macho militants of the Left.

Forrest Gump's affirmation of white masculine authority is enhanced by selective amnesia that ignores aspects of the decade's dissent that defy easy resolution in a return to traditional family life such as vivid news footage of the Tet Offensive, the My Lai Massacre, soldiers returning home in body bags, the brutal repression of black radicals, and Fred Hampton's heinous murder. After *Forrest Gump* confronts Jenny about Wesley's abuse, macho militant characters disappear, as do images of black political struggle. Byers (1996, 428) remarks that Forrest Gump's blatant omission of Martin Luther King's assassination is "simply astonishing" given that the film foregrounds other assassination attempts including John Lennon's murder. Byers concludes that the erasure of King's death "can only be understood" as a fantasy wish fulfillment to "attach victim status to white men" and "cover over any systemic exploitation of others by them."

A particularly insidious aspect of the film's amnesia is its refusal to acknowledge gay rights activism given that Jenny dies from a mysterious and incurable disease that implicitly references AIDS. Conveniently, the film ends in 1982, before AIDS received strong national attention as a public health crisis. Government inaction to the looming crisis was largely due to the perception that it was a disease primarily affecting gay men. Jenny's mysterious death gives cinematic form to conservative responses that dismissed the impact of the disease. According to Robert Self (2012, 401), many political leaders on the right including Jesse Helms, Newt Gingrich, Jerry Falwell, and Pat Robertson saw the AIDS epidemic as "an opportunity to discredit the entirety of the liberal worldview they associated with the Great Society and the equal rights movements of the 1960s." Even defenders of the sixties decade leveled this critique. As Camille Paglia (1992, 254) asserted, "Everyone who preached free love in the sixties is responsible for AIDS." *Forrest Gump* enacts a neoconservative fantasy and a warning; it imagines a world in which the GLBTQ+ community does not exist, and it instructs (presumably straight) audiences about the dangers inherent in sexual permissiveness and nontraditional family life.

Within Forrest Gump, macho militant Wesley's callous disregard for the ambivalent activist Jenny threatens the sanctity of the nuclear family and, by extension, the nation itself. Masculine authority is renewed through good citizen Forrest Gump's ability to win back Jenny's affections. Concomitantly, the militant's symbolic annihilation resolves an imagined threat to family values that conservatives have leveled against the Left since the rise of the Moral Majority. As Edward Morgan (2010, 199) observes, radical antiwar activists and black militants have become "media culture points of reference for those seeking to scapegoat the sixties" for national division that caused trenchant racism, sexism, and imperialist foreign policy. Thus, the macho militant's villainous behavior and eventual downfall reinforces political arguments that have called for the removal of radicalism from national civic life in order to secure national and family stability. The imperative to eradicate radicalism from public life is portrayed most vividly in the 1999 miniseries *The '60s*.

THE LIBERAL VISION OF THE BAD SIXTIES IN *THE '60S*

As the religious Right left its imprint on national policy in the mid-nineties, the memory of the bad sixties continued to appear in popular and political culture. Political figures and former activists spoke back to conservative critics with their own perspective on the decade. Rather than conflate sixties-era liberalism with the more radical movements of the late sixties, liberal memories of the bad sixties sharply distinguished the first half from the last half of the decade. While Clinton spoke nostalgically about the early sixties and John Kennedy, he described the mid-sixties as the start of a period of national decline. In a speech at the Pennsylvania State University in 1996, Clinton held the late sixties responsible for ongoing national division and for the "breakdown of community, family and work" (Clinton 1996). Bernard von Bothmer (2010, 171–75) notes that Clinton was intent on reframing the pejorative caricature of the Left created by conservatives. But rather than defend the sixties wholeheartedly, Clinton crafted his own memory of the bad sixties that reaffirmed traditional models of family and civic life. In an attempt to appeal to both moderates on the Right and the Left of the political center, Clinton reiterated the image of the radical sixties as a threat to the "heart and soul of a civilized society."

Released on February 7 and 8, 1999, NBC's miniseries *The '60s* gave televisual form to this bifurcated image of the decade. As its title makes plain, the miniseries makes the decade of the sixties the subject of its three-hour broadcast. A variety of visual and aural cues position the narrative within the broader context of the decade. Most of the dramatic scenes between characters occur in the context of tumultuous political events unfolding around them. These scenes intersperse archival news and documentary footage between recreated shots of actors. Some recreated scenes also include black-and-white shots, presumably to integrate the fictionalized narrative seamlessly with the historic documents of the decade. Cameo appearances by Carnie Wilson, the daughter of Beach Boys' musician Brian Wilson, and Hog Farm founder Wavy Gravy also signal the program's status as a source of memory about the decade. Familiar rock songs by sixties-era musicians including James Brown, Bob Dylan, Cream, Jefferson Airplane, Simon and Garfunkel, and the Doors give added drama to events. As it accompanies every important scene in which dramatic political and personal events unfold for the main characters, the soundtrack contributes to an affected portrait of the decade that drips with sentimentality. The sensory experience of the rapid cuts between shots, crosscutting of scenes about different characters, and the soundtrack invites audiences to immerse themselves in two competing impulses: overwrought nostalgia for the spirit of protest and anguish over the decade's excesses. Ultimately, the program reminds audiences of the imperative to get over the bad sixties as it reflects on the decade's broader legacy.

The miniseries' depiction of well-publicized events from the decade function as a plot device for an otherwise unremarkable and sentimental family drama about two families whose experiences were shaped by the turmoil of the decade. The central plot revolves around the Herlihys, a white middle-class Chicago family torn apart by conflicting values. Scenes of the Herlihy family are interrupted with scenes of the film's secondary narrative about Willie and Emmet Taylor, a black working-class father and son struggling in Los Angeles to overcome obstacles caused by civil rights injustices, inner-city riots, and racial profiling by law enforcement. Both the Herlihy and the Taylor children take dramatically different life paths from their parents and from one another.

The relatively little attention given to the Taylors illustrates the whiteness at the center of popular culture's selective amnesia about the sixties. (My next chapter offers a lengthier discussion about how the story of the Taylors contributes to film and television's memory of the Black Panthers that foregrounds black rage as a political threat to national safety and family stability.) In addition to its emphasis on whiteness, the miniseries highlights conflict over the legitimacy of the Vietnam War as the decade's defining issue. The National Teach-In Against the War in New York City is featured as one of the many defining events of the decade, even though the antiwar movement was relatively small until several years later. Likewise, the miniseries dramatizes student protesters' efforts to stop the troop trains in

Oakland, California, in 1965 despite its relatively low attendance of 10,000 protesters compared to later protest events that rallied over 100,000 people across the country. By featuring these events, the miniseries puts the New Left in the center of its narrative about the sixties. Thus, the white student movement is framed as a synecdoche for the decade itself.

As the program's central focus, each Herlihy sibling embodies a different variation of white youth culture's response to the sexual revolution and the Vietnam War. The eldest Herlihy son, Michael, is an earnest member of the civil rights and antiwar movements who participates in high-profile protest events including Mississippi Freedom Summer, the 1967 March on the Pentagon, the presidential campaign for Eugene McCarthy, and the 1968 Democratic National Convention protests. Michael's younger brother Brian enlists in the army and returns from Vietnam with signs of post-traumatic stress disorder. Meanwhile, their sister Katie runs away from home after she becomes pregnant, moves to the Haight-Ashbury district in San Francisco, and joins the Hog Farm commune in New Mexico before returning home to her parents for the film's dramatic conclusion.

Each sibling comes to realize that the late sixties counterculture and radical antiwar movements are ill-fated and dangerous. The miniseries illustrates the challenges of overcoming the legacy of the bad sixties in its central narrative about Michael. Much of Michael's antiwar activism is motivated by his attraction to fellow activist Sarah. The two find commonality in their political commitments and in their fondness for Bob Dylan, but their relationship is thwarted by a romantic rivalry between Michael and a more radical antiwar activist, Kenny Klein. Michael and Sarah have a long-distance romance until Sarah meets Kenny and becomes allured by his fiery rhetoric and daring strategies to end the war. Michael and Kenny's antagonistic relationship with each other rather obviously stands for the broader ideological divisions between liberals and radicals in the antiwar movement and among members of Students for a Democratic Society.

As the miniseries' central character, Michael is the good citizen. He idolizes President Kennedy and grounds his opposition to the war in terms of American ideals of democratic decision making and government obligations to protect innocent civilians. Michael is committed to supporting family members despite their ideological differences and is the only character who maintains close contact with all of them. Just as Michael strives to keep the peace in his home, he strives to find common ground across political division. When he is brought before a draft board, he explains that he burned his draft card because "peace is preferable to war" and that "love is better than hate." His commitment to pacifism is amplified during the march on the Pentagon. The scene depicts increasingly heated confrontations between National Guardsmen and protesters chanting, "Ho Ho Ho Chi Min! NLF is sure to win!" Alarmed, Michael redirects the crowd to a new chant: "We're not against the soldiers! We're against the war!" After the tension has diffused, he places a flower in the barrel of a guard's rifle. "Peace, brother," he tells the frightened-looking young man, "We mean you no harm."

This character is a departure from other depictions of committed activists that I have discussed thus far in the book. Unlike the accidental activism of Kevin Arnold of *The Wonder Years* or the sinister activism of radicals in *Forrest Gump*, Michael's actions project a positive image of dissent that affirms a nostalgic image of the good sixties. In many ways he is the fictional counterpart to the narratives constructed about early male leaders of the Students for a Democratic Society such as Tom Hayden and Todd Gitlin. In the decade before the release of the miniseries, both Hayden (1988) and Gitlin (1987) released their own memoirs about the New Left's promising rise and tragic decline. As Hayden described the movement, it was a period of "idealism rusted by tragedy" (Berman 1988, para. 1).

Gitlin and Hayden present the first half of the sixties as a positive movement for realizing social justice based on optimistic faith in democratic ideals and the last half as a radical movement driven by a cynical outlook on American society and an irrational drive toward violence and conflict. Like the miniseries, these memoirs incorporate the progressive ideals of the student New Left into a metanarrative of American national identity constituted by shared investment in the value of dissent. By valorizing moderate dissent, these memoirs and the miniseries call for a renewed vision of national civic identity that embraces civil disobedience in the wake of political ruptures caused by the Vietnam War and the repression of dissent at home. This renewed vision entails halting nostalgia for sixties-era militancy. Both Gitlin and Hayden express regret for their past support for the governments of Cuba and North Vietnam. Thus, their enthusiasm for dissent is tempered by their newfound quiescence regarding capitalist imperialism.

Gitlin's book could be the template for the miniseries' narrative structure and character development. As the *New York Times* review of his book notes, Gitlin described himself as a "studious and clean-cut" adolescent who became radicalized after falling in love with the "daughter of former Communists" who "introduced him to folk music" (Miller 1987). (In the miniseries, Sarah informs Michael during their first date that her parents discuss "politics from McCarthyism to civil rights," but they never do anything.) Like Michael, Gitlin was appalled by the image of police dogs attacking children in Birmingham, Alabama, and joined the SDS after becoming involved in a campus peace organization. Michael's constant desire to have activists vote to decide their next strategies also mirrors Gitlin's enthusiasm for participatory democracy in which individuals share in "those social decisions determining the quality and direction of his life" (Gitlin 1996, 107).[3] After he left the SDS, Gitlin pursued a career in higher education, teaching at prominent institutions including the University of California at Berkeley and Columbia University, and he has been a frequent contributor to the national press as an editor writer and expert source. Gitlin's work has become a foundational resource for several progressive and liberal accounts of the decade that retain some nostalgia for the movement's nonviolent direct action and grassroots organizing. But that nostalgia is matched with disdain for the movement's rising militancy. Gitlin takes particular umbrage with the Weathermen's takeover of the SDS. He concludes, "the Weathermen were a scourge, not an argument. They were the foam on a sea of rage" (Gitlin 1996, 397). This disdain is routinely echoed in popular culture's image of the sixties.

Gitlin's description of the relentless, enraged militant is most vividly portrayed in *The '60s*'s macho militant character Kenny. Kenny is a composite character drawn loosely from a variety of iconic New Left activists. Appearing as the leader of every major protest event depicted in the film, he stands in front of a train to prevent it from transporting troops to an army base (recalling Jerry Rubin's activism in Oakland, California), breaks into Columbia University's president's office (reminiscent of Mark Rudd's colleague during the Columbia University student protests), organizes the 1968 Democratic National Convention protests (drawing from any number of organizers of the Students for a Democratic Society), and builds a bomb in Greenwich Village, accidentally killing himself (recalling Ted Gold and Terry Robbins of the Weathermen). One scene during the first half of the film provides a brief glimpse into Kenny's political motivations. Over a dinner of Chinese takeout, Kenny explains to Michael and Sarah the lessons of Franz Fanon's *Wretched of the Earth*: the demands of capitalism have forced the people of the Global South to trade "good manners for efficiency." This scene provides an unusual effort by network television to acknowledge the Left's critique of Western imperialism. But the scene's focus on an international loss of manners was hardly the issue that motivated radicals at the time. Activists' more pressing concerns over capitalism's crushing control over the world's resources and its exploitation of people of color worldwide is excluded from the conversation.

As the miniseries continues, Kenny's motives become increasingly dubious. During the student takeover at Columbia, Kenny kicks in the door to the university president's office, distributes the president's cigars to other students, and urges other activists to start ordering pizza and burgers. His behavior models university administrators' and moderate politicians' description of sixties-era student protests as the childish antics of a generation that was reluctant to grow up. When police arrive on campus and begin to mercilessly beat Kenny and other protesters, Kenny is hardly a sympathetic character. Sarah tells news reporters that she and Kenny had peacefully assembled on the steps of the main hall before he was attacked, but she is clearly not revealing the entire truth.

Never expressing any remorse or ambivalence about direct action, Kenny seems to relish the prospect of violent confrontation. His zeal is highlighted in scenes depicting his leadership at the 1968 Democratic National Convention protests. During the scene, organizers express concern that the city's refusal to grant permits may lead to violence and to a split between liberals and radicals attending the rally. Kenny replies with a smirk, "What's better to polarize the center than a pig with a billy club?" The following scenes include archival images of Chicago city police beating and bloodying the dissenters. Given that the program never offers any additional context for the events leading to the bloodbath at the convention that year, its depiction of Kenny provides the clearest explanation for the disorder: militant radicals asked for it. The unsympathetic portrayal of Kenny neutralizes one of the more compelling arguments for protesters' confrontational tactics during the end of the decade; as police repression against nonviolent activists intensified, activists increasingly regarded the United States itself as a battleground. By foregrounding Kenny as the instigator of conflict, the miniseries echoes a common theme of earlier fictionalized television portrayals about the sixties: during the decade, no one had the moral high ground. Although law enforcement officers are portrayed throughout the miniseries using excessive force, activists are depicted as irresponsible and disrespectful provocateurs.

Kenny's condescending attitude toward Sarah invites viewers to dislike him even further. His brusqueness is a sharp contrast to Michael's soft demeanor. He consistently ignores Sarah's ideas and treats her as his personal assistant. When they first break into the president's office at Columbia, Kenny orders her to make sandwiches for the crowd. Later, to prevent her from seeing Michael at a protest gathering, he instructs her to make copies of a flyer. Sarah complains that Kenny refuses to appreciate her organizing experience and contributions to the movement, obliquely recalling gendered divisions within the New Left that prompted the formation of the radical strand of the women's liberation movement; however, Kenny's chauvinism does not prompt Sarah to pursue women's rights. Instead, she seeks the company and advice of good citizen Michael.

Sarah is an ambivalent activist throughout the miniseries. When she leaves Michael for Kenny, she tells Michael that she is "confused about a lot of stuff." Both personally and politically, she is torn between Michael's pacifism and Kenny's passion. When Sarah and Michael meet at the Pentagon, Sarah praises Michael for preventing impending violence between protesters and the National Guard. Yet, she adamantly defends Kenny's decision to put her and other women at the front of the crowd. "I truly believe he's going to save the world," she explains. Michael is nonplussed. "Yeah, while you get your head kicked in!" Michael worries that Kenny only cares about people in the abstract. The good citizen and unwavering romantic cannot imagine how Kenny could be trusted to lead a movement if he is willing to put his girlfriend in harm's way. Kenny's excessive machismo and sexism positions Michael as more sympathetic toward women's experiences.

The portrayal of Sarah as an ambivalent activist who has conflated political and romantic attachment illustrates how women's bodies were the turf and stakes of the nineties-era cultural wars. The struggle between the good citizen and the macho militant maps the ideological debate over national identity onto the controversy regarding patriarchal authority over women and the family. The miniseries positions viewers to understand that radical organizing and confrontational protest threatens women, and—by extension—the nation. To restore the nation back to its pre-sixties state of unanimity, *The '60s* and other programs like it suggest that women must also be sheltered from radical challenges to traditional values.

As the miniseries draws to a conclusion, Sarah realizes that Michael's concerns have merit. When she meets with Kenny for the last time, she finds him building a bomb in an apartment in Greenwich Village. Sarah is furious. Before leaving him, she declares, "Michael was right. You never cared about people. You only cared about ideas. And now you don't even have any ideas left." Ever the dismissive macho militant, Kenny snickers back, "Go ahead and run away, my little bourgeois princess." Sarah leaves his apartment building moments before Kenny accidentally sets off the bomb he is building, just in time to see it burst into flames above her. The scene dramatically reenvisions the history of the Weathermen's tragic bomb-making attempt that ended with the deaths of three of its members in a Greenwich Village townhouse in 1970. By many accounts, this event was the death knell of the New Left. For Gitlin (1996, 402), it meant that the movement's "innocence" and "larger logic" itself was destroyed. As one of its final scenes, *The '60s* confirms this conclusion. The lesson of this unfortunate periodization of the sixties is that the decade's dissent was doomed to fail, a victim of its own excess.

Once Kenny—the icon of the bad sixties—is removed from the narrative, the Herlihy family is able to reunite. In the miniseries' final moments, Sarah returns to Michael by attending his family's backyard barbeque. Michael's father, Bill, welcomes her by throwing her a football. When she catches it, he nods to Michael approvingly, "Nice catch. Nice girl. Nice tight end." The final scene depicts the Herlihy family playing a rousing game of football, the quintessential American pastime. Bill's double-entendre focuses not only on Sarah's athletic skill but on her attractiveness. Thus, the scene confirms that women's bodies themselves have been brought back under a nationalist form of patriarchal authority.

RETURNING TO THE NUCLEAR FAMILY, RESTORING THE NATION

Across both *Forrest Gump* and *The '60s*, the ambivalent activist's return to the security of the nuclear family stands in figuratively for the restored nation, protected from the threat of radical change. Both Jenny's marriage to Forrest Gump and Katie's return to her parents symbolically reaffirms patriarchal authority within the nuclear family after the challenges of the sixties posed by members of the counterculture. The ambivalent activists' rejection of radical militancy thus reaffirms the salience of women's roles as wives and mothers in the nuclear family.

The symbolic meaning attached to the ambivalent activist is most pronounced in *The '60s*'s depiction of Sarah. Torn between two lovers, one invested in nonviolent dissent and committed to the promise of liberal democracy and one radical invested in the possibilities of revolutionary social change, Sarah ultimately chooses liberalism. By choosing between the "good" and the "bad" sixties, Sarah functions as a metaphoric stand in for the divided nation itself. Conflicted over the choice between passive resistance and liberal reformism (the "good" sixties) and revolutionary dissent (the "bad" sixties), Sarah has to witnesses the horrors of terrorist violence to learn that revolutionary politics is morally bankrupt and ill-fated. Sarah's return to Michael in the closing scenes indicates that by putting faith in liberal democracy, the nation can find resolution to a decade of turmoil and dissent.

To a lesser extent, Michael's sister Katie is also the stakes of ideological conflict over the family and national identity. Her father is irate when Katie gets pregnant after having a one-night fling with a traveling musician. Like *Forrest Gump*'s Jenny, Katie finds no solace in California, where her drug-using boyfriend fails to help provide for her or their child. Katie's experience in San Francisco is fraught with difficulty. Desperate, Katie considers working at a strip club and gets mugged late at night. Before she leaves California for a commune in New Mexico she wails, "Peace and love my ass! I hate this damn city!" Echoing central themes of *Forrest Gump*, the miniseries derides the countercultural ideal of free love and drug culture as a threat to the nuclear family and dangerous for women and children. By the film's end, Katie leaves the commune to return home to her parents. Her function as a placeholder for the nation's imagined body is encoded on the front jacket of the DVD. In a close-up image of her face, one half is painted with the American flag; the other with a large purple flower. Ostensibly, her decision to reconnect to her traditional nuclear family restores national unity in the wake of challenges posed by alternative family structures and sexual liberation.

Across multiple mediated texts, the ambivalent female activist and the pregnant hippie drifter are a Hollywood fiction designed to propel a metanarrative of middle-class white men's experience of the decade. The narrative resolution of social conflicts from the sixties through heteronormative romance and reinvestment in the nuclear family symbolically restores white masculine authority over the family and secures liberal democratic capitalism in the nation. A synecdoche for the nation itself, the nuclear family cannot survive unless radicals and their challenges to liberal democracy are extricated from society. These movies reiterate Hollywood logics that, as rhetoric and film scholar Claire King (2012, 38) observes, "encourage the national body to restore itself to prior (imagined) states of unity and unanimity."

White women metaphorically represent the divided nation in narratives about the bad sixties. Poster for *The '60s*. DVD. NBC Studios, Inc., 1999.

The miniseries' conclusion invites a hegemonically masculine but nonetheless pluralistic understanding of the legacy of the sixties. Until her return, Katie's father, Bill, had consistently denounced his children's antiwar activism and countercultural lifestyles. His final acceptance of Katie reinforces a nostalgic image of the good sixties in which social change is haltingly embraced. In order to restore and reunite the family, Bill realizes he must accept their more liberal attitudes. This message aligned with Bill Clinton's own efforts to align the two major political parties under the banner of post-sixties unity at the time the miniseries aired. As Clinton asserted that the nation was stronger when both parties forged a consensus around shared values, *The '60s* presents a narrative in which a conservative father and World War II veteran has learned to appreciate his adult children. The lesson of both the miniseries and Clinton's own rhetoric is that the family and the nation succeed when political difference is constrained by moderation and contained under one roof.

Despite this moderately pluralistic vision of a post-sixties nation, the construction of the good citizen, ambivalent activist, and macho militant forgets the multiple constituencies who animated histories of activism and dissent over the past fifty years: people of color, socialists, feminists, and GLBTQ+ people. As they affirm the authority of heteronormative family relationships, both *Forrest Gump* and *The '60s* remove gay and lesbian activism from the public memory of the decade. Likewise, *The '60s* offers a reductive and false portrayal of late sixties black dissent. The miniseries provides no depictions or references to other radical movements that drew inspiration from the Black Panthers, including the Puerto Rican Young Lords, the Brown Berets, and the Young Patriots (a working-class white youth movement). As these examples suggest, Hollywood's construction of Black Panthers and radical antiwar activists erroneously implies that activists' political claims to rights and justice ended with the Panthers' decline and the war's end. Furthermore, both *Forrest Gump* and *The '60s* deny women radicals' political agency. We can find historical resonances to the macho militant in the constructed media personae of sixties-era activists such as Mark Rudd, Bill Ayers, and Jerry Rubin, but the ambivalent activist has no obvious real-world corollary; her function is to provide a source of narrative tension between good citizens and macho militants. In order for women to function as metaphors for national unity, female characters representing flesh and blood analogues are erased from Hollywood's collective memory of the sixties.

The family values rhetoric of the nineties helps to explain why the depictions of committed activists are, by and large, white, inevitably masculine, and driven by heteronormative desire. Movies foregrounding ambivalent activists who return to the nuclear family give cinematic form to political rhetoric that has called for traditional values and reduced government support for people who do not participate in the nuclear family. These texts contributed to the culture wars by inviting audiences to reinvest in the promise of American democracy without seeking radical political and social change. Beyond their rejection of radical politics, the confluences across these movies affirmed conservative responses to nineties-era controversies about women's rights. The worldview in which women are objects of masculine desire discredits women's claims for rights and public participation. More pointedly, cultural memories of the sixties contributed to the nineties-era backlash against feminism. The celebration of women's return to the nuclear family provided a welcome environment for religious conservative efforts to restrict abortion rights, block the passage of the Equal Rights Amendment, and restrict welfare support for single mothers. *Forrest Gump* and *The '60s* taught viewers that good citizenship is the duty of white men of means to bring women back into the nuclear family and away from the divisive politics of the Left.

This metanarrative of the bad sixties extends beyond *Forrest Gump* and *The '60s*. The scenario in which the ambivalent female activist leaves the macho militant because he has built a deadly bomb occurs elsewhere in fictionalized Hollywood narratives about the sixties. A 1990 episode of *Quantum Leap* offers a slight variation of this scenario. In this episode, main character Sam Beckett is the good citizen who is brought to a college campus in 1967 to convince ambivalent activist Elizabeth to defuse a bomb that she and a macho militant have set. Anticipating Forrest Gump's *Jenny*, Elizabeth's participation in radical dissent is a pathological response to her alienation from her parents. In the episode's final scene, Beckett concludes that Elizabeth was subconsciously motivated to get her bourgeois parents' attention. A good citizen till the end, Beckett reminds Elizabeth that activists will end the war—not through the use of violence but "by chipping away at it slowly over time."

The good citizen, ambivalent activist, and macho militant also appear in the 2007 movie musical, *Across the Universe*. The plot of this postmodern film revolves around the romance between Jude, an aspiring British painter, and Lucy, a student and antiwar activist. The film is more a hyperreal fantasy than earnest portrayal of the counterculture and antiwar movements. With characters and musical numbers inspired by Beatles songs, the narrative is driven by its clever integration of Beatles lyrics and melodies with choreography and video editing reminiscent of early music videos. Set primarily in Greenwich Village, characters play rock music in dark and crowded rooms, march against the Vietnam War, burn draft cards, and experience ecstatic hallucinations on LSD. Thus, the film's mise-en-scène, editing, and soundtrack is a pastiche celebrating Hollywood's nostalgia for the late sixties' music, protest, and culture.

Although he is not actually a US citizen, Jude is the film's good citizen. He passionately objects to the Vietnam War, but he is primarily concerned with building his career as an artist and fostering his romance with Lucy. As Lucy becomes increasingly consumed by antiwar organizing, she and Jude become distant. In a plot development that closely mirrors *Forrest Gump* and *The '60s*, Jude objects to her growing fondness for macho militant Paco. Jude concludes that Paco is nothing but a "seducer of beautiful young women." His condemnation of Paco positions the radical antiwar movement not solely as an ideological challenge to liberal democracy but as a threat to Lucy's virtue and to their normative sexual relationship. Singing "Revolution," Jude marches into the office of Students for Democratic Reform (a thinly veiled reference to the Students for a Democratic Society) where Lucy volunteers and declares his disdain for militancy. Echoing, if not directly inspired by the scene in *Forrest Gump* in which Forrest attacks Wesley, Jude punches Paco across the face, prompting a beret-wearing black activist to intervene while other activists throw Jude out of the office. Lucy breaks up with Jude and commits herself more fully to radical protest. She leaves Paco after she finds him building a bomb in the second floor of a Greenwich Village townhouse. Subsequently, Paco and his friends accidentally kill themselves during a homemade bomb blast, destroying the SDR office. The film concludes as Lucy finds her way back to Jude. As characters sing "All You Need Is Love," in the background, the two gaze longingly into each other's eyes. Thirteen years after *Forrest Gump* showed in theaters, *Across the Universe* reinforced the lesson that the political moderation of the nation's good male citizens is necessary to overcome the turmoil of the radical sixties.

Over and over again, Hollywood teaches viewers to envision women as objects of masculine desire and as the stakes of ideological conflict. This lesson has deeply troubling implications for women's rights today because it makes women's political agency and dissent unintelligible to the popular imagination. Celebrated depictions of white men who heroically bring white women back into the nuclear family in nineties-era film and television are a prelude to the current political climate in which Vice President Mike Pence refuses to be alone with a woman who is not his wife, even in professional settings. Pence's intimation that heteronormative desire threatens the sanctity of marriage makes sense in a cinematic context in which women's activism is fueled by their romantic attachments to men. Hollywood's ambivalent activist legitimizes concerns that women's political commitments are not to be taken seriously. Thus, the status of women's rights today calls for more nuanced and complicated depictions of dissent that reflect the motives and ambitions of radical women.

CHAPTER FOUR

Traumatic Victimhood or Black Rage? Contrasting Visions of Black Power

In 2016, Beyoncé's performance during the Super Bowl half-time show put the fiftieth anniversary of the Black Panther Party into the national spotlight. The popular culture icon led a team of dancers wearing black berets, Afros, and cropped black military-style jackets in almost perfect synchronization through a routine that paid tribute to the radical organization. After commanding her dancers to "get in formation," Beyoncé positioned herself in the middle of two intersecting rows of dancers to create an X on the football field. The performers also raised their fists in a Black Power salute, transforming the half-time entertainment show into a statement of protest against police violence and systemic racism. The half-time show elicited both support and outrage. Black Lives Matter activists and black political figures including Malcolm X's daughter Ilyasah Shabazz and Nation of Islam minister Louis Farrakhan praised Beyoncé (Colangelo 2016). Alternatively, conservative political figures viewed her celebration of black militancy with derision. Speaking on FOX News, former New York mayor Rudy Giuliani accused her of using her performance to attack police officers (Chokshi 2016, para. 3). The controversy surrounding Beyoncé's performance highlights deep national divisions regarding racial profiling by law enforcement.

The strong and disparate responses to Beyoncé's performance also illuminates how the memory of the Black Power movement is still associated with ongoing contestation about race and racism in the United States. Among racial justice advocates, the image of Black Power is a powerful symbol of collective resistance to systemic racism and brutal violence against black people. Unlike the civil rights movement, which favored working with mainstream political institutions to include black people into the structures of democratic capitalism, Black Power activists organized outside of those institutions to demand rights and justice. Black militancy in the late sixties posed the threat of radical collectivism and group demands, not just for equality of opportunity but for equal resources of health, safety, employment, and education (Omi and Winant 1994). The miserable conditions that animated Black Power activism during the late sixties continue to shape public life for many people of color in the United States. Given that the Black Panther Party began as an organization dedicated to protecting their community from the threat of police brutality, their memory may offer resources for envisioning empowered collective resistance to ongoing instances of police violence. It is unsurprising, then, that for many conservative groups and mainstream political figures, Black Power's symbolism is also associated with violence, civil disruption, and threats to the current racial order. For these groups, Black Power—and the Black Panther Party in particular—represents the worst excesses of sixties-era struggles, the memory of which should only serve to discredit contemporary claims for racial justice.

Hollywood film and television have contributed to ongoing public controversies about racial violence through their own portrayals of Black Power over the past several decades. In 1992, Spike Lee's biopic *Malcolm X* told the radical black leader's life story based on Alex Haley's best-selling biography. Three years later, Mario Van Peebles's movie *Panther* reviewed the history of the Black Panther Party's founding chapter in Oakland, California. These movies provided affirmative images of radical black leaders who empowered their communities to challenge the legacy of colonialism in the United States. By contrast, other mainstream media products including the film *Forrest Gump* and the television program *Law & Order* have depicted the Panthers as threats to racial harmony and civil society.

The interplay between affirmative and negative depictions about Black Power points to Hollywood's ambivalent relationship with US race relations; commercial media have sought to give meaning to black experience while maintaining its primary investment in white narratives and white audiences. Films by young black filmmakers in the early nineties point to the discontent among urban black communities in the wake of Rodney King's brutal beating by police officers in 1992. American Studies scholar Jane Rhodes (2007, 19–20) remarks that black youth looked to the black nationalism of the sixties and seventies for inspiration. She writes, "the Black Panthers and Malcolm X were appropriated as crucial symbols—reminders of an activist past to remedy an impotent and quiescent present."

Many pop culture depictions of Black Power appeared amid a period of political backlash against civil rights that continues today. Reagan's administration oversaw cuts in welfare benefits and a weakening of affirmative action policies, and these cuts were expanded under Clinton's presidency. Such policies were justified by postracial discourses that railed against "special interests," a code phrase that implicitly referred to women, people of color, the GLBTQ+ community, and other classes of people who benefited from the civil rights legislation of the Johnson era. Like other postracial discourses that have circulated since the rise of the New Right, the critique of protections for special interests presumed that racism no longer explained disparities in income and education; hence, policies that favored people of color were characterized as forms of reverse discrimination.

This logic ignores the material realities in which white communities have continued to reap the lion's share of the nation's wealth and resources. Black and Latinx communities living in segregated cities throughout the country during the eighties and nineties faced substandard schools and widespread joblessness. The effects of structural inequalities in education and employment have been compounded by systemic police abuse and criminalization of people of color. The war on drugs and tough-on-crime legislation prompted police campaigns that largely targeted black and Latinx neighborhoods, dramatically raising rates of black incarceration throughout the country.

Postracial rhetoric resolved the contradiction posed by the ongoing conditions of structural racism by celebrating what Herman Gray (1997, 353) refers to as "the civil rights subject." Gray describes this figure as the mediated representation of the middle-class benefactors of the civil rights era who affirmed the benefits of hard work and sacrifice for achieving material and status rewards. By valorizing the civil rights subject, critics of Great Society legislation have suggested that advancements made by individual black Americans are evidence of progress toward racial justice regardless of broader socioeconomic conditions for black communities (Bonilla-Silva 2009; Omi and Winant 1997). As Gray explains, "the civil rights subject performs important cultural work since it helps construct the mythic terms through which many Americans can believe our nation has now transcended racism" (356).

The popular family television sit-com *The Cosby Show* illustrates television culture's tendency to remember civil rights through a postracial lens. According to Gray (1997), the Huxtable family embodied the reformist agenda of the moderate wing of the civil rights movement. Portrayed in the context of the home, they affirm the liberal virtues of "individual responsibility and moral restraint" that grounds political life under post-industrial capitalism (35455). One episode in particular sutured memories of the black freedom struggle to the civil rights subject. In this season 3 episode, entitled "The March," adolescent son Theo learns about the history of the 1963 March on Washington from his parents and grandparents. Explaining that they had all attended the march, his grandparents describe their personal experiences walking to and from the National Mall. Notably, no one mentions the conditions of segregation, trenchant poverty, and racist violence that motivated the protests. Instead, the family recounts the friendly mood and diverse crowds who attended, "not to become part of history" but "to express how they felt." Claire concludes the discussion by telling Theo, "It was a friendly, peaceful day."

The depoliticized memory of civil rights protests provided by *The Cosby Show* illustrates how the civil rights subject depends upon the selective amnesia of contentious dissent and organized challenges to systemic racism. In *Cosby*'s vision of civil rights, even moderate demands for formal equality are excluded from memory. By forgetting the ongoing conditions that galvanized the black freedom struggle, hollowed-out memories of civil rights perpetuate the rhetorics of color blindness that insist that racism has been left to the past. Certainly, the potency of the civil rights subject depends upon amnesia of Black Power activism's calls for economic redress and black political agency outside of white-controlled institutions.

The rest of this chapter looks at how Hollywood's depictions of Black Power activism have responded to ongoing contestation regarding postracial rhetoric and the civil rights subject. Gray observes that the discourses of civil rights are still hotly contested because they fail to address ongoing conditions of poverty, institutional racism, and structural inequality that continue to plague poor and black communities. As the deliberating public remains divided over questions of race and policies to redress historic injustice, Hollywood has served as a site of contestation over public memories of Black Power. That is, entertainment media have transcoded ongoing debates over the legacy of civil rights into cinematic form.

I argue that Hollywood has provided an ambivalent response to the civil rights subject in the decades since *The Cosby Show* aired. The first half of this chapter explores how the movies *Malcolm X* and *Panther* offer alternative models of black political agency. Although these films defied nostalgic celebration of the civil rights era, they provide traumatic countermemories of black victimhood that anchor alternatives to the civil rights subject to the memory of the sixties. Thus, they envision limited opportunities for racial justice in the future.

The second half of this chapter critically reviews the variety of negative depictions of the Black Panther Party in brief scenes in Hollywood films and television since the mid-nineties. These scenes affirmed the civil rights subject through their portrayals of the angry black radical, a character type that serves as a foil for the civil rights subject. By espousing violence and hatred toward white people, this figure discourages audience identification with Black Power activism and presents a model of black political agency that must be avoided to affirm the legitimacy of existing political and economic institutions. Ultimately, the angry black radical provides implicit yet vivid support for postracial policies that insist that racism no longer hinders people of color. The contrast between these competing images of Black Power activists as figures of black victimhood or black rage reflects Hollywood's effort to appeal to diverse audiences with fundamentally different perspectives on US race relations. However, this ambivalence should not be overstated. By and large, Hollywood's memories of black victimhood and black rage discourage viewers from engaging in collective resistance to structural inequities and institutional racism.

TRAUMATIC COUNTERMEMORIES OF BLACK POWER

In many ways, Spike Lee's *Malcolm X* and Mario Van Peebles's *Panther* provided remarkable images of black political agency that countered the civil rights subject. Following the narrative framework of Haley's autobiography, Lee's film depicts Malcolm X's life transformation from a drug-addicted hustler to an influential advocate for racial justice. According to many critics, *Malcolm X* was the most conventional film of Lee's career. It was also his most commercially successful film at the time, earning $48 million at the box office. Three years after the release of Lee's film, Mario Van Peebles's movie *Panther* combined conventions of both the docudrama and blaxploitation film genres to tell the story of the Black Panther Party's founding chapter in Oakland, California. Although the film earned just $7 million at the box office and received chilly reviews from the mainstream press, several black film critics praised the film for recovering the memory of the Black Panthers (Dyson 1995; Hoerl 2007).

Malcolm X and *Panther* capitalized on a wave of renewed enthusiasm for Black Power memory in nineties-era popular culture. Music videos by Arrested Development, Public Enemy, and Boogie Down productions commercialized and marketed Black Power by including the iconic images of Malcolm X, Martin Luther King, the Black Panther Party, and Angela Davis into a variety of consumer goods.[1] Both movies were an outcome of rising prominence of black filmmakers in the early nineties and less a sign of Hollywood's enthusiasm for empowered black characters. Since Hollywood studios were reluctant to invest in these films, both Lee and Van Peebles raised outside money to maintain control over their projects (Turner 1995, 11).

These two films portrayed Black Power activists as individuals committed to improving black urban communities and establishing self-sufficiency for people of color to break from an oppressive social system that marginalized them. In this regard, both films provided cinematic countermemories. George Lipsitz (1990) describes countermemories as hidden histories excluded from dominant narratives that "force revision of existing histories" (213). Unlike dominant memories that purport to represent universal experience, countermemories offer narratives about local experiences that speak to the needs of oppressed groups and resist hegemonic narratives about the past. Thus, they may provide resources for viewers to critique and resist contemporary power relations.

During his lifetime, the mainstream press described Malcolm X as bitter, hate filled, and dangerous (Morgan 2010, 79–80). Likewise, national newspapers and magazines including the *New York Times*, the *Washington Post*, *Newsweek*, and *Time* routinely characterized the Black Panther Party as violent and criminal. Although the Panthers were frequent subjects of media reports, the press gave little substantive attention to the organization's concerns about systemic racism and injustice. For instance, the *Washington Post*'s coverage of the 1969 raid on Chicago Panther headquarters that involved the deaths of Fred Hampton and Mark Clark dismissed claims that the raid was part of a broader effort to destroy black political organizing. A few years later, the discovery of the FBI's counterintelligence program (COINTELPRO) files revealed that the destruction of the Panthers was precisely on the agenda of state law enforcement and the FBI. The FBI helped Chicago police gain access to Hampton's bedroom because FBI agents shared information gathered from informant William O'Neal, who was posing as Hampton's bodyguard.[2]

Lee and Van Peebles countered dominant culture's depictions of black radicals as violent criminals by evoking the perspective of black communities for whom Malcolm X and the Black Panthers symbolized self-determination and political empowerment. These films also challenged the dominant culture's image of dangerous black militancy by depicting Black Power activists as victims of endemic racism. Thus, they invited oppositional consciousness about Black Power's contributions to racial justice.

RADICAL CHALLENGES TO POSTRACIAL DISCOURSE IN SPIKE LEE'S *MALCOLM X*

The first half of *Malcolm X* explores how the experiences of racial brutality and injustice influenced the title character's radical outlook. An early scene depicts the death of his father, presumably at the hands of Ku Klux Klan members. Following scenes illustrate how Malcolm faced a variety of obstacles due to racist assumptions about black inferiority. Although he is considered to be a smart and popular student, Malcolm's instructor tells him that his goal of becoming a lawyer is unrealistic and that he should be a carpenter instead. Several years later, he is sentenced to eight to ten years in prison for conspiring to rob a house with his girlfriend, a white woman named Sophia. When Sophia receives a sentence of one to five years for the same crime, Malcolm concludes that his real crime was "sleeping with white women." He also laments that many black men were forced into lives of crime and drug abuse because they were "victims of whitey's social order." These early scenes contextualize Malcolm X's later rhetoric and activism as a justified response to institutional racism that thwarted achievement for black men.

According to the film's narrative, these early experiences prompted Malcolm X to study the history of US race relations, which led him to the conclusion that racism is embedded within US politics and economics. The second part of the three-hour film portrays Malcolm X's conversion to the Nation of Islam while in prison. Enlightened by newfound knowledge about the history of racial oppression, he adopts the last name X to renounce Western control of African Americans' identities. After his release from prison, Nation of Islam leader Elijah Muhammad names him the Nation's minister of information. Throughout the last half of the film, Malcolm X gives rousing speeches highlighting the entrenched racism within American politics and capitalism. He reminds one crowd, "We didn't land on the Plymouth Rock. Plymouth Rock landed on us!" The film also features Malcolm X's incendiary statements warning white-governed institutions of a "racial explosion" from the black community if economic and political subordination continued unabated.

The film's visual footage of police violence against black people affirms Malcolm X's indictment of the legal system in the United States. The film's opening shots contextualize Malcolm's activism by presenting archival television footage of police dogs and fire hoses set on young protesters in Birmingham, Alabama, as well as Martin Luther King's arrest during that rally. The sequences of images end with Malcolm X's famous statement: "To love the enemy is not intelligent. We have a right to defend ourselves." The sympathetic portrayal of X's virulent response to racist violence challenges postracial politics by framing black activists' demands for political redress as a just response to systematic exploitation and violence against communities of color.

Lee's film also challenges the postracial emphasis on individual success as the chief marker of black advancement; instead, it portrays black solidarity and collective organizing as an empowering means for achieving racial justice. A particularly evocative scene, including the screen image that appears below, highlights Malcolm X's influence during his years with the Nation of Islam. In the scene, Malcolm X mobilizes members to protest the brutal police beating of Brother Johnson. Malcolm leads several Nation of Islam men in an orderly march to police headquarters and then to a local hospital. Local Harlem residents take notice and follow them, chanting, "We want justice," until they receive assurances that Johnson has received medical treatment. By depicting the Nation of Islam's strategy of working outside of mainstream politics to resist state-sanctioned violence, the movie offers a defiant image of black political agency that refuses to honor the civil rights subject.

Later scenes depicting his final transformation after his expulsion from the Nation of Islam elaborate on Malcolm X's efforts to build coalitions against endemic racial injustice. After his holy pilgrimage to Mecca, he decides that people of all races should unite on the basis of divinely inspired love. He also concludes that Western nations' control

Malcolm X demands justice for Nation of Islam member Brother Johnson. *Malcolm X*. DVD. Directed by Spike Lee. Burbank, CA: Warner Home Video, 2000.

over the world's resources is a fundamental cause of racial subordination and calls upon the United Nations to bring charges against the United States government for human rights abuses against African Americans. This scene subtly points to Black Power's growing interest in Third World activism, as the movement's framework for envisioning racial justice expanded to include coalitional, global efforts to resist Western exploitation of colonized people's resources and labor.

In addition to offering a resistant image of black political agency, Lee amplified the film's counterhegemonic potential by drawing explicit connections to contemporary racial justice issues. The film's prologue includes footage of police violence that would have been familiar to early nineties audiences. The opening credits appear alongside film footage of four police officers beating Rodney King in 1991. Malcolm X's words spoken to a cheering crowd accompanies the images. Taken from his most widely recognized speech, he indicts the American political system for its historic and violent racism. "You are the victim of America . . . We've never seen democracy. All we've seen is hypocrisy. . . . We don't see the American Dream. All we see is the American nightmare." This scene connects racial profiling during the nineties with the circumstances that motivated Malcolm X's radicalism. Footage of police officers beating King was a visual commonplace for thinking about racial violence at the time Lee's film was released. It put Malcolm X's fiery condemnation of the American political system in the context of ongoing police violence and racial targeting of black people. Thus, footage of King's beating explains Malcolm's disavowal of nonviolent protest for nineties-era audiences and frames the life story of Malcolm X as a political lesson for the present: black people are still the victims of white violence and black people must work together to demand justice.

RESISTANT IMAGES OF EMPOWERED BLACK YOUTH IN MARIO VAN PEEBLES'S *PANTHER*

Van Peebles's *Panther* also counters postracial discourses and sanguine celebration of the civil rights subject by highlighting law enforcement's systematic repression against black citizens. The movie integrates recreated and actual footage of events involving the Oakland chapter through a narrative revolving around a fictional character named Judge. As the film's narrator, Judge explains that the Panthers sought to support their community and fight back against the FBI's efforts to destroy their organization. The movie also foregrounds the Black Panther Party's efforts to defend the Oakland community from trenchant police abuse.

The opening sequence establishes the film's depiction of the Black Panther Party's militancy as an understandable response to brutal violence of the civil rights era. The prologue includes archival newsreel footage of Martin Luther King facing angry white southerners, the assassinations of Malcolm X and Robert Kennedy, and police beating black citizens. The movie asserts its meaning as a resource for remembering the Panther's contributions to black identity and agency as it crosscuts news-reel footage with recreated scenes. Montage sequences depict the organization's free breakfast program for children, sickle-cell anemia testing, and community meetings to raise awareness of racial oppression. In addition to these montages, the film depicts the group's armed patrols of law enforcement to prevent police from assaulting members of the community. In one dramatized scene, party leaders Huey Newton and Bobby Seale approach white police officers who are beating an indigent black man and demand that they leave him alone. Other scenes include the Panther-led protest against the shooting death of Denzell Dowell, the march into the California state capitol in Sacramento to protest the Mulford Act, and the rally at the Alameda County courthouse to free Huey Newton from prison. Ultimately, these scenes portray the Black Panther Party as a volatile organization that empowered their community by demanding an end to violence against black citizens. The film's depiction of the Panthers as protagonists who struggle against racist and corrupt FBI agents and police officers vividly counters the dominant memory of black militancy as a threat to civil society. In contrast to mainstream characterizations of the Black Panther Party as violent criminals, Van Peebles's movie represents the Black Panther Party's militancy as a force for racial justice.

Panther also reverses mainstream characterizations of the Panthers as murderous thugs by portraying state and federal law enforcement agencies as menacing villains. The film foregrounds Federal Bureau of Investigation and police efforts to suppress the Panthers, depicting police assaults on Black Panther Party offices in cities across the country between 1968 and 1969. The FBI and local police antagonize the Panthers throughout the film by firebombing Panther offices and engaging in shoot-outs with Panther members. One pivotal scene depicts the April 6, 1968, confrontation between the Panthers and Oakland police officers that ended in the shooting death of eighteen-year-old Panther Bobby Hutton. By following the conventions of the action crime drama, audiences without historical awareness of this period in history might have understood the film as an outlandish spectacle. However, the crime thriller portrays many of the outrageous tactics that FBI agents actually used to repress the Panthers and other radical organizations.

Between 1967 and 1971, the FBI launched 233 illegal operations against the Black Panthers in its effort to minimize the organization's influence. Their operations included using informants to help police arrest Black Panther Party members on dubious charges that could not be substantiated in court and helping police raid party offices on

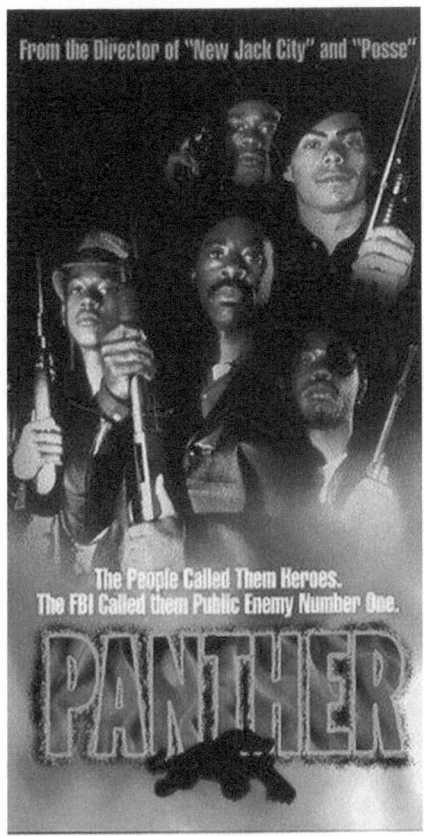

Panther glorifies the Black Panther Party's armed patrols and shoot-outs with law enforcement. Poster for *Panther*. DVD. Directed by Mario Van Peebles. New York: PolyGram Video, 1997.

false pretenses. In 1976, a Senate report concluded that these "lawless tactics" fomented "violence and unrest" (Self 2006, 45). US district judge Thomas Griesa ruled against the FBI in a lawsuit filed by the Socialist Workers Party and the Young Socialist Alliance, finding that the bureau's operations were "patently unconstitutional" (Blackstock 1988, 8). *Panther* is one of few popular culture texts to portray the FBI's lawlessness. According to black studies scholar Michael Dyson (1996, 115), the *Panther*'s focus on FBI repression "faithfully evoked the spirit of police terror of the 1960s and 1970s" and told "neglected truths" about black struggles.

Van Peebles's film accentuates the memory of law enforcement's illegal efforts to suppress the Panthers by intertwining historically inspired scenes with a fictional narrative about Judge's participation in the Oakland chapter. After Judge joins the Panthers, he poses as an FBI informer in order to give the Panthers an advantage in their war with local and national law enforcement. Much of the film's drama involves Judge's interactions with Detective Baker, who asks Judge to set the Panthers up for robbery, and Judge's relationship with fictional Panther member Tyrone, who suspects Judge is working for the police. In the film's climax, FBI director J. Edgar Hoover urges agents to collude with the Mafia to bring cheap cocaine and heroin into black urban ghettos. The scene's climax ends when fictional main characters Alma, Tyrone, and Judge destroy a warehouse filled with drugs as a last act of defiance against the FBI. In the film's denouement, a voiceover from Judge accompanies images of an Oakland city street and still photos of Huey Newton and Bobby Seal. Judge blames the epidemic of drug addiction in black inner cities on federal officials:

> They pumped in the dope to neutralize the black community and to destroy the Black Panthers' power base. But drugs overflowed the borders of the ghetto and ended up on all America's doorsteps.... In 1970, there were 300,000 addicts in the United States. Yesterday, there were three million. The way I see it, the struggle continues.

As Judge's closing dialogue suggests, the suppression of black radicals during the late sixties has direct bearing on the challenges facing black communities in the early nineties.

The film's closing lines address central issues that belied postracial discourse at the time the film showed in theaters. Although there is no strong evidence that the FBI brought drugs into black communities to shut down collective activism among the black urban poor, the drug epidemic of the eighties and nineties had devastating consequences for people of color. This was exacerbated by antidrug legislation during Reagan's administration that disparately penalized those possessing crack cocaine and those with powder cocaine, leading to a disproportionate number of black people in prison for drug-related offenses. The death of University of Maryland basketball star Leonard "Len" Bias precipitated the quick passage of the 1986 Anti-Drug Abuse Act. Although Bias died from a cocaine overdose, rumors that he died from smoking crack inflamed the social panic over the drug epidemic. The law garnered bipartisan support with little research or discussion about its implications (Schuppe 2016). Racially uneven rates of incarceration became more pronounced under Bill Clinton's administration, due in part to legislation that enhanced penalties on those convicted of drug-related crimes. Donna Murch (2016, para. 21) observes that as multiple generations of African Americans, Latin Americans, and the poor faced long-term prison sentences, "incarceration became *de facto* urban policy for impoverished communities of color in America's cities."

Policy rhetoric largely avoided explicit discussions about race, but it was an absent presence in discourse advocating "tough-on-crime" legislation. Coverage about the crack crisis during the early nineties foregrounded images of "black youth running wild in the streets" (McCann 2010, 400; Reeves and Campbell 1994, 90). In 1994, Hillary Clinton defended her husband's Violent Crime Control and Law Enforcement Act, which included the "three strikes" law, elimination of early parole for a large number of prisoners, and a variety of other measures that expanded punitive measures. She explained that the law was necessary to "put to heel" the "superpredators" who lacked conscience or empathy. Discourse about superpredators invariably referred to black youth (Gearan and Phillip 2016).

Appearing in theaters a year after passage of Clinton's crime bill, *Panther* rebukes the rhetoric that holds black youth accountable for rising crime rates and drug use in inner cities. Instead, it directs political anger toward the legal justice system and locates the drug epidemic within the structures of white supremacy. In this regard, the film is a representative anecdote for the crisis in which members of the black community envision themselves as under attack by white power structures. A similar conspiracy appeared in the mainstream news media one year later, this time accusing the CIA of colluding with Nicaraguan drug traffickers to distribute crack cocaine on the streets of Los Angeles in order to support the Contra rebels fighting to overthrow the Sandinista government. As Bryan McCann (2010, 400) notes, this narrative was a resource for members of the black community to articulate the drug epidemic with the histories of institutional violence against African Americans. Both *Panther* and the CIA crack conspiracy give expression to black communities' deep suspicion of party politics and law enforcement. They also confirm foundational beliefs among Black Power activists that mainstream institutions cannot be trusted to provide justice for people of color. Ordinary people must organize themselves instead.

THE LIMITATIONS OF TRAUMATIC MEMORY FOR CONTEMPORARY PROTEST MOVEMENTS

Although *Malcolm X* and *Panther* provide countermemories that defy postracial constructions of racial progress and national unity, their radical potential is contained by their use of film and narrative conventions that make the legacy of black radicalism less threatening to mainstream audiences. Emmett Winn observes that *Malcolm X* is the product of negotiation between the mainstream Hollywood industry and Lee's desire to challenge racist depictions of black experience. By framing Malcolm X's story in terms of one individual's overcoming obstacles to achieve greatness, Lee relies upon the narrative framework of the American Dream myth central to liberal ideology. Consequently, this version of Malcolm X is a less volatile, less radical figure than the speaker who inspired the Black Power movement. The film avoids many of his controversial statements that condemned capitalism as "vulturistic; it also obscures the larger context of Black Nationalism in the United States that shaped Malcolm X's thinking" (Bogle 1996; Dyson 1995; Hoerl 2008, 355–70; Lyne 2000, 39–59; Marable 1995; Winn 2001, 452–65). Likewise, *Panther* ignores the philosophy underlying the Black Panther Party's activism that was rooted in a Marxist critique of capitalism and Western colonialism. Both films glorify black masculine agency, ignoring the central role that women played in the Black Power movement. Lee's and Van Peebles's depictions conform to a broader trend in Hollywood's portrayal of late sixties activism that imagines social protest as a predominantly masculine enterprise. This version of the decade reinforces public amnesia about women's involvement in anticapitalist, antiwar, and antiracist movements from the decade.

The movies' political edges are also blunted by their emphasis on the violent murders of iconic Black Power leaders. Lee's film culminates in Malcolm X's assassination during his final speaking engagement on February 21, 1965, in Harlem's Audubon Ballroom by three mysterious assailants. Similarly, the last dramatic scene in *Panther* ends with images of the fictional character Tyrone's body being riddled with police bullets as he stands in front of a blazing warehouse to distract police from Alma and Judge as they make their getaway. Both movies suggest, tacitly if not explicitly, that some of the highest levels of governmental office were involved in these murders.

By concluding their narratives with the murders of committed Black Power activists, Lee's and Van Peebles's films foreground the tragic consequences of radical black dissent. In this regard, they contribute to the legacy of physical violation that is intrinsic to the black experience in the United States. Elizabeth Alexander (1995) argues that video footage of Rodney King's beating activated a collective memory of pervasive violence against African Americans. She observes that such images terrorize when they are made public because they foreground traumatic experience as a key source for collective identification. Alexander also remarks that stories about white violence against blacks are necessary for their survival, reflecting that "black people have paradoxically had to witness their own murder and defilement and then pass along the epic tale of violation" (94). These observations point to what may be an inescapable limitation of countermemories of Black Power. Although they offer radical alternatives to hegemonic narratives about racial uplift, memories inspired by the traumatic murders of black dissidents remind viewers of the dangerous and deadly consequences of radical black organizing. These are memories that must be shared even though they are part of the traumatic legacy of African American life. Thus, narratives that foreground the tragic demise of some of Black Power activism's most charismatic figures offer crucial yet limited resources for envisioning collective challenges to racial exploitation and violence at present.

By positioning radical black dissent within the memory of a traumatic past, *Malcolm X* and *Panther* offer ambiguous lessons about how racial justice organizing might proceed in the future. Thus, these films illustrate the drawbacks of Hollywood's tendency to periodize radical black dissent in the sixties. Both *Malcolm X* and *Panther* evoke a crisis of radical political knowledge in which the racism embedded within liberal capitalism is neither sustained nor actively challenged; rather, it is enshrined within traumatic cultural memory. The tragic endings to these films foreclose possibilities for envisioning a long history of racial justice struggles that have persisted beyond the lifetimes of particular leaders or specific organizations.

The tragic demise of the Black Power movement is the focus of films outside of Hollywood as well. The 1990 documentary series *Eyes on the Prize II: America at the Racial Crossroads, 1965–Mid-1980s* and the more recent Swedish documentary *The Black Power Mixtape, 1967–1974* also revolve around the martyrdom of black leaders and movement leaders' despair over the pervasive drug culture in US urban centers (Hoerl 2014). The recurring image of assassinated black leaders and racist violence of law enforcement solidifies a black countermemory that consigns dissent itself to the past.

The articulation of radical protest to trauma contributes to an environment in which progressive causes for racial justice are channeled into electoral politics. The conclusion to Spike Lee's film does so directly by connecting Nelson Mandela's own life story as part of the slain leader's legacy. The movie concludes with an extended shot of a nineties-era Mandela repeating Malcolm X's declaration of black people's rights to be respected as human beings and to bring this right into existence "by any means necessary." Mandela's own career was one of political transformation. The antiapartheid leader of South Africa was imprisoned for treason after his militant resistance to apartheid, including his role in the bombing of military infrastructure and power plants. After his release from prison, he went on to become the first president of postapartheid South Africa. Audiences familiar with Mandela's history might appreciate the connection between the two leaders who both advocated armed resistance as necessary to ending racial exploitation of black people in their countries. Insofar as Mandela rejected nonviolence in favor of militant resistance to the inhumane conditions of apartheid, this closing scene suggests that there is in fact a longer history of militant antiracist dissent that has continued into the present. However, I am not entirely convinced that the brief clip of Mandela does enough to break from the traumatic narrative that the rest of the biopic film constructs. Given Mandela's acceptance by many mainstream political figures in the United States and his celebrated history as a human-rights advocate worldwide, Mandela's appearance in the film also helps to mainstream the memory of Malcolm X. Although historically astute viewers might infer a counterhegemonic message, the movie's radical implications would be obscured for audiences unfamiliar with Mandela's history prior to his release from prison in 1990.

By consigning radical activism to the traumatic memories of black victimhood, *Malcolm X* and *Panther* implicitly suggest that radical dissent offers little recourse for African Americans seeking racial justice. Even as they provide countermemories that question the legitimacy of the civil rights subject as a model of black political agency, these movies obscure how activism for fundamental change has been advanced due to the collective efforts of activists throughout the United States. The selective amnesia created by narratives of traumatic loss teach viewers to forget that radicalism among people of color in the United States has evolved and continues to respond to different exigencies and goals.

POSTRACIAL CONSTRUCTIONS OF THE BLACK PANTHER PARTY

Although the early to mid-nineties witnessed a proliferation of popular music and movies that celebrated Black Power icons as symbols of black empowerment and resistance to white power structures, many other prominent Hollywood products have provided caricatures of the Black Panther Party as comically paranoid or as menacing threats to white society. These one-dimensional depictions of the Black Panthers extend routine press characterizations of black radicalism as a threat to civil (white) society. Such depictions affirm the authority of the civil rights subject and the dismissal of radical black politics that bolsters postracial assumptions that racism no longer impedes black people's achievements.

The Black Panthers' appearance in one brief scene of *Forrest Gump* illustrates how Hollywood has continued to derogate black radicalism. As I explain in the previous chapter, the Panthers' presence punctuates the callous violence of Jenny's boyfriend, Wesley. In this scene, Jenny brings Forrest to a Black Panther meeting. The Panthers' cartoonish costumes and clichéd language resembles a parody of mediated depictions of late sixties activism. Since the film never depicts racist brutality, this speech might seem abrasive and irrational to viewers with limited knowledge of US histories of racial violence. The caricature might prompt viewers to disregard the entire scene as a comically hyperreal take on radical sixties memory; however, the film prompts viewers to view Gump's naiveté with sympathy and affection and offers no cues to prompt viewers to view its depictions of social and political turmoil with critical distance.

With its focus on white masculine struggles over women's political agency, the scene directs viewers to understand the Panthers' priorities as dangerously misguided. Jenny and Wesley begin to argue while another Panther, oblivious to the conflict, confronts Forrest. As this Panther provides a lengthy rant about the organization's mission to end the war in Vietnam, the camera zooms in on Forrest's face. Forrest is the only person to react when Wesley smacks Jenny across the head. By focusing on Forrest's reactions, the scene positions the Panther's speech as background noise. Forrest pounces on Wesley, bringing him to the floor with a series of punches. After Forrest attacks Wesley, a Panther wearing a bulleted belt opens the door, indicating that Forrest should leave. Clearly, the Panthers are indifferent to Wesley's abusive behavior and distrustful of Forrest. Forrest turns to see a crowd of stern-faced Black Panthers staring back at him. One holds a pistol in the air. Forrest offers an apology that provides a moment of levity into the tense scene, "Sorry I had a fight in the middle of your Black Panther

Party." Despite the humorous quip, the Panthers appear as menacing threats to Forrest and to the family values that Forrest represents.

While *Forrest Gump* portrays the Panthers as irrational, misguided, and misogynist, other Hollywood products since the late nineties including the 1999 NBC miniseries *The '60s*, a 2000 episode of *Law & Order*, the 2004 movie *Barbershop 2: Back in Business*, and the 2013 film *The Butler* depict black militancy as an impediment to social and economic progress. These texts provide more context to explain the emergence of black militancy than *Forrest Gump* offered, but they all focus on black rage as the problem that imperils black communities and national unity.

CONTRADICTORY LESSONS ABOUT THE BLACK PANTHERS IN *THE '60S*

In the 1999 NBC miniseries *The '60s*, the central narrative involving the Herlihy family is interrupted with scenes about Willie and Emmet Taylor, a black working-class father and son struggling to overcome obstacles caused by civil rights injustices, inner-city riots, and racial profiling by police. The miniseries' investment in whiteness is highlighted by its depiction of the Taylors' struggles as secondary to the Herlihy family's problems. Their portrayal is as reductive as the depiction of the Herlihys. Willie Taylor stands in for the perspective of more moderate civil rights organizations such as Martin Luther King's Southern Christian Leadership Council, and Emmet represents the activism of younger Black Power activists who belonged to organizations such as the Student Nonviolent Coordinating Committee and the Congress for Racial Equality. After Malcolm X is assassinated, Willie observes that his son has become increasingly angry and cautions him to avoid becoming bitter. Looking sternly at his son, Willie warns him, "bitterness will only bring you down." Several scenes later, Emmet's anger has tragic consequences. Willie stops his son from stealing a television during the 1965 Los Angeles riots. Mistaking Willie for a looter, a police officer shoots him. Moments later, he dies in Emmet's arms. By framing it in the context of a familial argument over the merits of nonviolent civil disobedience, the scene focuses on Emmet's culpability for Willie's death. The central problem facing black communities throughout the miniseries is black anger, not the racist brutality of law enforcement.

During the second half of the miniseries, Emmet retreats into drug use to cope with his loss, and then becomes a committed member of the Black Panther Party. Echoing their portrayal in *Forrest Gump*, this scene depicts Black Panthers as angry and misogynist. Huey Newton and Bobby Seale recruit Emmet on Haight Ashbury Street in San Francisco. During the scene, Emmet meets Katie Herlihy. Seale calls Katie a "white bitch" and castigates Emmet for dressing like a "white clown." They instruct Emmet to take pride in himself by joining them. Later scenes crosscut actual and recreated footage of the Panthers in training, wearing black berets and carrying rifles. This depiction imagines the Panthers in ways that correspond more closely to the rhetoric that promulgated the moral panics over crime and gangs in the eighties and nineties than to Black Panther Party histories. By fusing the selective amnesia of the Panthers with nineties-era tough-on-crime legislation, the miniseries stokes fears about radical black collectivity. Presumably, organized radicals, like gangs, endanger white women and threaten civil society.

This lesson does not cohere with the miniseries' final depictions of the Panthers, which are more positive. Inexplicably, the miniseries concludes its narrative about Emmet by placing him in Chicago, where he volunteers for the Panthers' free breakfast program for children alongside Fred Hampton. Hampton encourages the children to eat and empower themselves to help free now-imprisoned Huey Newton. (The miniseries offers no explanation for Newton's incarceration; given the earlier menacing portrayal of him, viewers with little familiarity with this history might easily infer that he was engaged in criminal activity.) By jumping between scenes of Panther activism in San Francisco and Chicago, the miniseries lacks internal coherence and offers a confusing account of the movement. Toward the end of the film, Hampton explains that the Panthers' community service was the organization's most important contribution to black empowerment. He then counsels Emmet to let go of his hatred exacerbated by his father's death. "Hatred will fool you, trick you into looking for the cop who killed him . . . trick you into looking for any white man." Hampton concludes his lecture by noting that, "come the end of the day, you ain't going to be any closer to your father." This scene ends with a caption informing audiences, "Fred Hampton was assassinated in his sleep on December 4, 1969."

The miniseries' attention to Fred Hampton provides an ambivalent response to popular culture's almost wholesale amnesia regarding Hampton. By acknowledging Fred Hampton's contribution to the Black Panther Party, the miniseries offers a somewhat more developed depiction of the organization than most televised programs. Yet, its portrayal of the Panther leader is egregious nonetheless. The miniseries offers no clues that the Chicago police were responsible for Hampton's murder. The emphasis on Hampton's unexplained assassination as the end of the story about black activism contributes to memories of dissent that consign black radicalism to a traumatic past without explaining the context for radical organizing. During his life, Hampton regarded revolutionary action as foundational to the Panthers' mission, as community service programs were designed to promulgate popular support for the "revolution." Hampton was particularly effective in building coalitions with other radical groups in the Chicago area, which made him a central target of concern for the FBI. Given that the Black Power movement was a response to the failures of early civil rights activism, Hampton's murder heightened the political Left's anger and contributed to growing militant activism in the early seventies.

The lack of information regarding the circumstances of Hampton's assassination positions his death as one among a myriad of tragic iconic moments that has given meaning to the sixties. Thus, the portrayal of Hampton as a critic of black political anger enjoins audiences to mourn Hampton's death as a civil rights tragedy, not as the horrendous violation of civil rights that it was. Further, the depiction of Hampton as a politically moderate figure realigns the memory of Hampton with the civil rights subject who has exchanged collective demands for justice with hard work and philanthropy. It is telling that the miniseries does not identify law enforcement as Hampton's killers; clearly, the miniseries sought to avoid complicating a story of the sixties that ends in family unity and national redemption. Information that he was killed by police in his sleep would obstruct a narrative in which Emmet learns to overcome his anger and hatred toward the white establishment.

Overall, *The '60s*'s depiction of the Panthers contradicts much of what the organization stood for. Although many aspects of the Black Panther Party reinforced sexism, the organization recognized that women's liberation was important to their movement (Matthews 1998, 268–304). The Panthers parted ways with other Black Power organizations by coalition-building with white radicals. They also diverged from Black Nationalist organizations by identifying capitalism as the primary cause of people's oppression and viewing their own organization as the vanguard party that would lead the global masses in a revolution against Western imperialism. *The '60s* dissolves the radical potential Black Panther Party memory by imagining the organization as a white hate group, by restaging and exaggerating its early sexism, and by articulating the party's progressive contributions to the black community to Fred Hampton's assassination. This construction forgets crucial elements of Panther history including the Panthers' commitment to interracial coalition building, its inclusion of women in leadership positions, and the FBI's illegal campaign to destroy them through overt and covert methods. *The '60s* flagrantly avoids nuanced understanding about the role of black radicalism in recent history. It is a vivid example of the troubling consequences of selective amnesia surrounding the bad sixties.

THE PROBLEM OF BLACK RAGE IN *LAW & ORDER*

A year after NBC aired *The '60s*, an episode of the long-running NBC police procedural *Law & Order* portrayed a former Black Panther as an illustration of destructive black anger that undermines the cause of justice. The state prosecutors of *Law & Order* repeatedly put late sixties militancy on trial over the course of its twenty-year run. A 2000 episode was loosely inspired by events surrounding the arrest of Jamil Abdullah Al-Amin, a Muslim cleric who led several radical black political organizations including the Congress on Racial Equality and the Black Panthers during the late sixties, when he went by the name of H. Rap Brown. As H. Rap Brown, he became infamous for remarking that violence is "as American as apple pie," and for stating, "If America don't come around, we're gonna burn it down." In 2000, Al-Amin was arrested for shooting two Atlanta sheriff's deputies who tried to serve him with an arrest warrant on minor charges. One of the deputies, Ricky Kinchen, died of gunshot wounds. A jury found Al-Amin guilty and sentenced him to life in prison despite Al-Amin's insistence that the charges were part of a government conspiracy to punish him for his earlier activism.

Released before Al-Amin's trial, the *Law & Order* episode entitled "Burn, Baby, Burn" depicted detectives' and state prosecutors' efforts to apprehend and convict fictional character Latiffe Miller for the murder of a New York City police officer. Although he is now a Muslim cleric and community leader, detectives recognize Miller as former Black Panther Party member Bobby Miller. Like Brown, the fictional Miller served five years in jail for a robbery he committed decades earlier. The episode does not anticipate Al-Amin's defense that the FBI was intentionally trying to set him up. Nor does the episode foresee Al-Amin's conviction. Instead, *Law & Order* prosecutors fail to win a conviction because the jury is wary of law enforcement's record of violence against black people. The episode builds tension by creating moral ambiguity over Miller's guilt. Although strong evidence connects Miller to the crime, the defense argues that the history of police violence in the United States provides Miller with an understandable motive. The defense highlights a series of violent police assaults of black suspects, including the real person Amadou Diallo, a twenty-two-year-old migrant from Guinea who was shot and killed by four New York City police officers in 1999. When he is questioned, Miller states that police constantly harassed the Panthers and that "several brothers were outright murdered by police raids." Miller explains that his nephew was shot by a police officer in a case of mistaken identity, and he instinctively viewed all police officers as potential threats since then.

The program crafts a negative public memory of the sixties during the scenes of Miller's trial. The defense attorney characterizes Miller as a product of the sixties, noting that his worldview was "shaped by the political foment of the sixties and then crystallized by current events, a never-ending list of African Americans that have been murdered and attacked by white police officers." *Law & Order* goes further than other television depictions of the Black Panthers by referencing the FBI's corrupt efforts to destroy the Panthers; however, Assistant District Attorney Jack McCoy is nonplussed. He recalls that Miller "incit[ed] his followers to kill police officers" during the sixties and notes that Miller might also have been motivated to shoot the officer because he was under investigation for fraud. Here, and for other sixties-era radicals that *Law & Order* has put on trial, former activists' stated principles are not to be trusted. As I explain in the next chapter, the image of the former radical with self-interested motives is a key message that has contributed to the criminalization of dissent in television programming.

In the case of fictional Latiffe Miller, the attorneys' competing explanations for events negotiates between mainstream and oppositional understandings of law enforcement. However, the program implicitly urges audiences to identify with the prosecutor's perspective. After all, the program revolves around the perspectives of New York City detectives and prosecuting attorneys featured in each episode. Routinely, these characters express their commitment to serving the cause of justice, and episodes usually end with successful prosecutions based on strong evidence of the defendant's criminal wrongdoing. In "Burn, Baby, Burn," McCoy enjoins the jury (and the audience) to understand Miller's actions as a result of black rage that threatens to destroy the legal justice system. During his closing argument, McCoy states that Mr. Miller's "anger and racial mistrust" has "contaminated the truth." While the camera cuts to an image of Miller's adolescent son, McCoy asserts that Miller has avoided taking accountability for his own actions. McCoy concludes that experiencing racism is not a "free pass to commit murder." Miller's son appears to listen attentively to McCoy; ostensibly, he is the stakes of the controversy, a pre-political subject on the verge of developing his own civic identity. The close-up on this young black man implies that he may be moved to diverge from his father's radical critique under the influence of

McCoy's seemingly reasonable argument. By focusing on Miller's son during the closing arguments, the program suggests an ideal future of race relations in which black distrust of white institutions and law enforcement has been overcome. This distrust is ostensibly overcome through the black youth's understanding of a presumably impartial legal justice system (despite all real-world evidence to the contrary), not by the end of police abuse against the black community.

Although the jury finds Miller, and by extension, the sixties, innocent, the police detectives and the prosecutor's office understand that the sixties has sown decades of racial distrust and violence. McCoy and Lewin lament that black radicals have influenced the community to view white police officers as threats to the black community. After the jury finds Miller innocent of charges, District Attorney Lewin assesses the outcome with McCoy and concludes, "Enough of the jury identified with Miller's fear of cops." McCoy retorts, "used to be a fear of cops didn't justify shooting them." As Lewin turns to leave the office, she sighs, "it used to be a lot of things." The episode's conclusion reveals that the memory of the Black Panthers was deployed to usher in nostalgia for a pre-sixties past when police officers were well-respected members of the community. Given that the program positions Miller's worldview in "the sixties," the program's conclusion infers that black radicals from the sixties era have corrupted the justice system. The episode absolves the legal justice system from responsibility to restructure law enforcement policies and practices by suggesting that the solution is for black men to abandon their sixties ideology, trust cops, and have faith in the legal system. Ostensibly, we would all do well to hold the sixties accountable for corrupting our civic duty and ethical obligations to others.

CELEBRATING THE CIVIL RIGHTS SUBJECT IN *BARBERSHOP 2*

While *Law & Order* blames Black Panthers for damaging the citizenry's faith in law enforcement, the popular 2004 movie *Barbershop 2: Back in Business* faults them for jeopardizing African Americans' economic progress. The sequel to 2002's *Barbershop*, *Barbershop 2* features an all-black cast. It earned nearly $65 million at the box office, and ranked first among new releases during its opening weekend (Germain 2004, D5). The movie's large audience highlights its prominent role as a source of public memory about the Black Panthers. This memory suggests that the Panthers posed a threat to black advancement. As Roopali Mukherjee (2006, 613) argues, the *Barbershop* films champion black entrepreneurship as the basis for black political and economic progress. The film's narrative revolves around a family-owned barbershop that is a center of community life for an urban neighborhood. The business is threatened by the opening of a national barbering enterprise that has opened across the street. In solidarity with the local members of his community, the main protagonist Calvin Palmer refuses to partner with developers. Calvin also resists a local alderman's desire to use the barbershop as the location for his own public relations stunt. The movie expresses black communities' disillusionment over electoral politics, suggesting that black politicians have just as much potential to exploit working-class blacks as whites. But they also indicate that community organizing is useful only insofar as it enables small black businesses to succeed.

Opening and closing scenes reinforce *Barbershop 2*'s emphasis on black entrepreneurship as a means to black self-determination. The film opens with flashback images of supporting character Eddie being pursued by baton-wielding police officers on July 4, 1967. He escapes by running into the barbershop. Instead of exposing him to the cops, Calvin's father harbors Eddie and offers him a job in exchange for good civic behavior. Hard work, not activism, was the solution to police repression. During the conclusion, Calvin asks Eddie, "Is this the life you wanted or did you think you could do better someday?" In response, Eddie recalls the city's riots after Martin Luther King's assassination, less than a year after he started working at the barbershop. Eddie explains that he warded off an attempted attack by a young black man threatening to throw a flaming brick through the store window. After that moment, Calvin's father never made him pay for a chair in the store again. Eddie concludes that he didn't save the store. On the contrary, he tells Calvin, "the shop saved me. As far as I'm concerned, my life began on July 4, 1967, when I got this job working in the barbershop."

Eddie's response to Calvin suggests that he would have perished had he succumbed to pressures to embrace black militancy. The movie's lessons are that black politics geared toward fundamental economic transformation leads to tragic consequences and that one would be a fool to question the merits of capitalism. Presumably, even if capitalist enterprises breed injustice, movements to transform American society will ultimately get black people killed. If capitalism is the lesser of two evils, it is best to embrace it. The movie amplifies the dangers of black organizing by pitting characters against radicals and politicians who seem to have lost touch with the community. Midway through the film, commentary by senior barber Eddie punctuates the importance of black private enterprise as a means of empowerment. When Calvin expresses his resentment toward an alderman's desire to use the shop for a public relations stunt, Eddie recalls another time in which black radicals used the shop as a home base for political organizing. A flashback scene of black-and-white film depicts a much younger Eddie surrounded by men wearing black berets and leather jackets reminiscent of the Black Panthers. The scene opens with shots of Eddie and Calvin's father nodding their heads as a Panther encourages the group of patrons and fellow Panthers to support the community. Then, the radical leader adds, "When the pigs show up, they gonna show up with their guns. We gonna show up with OUR guns. Then they gonna start shooting. Only we gonna start shooting. I tell you, if only one of them gets shot, all of us is gonna get shot!" The camera cuts to Eddie, who begins to furrow his brow and lowers his raised fist, demonstrating his less-than-enthusiastic response to what he is hearing. The radial leader then shouts, "All of us is gonna die together!" The crowd exits the barbershop shouting, "Black Power!" Eddie pretends to follow them, but locks the door instead. He mutters to the remaining patrons and fellow barbers, "Shit. Man, those fools crazy." This hyperbolic depiction of black militancy makes the Panthers appear dangerous and foolish. The next shot signals its return to the present day through color footage of Calvin being greeted by the alderman who has arrived at his shop to win support for his campaign. The inference is that both family business owners and audiences should be suspicious of all political organizing, including the Black Panthers of the past and self-serving politicians of the present. Presumably, both would use black-owned businesses to the detriment of the community.

By marginalizing black organizing in favor of private enterprise, *Barbershop 2* confirms the logics underlying the welfare reforms eight years prior to the film's release. Clinton's Personal Responsibility and Work Opportunity Act of 1996 replaced the federal welfare system with a program that restricted some benefits and left administration to the states. As the bill's name makes plain, supporters of the change insisted that putting individuals to work was preferable to entitlements for the very poor. Arguments promoting welfare to work invoked the specter of blackness without naming it directly. Politicians on both sides of the aisle alluded to historic racial stereotypes of black people as lazy dependents on the state. For example, the White House spotlighted Ronda Costa, who purportedly stated that she left the welfare rolls after her daughter said, "Mommy, I'm tired of seeing you sitting around the house doing nothing. Why don't you get out and do something with yourself?" ("Clinton Marks" 1998, 6). This quote evokes the mythic image of the welfare queen made famous by Ronald Reagan during his 1976 presidential campaign. News coverage made the presence of blackness in discourses about welfare visible by featuring black recipients in reports about the welfare debate, even though the majority of welfare recipients were white (Gilens 2009).

At the time *Barbershop 2* showed in theaters, the nation's most vulnerable populations had been deeply impacted by the reforms. The number of families receiving benefits had declined even though the number of families with children living in extreme poverty had risen. People who were unable to work and who could not meet eligibility requirements for benefits were hit particularly hard ("Chart Book" 2016; Ehrenfreund 2016). Arguments favoring welfare reform overlooked factors such as urban deindustrialization that contributed to black unemployment and low wages for low-skilled jobs. Such wages have failed to rise alongside inflation rates and the rising salaries for the professional class. These are structural issues tied to the neoliberal trade economy that groups including organized labor have rallied against. Ignoring these structural constraints, *Barbershop 2* suggests that the fortunes of black lives depend on this economy, not to the coalitional organizing efforts of groups protesting global trade policies.

DISCOURSES OF DISTRACTION

Contrasting visions of the Black Power movement in Hollywood film and television illustrate how popular memories are cultural sites for carrying out political struggles in the present. The competing images of radical black political agency are a synecdoche for broader national divisions, not only over who should have access to the American Dream but whether it is a dream at all. As Malcolm X told an audience in 1964, "I don't see any American dream; I see an American nightmare." Since Black Power activists foregrounded the injustices embedded within the fabric of the nation, film and TV memories of the movement speak to contemporary political agendas for racial justice and the prospects for fundamental transformations in the racial order.

Hollywood's ambivalence regarding Black Power memory also illustrates the industry's struggle to remain relevant to a diverse audience without alienating dominant viewing audiences. Popular portrayals of the Black Panthers in products targeting broader—whiter—audiences implicitly confirmed neoconservative arguments favoring "tough-on-crime" legislation and free-market individualism. The proliferation of these more pejorative portrayals of the Black Panthers contributes to a backlash against civil rights and Great Society legislation by using Black Power as a symbol for the excesses of black activism. Thus, Hollywood memories of the Black Panthers rearticulated racial tensions in terms amenable to postracial logics. By depicting Black Panthers' rage as a social problem, Hollywood films and television blame those opposing racial inequity for perpetuating racism. Presumably, discrimination against people of color has been left in the past.

Hollywood portrayals of radical black rage illustrate what Omi and Winant (1994, 117) have referred to as "discourses of distraction" from the realities of virulent forms of racism with harmful consequences for people of color. Consequently, they help neoliberal policymakers deny claims for structural recourse. During the late 1990s and the early twenty-first century, postracial politics were evidenced by the elimination of Affirmative Action programs by state referenda in California, Texas, and Michigan. In each of these states, the demands of black communities for proactive policies to redress the consequences of racial discrimination were characterized as a threat to individual rights and equal opportunity. More recently, Louisiana's legislature brought color-blind policies to bear in hate crimes legislation by passing the "Blue Lives Matter" bill that includes police officers and firefighters as categories of people deserving special prosecution for violent crimes committed against them. This move dilutes the legislation's protections for black people who have been historically subjected to violence on the basis of historic prejudice and discrimination.

Hollywood has reinforced the civil rights subject and its foil of the angry black radical most recently in Lee Daniels's 2013 movie *The Butler*, a film inspired by the story of an African American butler who served the White House during and after the civil rights struggle. The film's central conflict involves main character Cecil's tumultuous relationship with his oldest son Louis. While Cecil diligently serves multiple presidential administrations, his son becomes involved in activism. Louis is a synecdoche for young black people's participation in the civil rights movement. Similar to the character portrayal of *The '60s*'s Kenny, who participates in most of the major antiwar protest events of the decade, Louis attends almost every major civil rights protest event of the mid- to late sixties. Later, disenchanted with the slow pace of integration, Louis briefly joins the Black Panther Party. When he shows up at his father's home wearing a black beret, Cecil throws him out. Although Louis is enthusiastic about the Panthers' commitment to community service, he leaves the organization when he learns that it is prepared to murder white people to achieve their goals. Cecil and Louis reconcile many years later, after Louis has focused his energies on electoral politics. In the film's final scene, the two attend a celebration of Obama's first presidential inauguration.

I provide this brief plot summary to explain how *The Butler* expands upon the selective amnesia about Black Power that has been cultivated by previous depictions of black radicalism. This movie exaggerates the Panthers' commitment to violence, failing to recognize that the Panthers' bravado was a performance designed to empower black youth to organize against racial discrimination (Rhodes 2007). This reductive caricature of the Black Panther Party amplifies the virtues of civil rights subjects, Cecil—and a middle-aged Louis—whose political moderation and hard work lead to success. Further, the film's narrative gives cinematic form to postracial rhetoric about Obama's election as the conclusion to the civil rights struggle (Hoerl 2012). By depicting Obama's presidency as the fruits of the civil rights struggle, the movie negates and silences those who have contested hegemonic narratives of national unity by highlighting ongoing systems of oppression in the United States.

Fictionalized depictions of enraged black militants also provide a common-sense understanding about the threat of black radicalism that the Right has continuously drawn upon to stir up resentment toward political liberals. On the night of the 2008 presidential election of Barack Obama, the FOX News network diverted attention from Obama's impending victory toward the image of two members of the New Black Panther Party who were intimidating voters at a Philadelphia polling station. While the rest of the nation was focused on long lines of voters who were excited about the prospect of electing a black president, FOX raised the specter of black boogeymen as a threat to democracy. Two years later, the network's pundit Bill O'Reilly lambasted the Department of Justice for not pursuing criminal charges against the men, suggesting that the department's response was evidence of political corruption. Paradoxically, the outrage obscured the controversy of voter ID laws across several states that suppressed voter turnout among minorities. Talk about a discourse of distraction! (Cullen 2008; Farley 2010; Ferns 2007).

Selective amnesia of Black Power occludes the public memory of radical black dissent by omitting significant events in the history of antiracist struggles, particularly those occurring after the passage of the 1965 Civil Rights Act. Toward the end of the decade, activists including not only Black Power figures but also more moderate voices such as Martin Luther King's brought attention to structural conditions that perpetuated racial disparities throughout urban centers in the North and the West Coast. The civil rights subject is affirmed by memories of the freedom struggle that forget or deride the activism that challenged racial injustice beyond the segregated spaces of the Deep South. Certainly, postracial portrayals of Black Power have not prevented racial justice movements from seeking political redress in recent decades, but they do contribute to an environment in which political figures and the press can offer simplified and dismissive commentary about black activism at present. By imagining Panthers' activism primarily via images of black victimhood or black rage, Hollywood shrinks our resources for understanding how urgent problems of our day connect to US histories of black struggle.

CHAPTER FIVE

The Criminalization of Late Sixties Militancy in Television Police Procedurals

Few aspects of late sixties activism have received as much critical and ongoing attention in popular culture as the militant movements of the late sixties and early seventies. The Weathermen organization has been a particular source of fascination. During the 2008 presidential campaign, former Weathermen activist Bill Ayers received persistent television news coverage after it was reported that he and then candidate Barack Obama were friends. During the last primary debate between Barack Obama and Hillary Clinton, moderator George Stephanopolous asked Obama to explain his relationship to Ayers. Stephanopolous reminded audiences that on 9/11, the *New York Times* quoted Ayers as saying, "I don't regret setting bombs. I feel we didn't do enough." Obama replied that Ayers was "a guy who lives in my neighborhood, who's a professor of English in Chicago, who I know and who I have not received some official endorsement from" ("Obama and Clinton" 2008). (The press reported later that Ayers was a University of Chicago professor of education and that Ayers hosted a fundraising event at his home to support Obama's first campaign for the Illinois state senate in 1995. In later years, they worked together on the Woods Foundation charity and Chicago Annenberg Challenge service organizations.)

Despite his decades of work as an education scholar, broadcast news coverage repeatedly displayed the mug shot of a much younger

Ayers, implicitly validating political claims that any association Obama might have with the former sixties-era radical could potentially discredit him from holding the presidential office. The sixties-baiting of Barack Obama—the attempt to tarnish him with the brush of Leftist politics and antiwar sympathy—illustrates how the memory of radical politics from the Vietnam War era has been a lightning rod even forty years later, generating intense feelings against moderate or (presumably) left-of-center political candidates.

Beyond news reports, a broad range of representations in popular culture have contributed to media memories of leftist militancy from the late sixties and early seventies. Several memoirs of former Weathermen and other late sixties radicals have been published as recently as 2011 (Albert 1990; Ayers 2001; Gilbert 2011; Rudd 2009; Stern 2007; Wilkerson 2007), and the Weather Underground is the subject of a 2003 Academy Award–nominated documentary. Conservative news media and print culture continue to publish reports and books about the history and current projects of former Weather Underground activists (Burrough 2015; Collier and Horowitz 2006). The memory of radical sixties-era militancy has also inspired novels, plays, and Hollywood films.[1]

Many fictionalized narratives have revolved around sixties-era fugitives who evaded law enforcement after committing violent crimes to advance a leftist antiwar agenda. Based on Neil Gordon's 2003 novel, Robert Redford's 2012 thriller *The Company You Keep* depicts a fugitive from the Weather Underground who stayed underground decades after he was wrongly accused of murdering a security guard. Late sixties militancy is also referenced in scripted television programs.[2] The animated half-hour comedy program *The Simpsons* modeled the character of Homer Simpson's mother, Mona, after Weathermen activist Bernardine Dohrn (Appel 2005). More recently, Comedy Central's television program *Drunk History* featured the Symbionese Liberation Army, offering a comedic portrayal of Patricia Hearst performed by the well-known comedic actress Kristen Wiig.

A wide variety of television police procedural programs have also drawn inspiration from events surrounding the actions of the Weather Underground, the Black Liberation Army, the Symbionese Liberation

Army, and other unaffiliated fugitives. They include well-known, long-running series including *Hill Street Blues* (which ran from 1981 to 1987), *Law & Order* (1990–2010), *The Practice* (1997–2004), *Cold Case* (2003–2010), and *Bones* (2005–present). They also include more recent but less popular programs that lasted only one season: *Life on Mars* (2008–2009) and *The Chicago Code* (2011).[3] Although much could be said about the recurring messages that run across the wide range of mediated portrayals of late sixties militants, this chapter focuses on these police procedurals because they provide some of the most widely accessible and patterned depictions of radical Left militancy for film and television audiences.

Spectacular events surrounding late sixties militancy have surely motivated popular culture's investments in remembering radical Left violence. The Weathermen became notorious after a Greenwich Village townhouse explosion on March 6, 1970, killed three of its members during a failed bomb-making attempt. Surviving members changed the organization's name from the Weathermen to the Weather Underground, cut all ties to former friends and family, and implemented the policy of strictly targeted inanimate structures as dramatic but largely symbolic gestures of political opposition to capitalist imperialism and US occupation overseas. Between 1970 and 1975, the clandestine organization took responsibility for bombing twenty-five inanimate structures including the US Capitol and the Pentagon in retaliation for the ongoing war in Vietnam and political repression of black radicals. The Weather Underground disintegrated by the mid-seventies, and many members were arrested or turned themselves in during the following decade. The Weather Underground received renewed political attention in 1981 when several former members were convicted for their involvement in the robbery of a Brinks armored car in New York that ended in the murders of a Brinks guard and two patrolmen.

Although the Weathermen are the most familiar clandestine radicals from the late sixties, they were not the only leftists who viewed themselves as at war with the US government. Others involved in the Brinks robbery were members of the Black Liberation Army, the guerilla arm of the Black Panther Party dedicated to armed resistance to fight colonialism in the United States. The mainstream press continues to report on the whereabouts of its most famous member, Assata Shakur, who escaped to Cuba after being convicted for killing a New Jersey state trooper in 1977.[4] The Symbionese Liberation Army also garnered national media attention after the group kidnapped Patty Hearst in 1973 and committed a series of bank robberies and murders between 1973 and 1975. A large shoot-out with Los Angeles police that ended with the deaths of six SLA members was broadcast live on local television in 1974.

In what follows, I situate my analysis within the media context that contributed to the meaning of episodes of television police procedurals about radical fugitives at the time they initially aired. Then, I explain how episodes from three programs—*Law & Order*, *Life on Mars*, and *Chicago Code*—have portrayed former sixties-era radicals as suspicious and criminal. The narrative patterns and recurring character portrayals occurring across these and episodes of other programs invite viewers to understand dissent through a law and order frame that carries not-so-subtle messages about the moral turpitude of radical militancy. Recurring themes across these episodes teach viewers that radicals have selfish motives and endanger civil society. These themes cultivate norms of democratic citizenship that call for suspicion toward dissidents and welcome police surveillance and detentions of activists.

My analysis draws particular attention to the ways in which police procedurals have foregrounded women radicals as a threat to civil society. The broad range of programs I observed for this study provide a bifurcated image of radical womanhood. On the one hand, former radicals who regret their past activism are portrayed as loving and supportive wives and mothers in programs including *Law & Order* and *Bones*. On the other hand, radical women who remain committed to ending structural racism and the Vietnam War seem unconcerned about the welfare of their children and express callous disregard for human life in programs including *Hill Street Blues*, *Cold Case*, *Life on Mars*, and *The Chicago Code*. This bifurcated image of women as either loving mothers or committed radicals suggests that public memories of radical women are bound up in ongoing contestation over traditional family structures and the belief that the nuclear family is the cornerstone of national civic identity. Ostensibly, women cannot simultaneously be committed radicals and caring nurturers because no kind-hearted woman would willingly participate in radical action. This presumption is affirmed by several programs' depictions of women radicals as guilty of murdering civilians. The construction of radicalism as a threat to children and the nuclear family points to a broader national investment in the memory of women's patriotism as inherently connected to their roles as wives and mothers. That is, it reveals how our sense of the nation is tied to beliefs about normative family structures. While challenges to the traditional family values have been taken as threats to the national order, radical challenges to the nation's militarism and foreign policy are, concomitantly, considered threats to the very fabric of society.

MEDIATED CONTEXTS OF TELEVISION CRIME DRAMA PORTRAYALS OF SIXTIES-ERA MILITANCY

I focus on police procedurals because television crime drama is a ubiquitous and popular genre. Now in syndication, episodes of *Law & Order*, *Bones*, and *Cold Case* repeatedly air on basic and cable television networks, often with episodes running back to back on weekdays, evenings, and weekends; thus, it is likely that many television audiences have viewed several of the episodes featuring sixties radicals. (As a case in point, I identified most of these episodes during a year in which I left the television on in the background when I was working on other projects.)

Across all of the television crime dramas that have featured sixties-era radicals, fictionalized versions of "ripped from the headlines" events are taken up as the subject of a single episode. In the episodes discussed here, organizations resembling the Weather Underground and/or the Symbionese Liberation Army are featured for their involvement in a violent crime. During the course of an investigation, the program's central characters encounter a former sixties-era radical. This encounter prompts police officers and attorneys working the case to recall the organization's destructive tactics, violent rhetoric, and physical confrontations with police.

The main characters' investigations and dialogue draw upon journalistic news frames of the real-life cases that inspired each episode. Characters and events cue audiences to the episode's political and historical relevance. The episodes identify actual activist groups or leaders as suspects, or they provide fictionalized identities that are thinly veiled references to late sixties and early seventies militant groups. Most of the episodes offer a bricolage of news events that have come to stand in for late sixties militancy in American popular culture; however, this bricolage does not reflect any concerted attempt to put historical events in televisual form. For instance, *Law & Order*'s episode is inspired by the case of Katherine Ann Power. The episode cast real-life attorney William Kunstler to play the defendant's counselor. Although Kunstler is well known for defending a variety of antiwar activists, he never represented Power. *Law & Order* also characterized the defendant as a member of the Students for a Democratic Society at Columbia University. The reference to Columbia enabled writers to set events in New York and relied upon baby-boomer audiences' possible familiarity with the publicity surrounding the 1968 student takeover at Columbia University led by SDS leader Mark Rudd, who later joined the Weather Underground in 1970. However, Power was not a member of the organization. This bricolage amplifies the episode's contribution to the intertextual construction of late sixties memory in popular culture. Although these programs do not explicitly attempt to mirror actual cases, their references to historic and current events position the episodes as commentary and reflection about radical politics.

These episodes also replicate and exaggerate the framing devices provided by mainstream press coverage of the anti–Vietnam War movement. As Todd Gitlin (2003, 182) explains, the mainstream press covered the antiwar movement selectively, foregrounding the "most violent, bizarre, and discordant actions and, within the boundaries of any action, the most violent segments." Gitlin attributes the "violence-on-the-Left" frame to the press convention of "describing an exceptional event rather than explaining its sources in normal, everyday social life" (185). As the decade of the sixties progressed, the press increasingly characterized dissent itself as the social problem requiring a solution. As a further consequence of news emphasis on the exceptional event, the press routinely decontextualized protest events and police busts from the political conditions that prompted them. News routines of *amplification* (depicting radical activists as the problem requiring solution), *personalization* (focusing on dynamic and outrageous individuals), and *decontextualization* (backgrounding the consequences of the war for human lives) resonate across these television episodes (185). Although they acknowledged that radicals were motivated by their commitment to ending the war, the context of the Vietnam War was given brief, if any, mention.

Television crime dramas complemented these news routines. Episodes across ten separate programs portrayed dissidents as perpetrators of criminal activity, included spectacular scenes of dissident violence and other forms of outrageous radical behavior, and omitted mentioning events that motivated activist militancy such as the My Lai Massacre, the invasion of Cambodia, and the police killing of Chicago Black Panther Party leader Fred Hampton. The episodes also ignored the FBI's extensive and illegal investigations of nonviolent dissent during this time period. Given that the FBI frequently colluded with local police departments to disrupt and discredit New Left and Black Power activism, the episodes' valorization of law enforcement largely affirm hegemonic assumptions about the inherent justness of the legal system. Consequently, their narratives contribute to a structured message system in mainstream culture that has encouraged citizens to dismiss activists who have demanded the end of police abuse and deadly violence against people of color in the United States. In this regard, these episodes not only have implications for public memories of late sixties radicalism but also for contemporary protest movements for police reform and racial justice such as Black Lives Matter.

The selective amnesia constructed by the news accounts that decontextualized protest events from systemic problems of war and racism created a vacuum for imagining the radical sixties that entertainment television could help to fill. Beyond replicating hegemonic news coverage of radical dissent, these programs invariably exaggerated the criminal behavior of the actual activists who inspired the episodes. Having a limited imperative to depict events with fidelity to historical accounts, these programs invented events, groups, and characters that complemented the conventions of the television crime drama in which police officers and prosecutors seek justice on behalf of those victimized by violence. The conclusions to most of these episodes exemplify Elayne Rapping's (2003, 46) observation that in crime shows such as *Law & Order*, prosecutors—not defenders—are the heroes, and the suspects are presumably guilty, rather than innocent or socially powerless." In episodes about sixties-era radicalism, investigators' recollections lead them to single out former activists as suspects in a homicide case. Although the investigations lead to various outcomes, former activists are always guilty of contributing to the deaths of civilians or police officers. The episode's criminalization of dissent amplifies the lessons provided by other films and programming discussed in the previous chapters of this book that sixties-era politics must be eradicated from public life.

CONTAINING THE THREAT OF RADICAL WOMEN'S MILITANCY IN *LAW & ORDER*

The long-running series *Law & Order* is the most widely recognized crime drama that has prominently featured late sixties militancy. Airing from 1990 to 2010, the NBC program blended the police procedural and courtroom drama to follow a case from the moment the crime is reported to the state's efforts to prosecute the accused. Set in New York City, *Law & Order* created story lines based on actual legal cases covered by the national press. While some early seasons stuck closely to case histories, later seasons were loosely inspired by actual events. Although the cast of characters and actors changed over time, the series routinely featured two detectives who investigated the case and two prosecuting attorneys who worked with the state attorney's office. The program earned multiple Emmys during its twenty-year run, including Outstanding Drama Series in 1996; its success prompted four spinoffs.

A 1994 episode entitled "White Rabbit" chronicles legal proceedings after a former sixties-era radical who evaded the law for twenty-three years is finally apprehended. The episode begins when an investigation of an explosion at a bank unexpectedly leads detectives to a conservative suburban wife and mother who is revealed to be Susan Forrest, a former student radical who was involved in the 1971 robbery of a defense contractor, Newcon technologies. Forrest and three other antiwar radicals explain that the robbery was designed to "strike a blow against the war machine," but their justification rings hollow because one of the robbers killed a police officer in the process. Further investigation reveals that Susan warned the shooter about the police officer's presence on the night of his murder. To avoid a steeper sentence, Susan pleas to the charge of manslaughter and goes to prison.

"White Rabbit" drew its inspiration from news coverage of Katherine Ann Power. In 1993, Power made national headlines when she turned herself in to authorities. Twenty-three years earlier, she drove the getaway car in a robbery of a Brighton, Massachusetts, bank that netted $27,000. One of her accomplices shot and killed police officer Walter Schroeder during the robbery. Afterward, Power assumed the name of Alice Metzinger and moved to Oregon, where she got married, raised a son, and worked as a chef outside of Eugene. After pleading guilty to robbery and manslaughter, she served five years in prison. Power's story is among a variety of stories about white women who garnered extensive media attention after their arrest for criminal activities motivated by revolutionary goals. Certainly, male counterparts such as Weathermen Bill Ayers and Mark Rudd have received intensive media scrutiny, but women radicals have received more ongoing and consistent mainstream press coverage. Other radical fugitives featured by the press include Marilyn Buck, Sara Jane Olsen, Judith Clark, Kathy Boudin, Susan Rosenberg, Linda Sue Evans, and Patty Hearst. They all served prison sentences for using firearms, explosives, harboring fugitives, or murder after they were apprehended or turned themselves into authorities.

The media fascination with these women radicals is likely driven by the ways in which their stories dramatically disrupt essentialist narratives about white femininity. Although liberal feminist movements have challenged the Victorian image of women as nurturers within the domestic sphere of the home, popular culture has continued to foreground images of women as more pacifist and diplomatic than their hawkish male counterparts. Depictions of white women voluntarily taking militant actions to advance revolutionary aims shatters this stereotype. Their actions pose a crisis to the gender order because they enact their agency outside of the nuclear family and do not seek to gain entrance within the halls of mainstream politics. Of course, male militants also worked outside of conventional politics; but women radicals compound the challenge to mainstream culture by refusing to embrace normative expectations for women.

Several media portrayals of women radicals have contained their threat to hegemonic femininity by softening their images, highlighting their remorsefulness or vulnerability. *Law & Order* softened its depiction by inviting sympathy for Forrest and creating some doubt about the extent of her guilt in the police officer's death. Echoing news coverage of Power's surrender, Forrest expresses deep remorse for her actions. In an attempt to have her plea reduced to manslaughter, she makes a statement to the New York district attorney's office to explain that she had not come forward because she was "so ashamed." Then she added, "and all these years, I am so sorry."[5]

On its surface, the episode's main conflict is whether Forrest, and Power by extension, deserves a stiff sentence. The prosecutors face a moral dilemma as they consider the circumstances surrounding the robbery and the state's own repression of nonviolent dissidents. Initially, District Attorney McCoy is hesitant to seek a murder conviction. His office is challenged to win a conviction, in part, because much of the evidence that could be used against Forrest was obtained illegally by the FBI. The developments in the case cast some doubt that Forrest should be convicted for murder. However, outrage from the widow of the slain police officer convinces McCoy to seek a conviction for first degree murder anyway.

The episode suggests that Forrest's contrition might be sincere by situating her actions in the context of the atrocities committed during the Vietnam War. When she is questioned, her accomplice Margaret Pauley explains to detectives that she and Forrest "were trying to save lives." Then she asks them, "Do you know how many people were being killed every day in Vietnam?" In another scene, a former

SDS-member-turned-Marxist-professor reminds detectives of the traumatic national events at the time of the robbery, "What I remember is the United States government sending half a million troops to fight in a war it had already decided it couldn't win. I remember the National Guard killing four college students whose only crime was protesting the illegal invasion of Cambodia." Although detectives seem to appreciate the professor's comments, they are skeptical. After they question him, Briscoe and Logan snicker when they read the title of his latest publication, "The Whale is Red: A Neo-Marxist Criticism of *Moby Dick*." By combining Marxism with one of the most well-known pieces of American literature, the incongruous title signals to audiences that radical professors are disconnected from the rest of society. Thus, the episode maintains an ambivalent stance regarding antiwar dissent on college campuses.

Detectives Logan and Briscoe are uncertain about the culpability of law enforcement officers during the war, and this gives them some sympathy for Forrest. During their investigation, they remark that the FBI arrested nonviolent antiwar protesters, including Catholic clergy and Dr. Spock. In a later scene, other characters amplify the ambiguity over Forrest's guilt. Defending his client, Bill Kunstler tells McCoy that what happened on the night of the Newcon robbery was that "the violence committed against the people of Vietnam finally rebounded to the home front. A tragic confluence of events." Ostensibly, Forrest was motivated by her commitment to social justice, which might exonerate her from charges stemming from the belief that the police officer's death was premeditated.

Uncertainty about Forrest's guilt amplifies messages from other narratives that craft sixties-era conflicts as morally ambiguous. The program's ideological balancing act invites mainstream viewers from both sides of the political aisle to become invested in the program's outcome. Deliberation about Forrest's culpability resonates with the first season of *The Wonder Years*. Just as Kevin Arnold admits that he still cannot decide whether the war was right or wrong, McCoy is dubious about the extent of Forrest's wrongdoing. Both programs suggest that criticisms of US foreign policy during the sixties were justifiable and that state repression against activists contributed to the decade's violence, affirming mainstream critiques of US policy during the late sixties that have been broadly accepted since the Vietnam War ended.

The episode also builds sympathy for Forrest by providing a more scathing portrayal of Forrest's male accomplices. Detectives learn that Forrest and her friend Margaret Pauley were influenced by ex-convicts who convinced them to rob the armored car to help finance the Black Panthers. These details roughly parallel the press coverage about Power. Power was radicalized during her years as a student at Brandeis University, where she and her roommate Susan Saxe planned the robbery with three male accomplices, William Gilday, Robert Valeri, and Stanley Bond, in order to buy arms for the Black Panthers.

News coverage intimated that the men manipulated Power and Saxe. The *New York Times*'s coverage of Power included an interview with Brandeis professor Jacob Cohen, who suggested that Power and other young women were "mesmerized" by Stanley Bond. Cohen stated that Bond was "thrilling, like Othello to Desdemona ... from Kathy's point of view, there was something exciting and romantic and even revolutionary about a criminal" (Rimer 1993). Likewise, *Time* magazine explained that Power had "fallen under the spell of Stanley Bond" (Carlson and Attinger 1993).

Law & Order also suggests that the fictionalized radical women were enchanted by their male accomplices. Dialogue from "White Rabbit" frames the allure of radical men bluntly. District Attorney Jack McCoy considers a plea from defense attorneys because Forrest was "duped by a couple of convicts who pretended to love Ho Chi Min so they could get in to her pants." Detectives interview Forrest's accomplice Sam Burdette, who confirms McCoy's interpretation. Recalling Forrest and Pauley, Burdette chuckles, "Those girls, they were live wires!" Recalling their plan to give the stolen money to the Black Panthers, he admits that he had really planned to keep the money for himself. Both news accounts and the *Law & Order* narrative indicate that Power/Forrest was a vulnerable young woman who was exploited by crooked con artists. The episode's references to the Vietnam War and to her male accomplices suggest that Forrest's actions were the product of her altruism and naïveté.

Although the television program draws from Power's relationship to male accomplices with criminal pasts, "White Rabbit" makes a conspicuous departure from the press accounts. Power's accomplices were white, but in *Law & Order*'s version of the events, the fictionalized con artists are black. This choice extends the racist stereotype about dangerous black masculinity by suggesting that Forrest was corrupted by lascivious black radicals who delighted in exploiting white women. The program's construction of Burdette is a rather obvious attempt at race-baiting in an effort to blame black men for white women's militancy. It also expresses anxiety about the potency of black radicalism that conflates white fears of black male sexuality with the threat of radicalism. While the former challenges the racial order, the latter compromises political hegemony.

The portrayal of Forrest's relationship to Burdette contributes to Hollywood portrayals of women radicals as metaphors for the contests over national character and identity. As white women signify national character that must be protected, black men represent the threat to national stability. Concomitantly, the bodies of black men stand for the threat to white masculine hegemony and as conduits for radical ideas to corrupt the sanctity of liberal democracy. By depicting black activists as con men, the program invites viewers to disregard radical black activists' historic claims for racial justice.

The characterization of Forrest as manipulated by charismatic macho militants illustrates what Dana Cloud (1998, 85) refers to as the "domestication of dissent." Looking at news coverage of the Persian Gulf War, Cloud observes that the press muted dissident voices by framing criticisms of the war within the gendered domestic sphere of the home. In "White Rabbit," the episode's attention to antiwar protest is obscured by a lurid tale of romantic deception. The domestication of women radicals appears in other crime dramas that aired in the following years. A 2007 episode of *Bones* entitled "Soccer Mom in the Mini-Van" revolves around the mysterious death of a suburban woman who was a former member of the National Liberation Association. While the episode focuses on her history as a loving wife and mother, it never explains her politics. That same year, an episode of *Cold Case* focuses on a radical fugitive who convinces her husband to plant a bomb in order to prevent one of their former accomplices from turning himself in to the authorities. An episode of *Life on Mars*, the subject of the next section of this essay, also foregrounds women's personal motives for their radical actions. These episodes' narratives about these pseudo-radicals, whose real-life counterparts defied the image of the national womanhood, ostensibly close the chapter on radical sixties-era challenges to American narratives of law and justice.

Although *Law & Order* acknowledges that public officials and law enforcement bore some of the blame for political turmoil during the sixties, this does not meaningfully influence the verdict against Forrest. The conclusion resolves uncertainty over Forrest's guilt by revealing details that put her altruistic motives in doubt. Amplifying Forrest's criminal intentions, the episode suggests that she stole $200,000 from an armored truck, an amount far greater than the $27,000 that Power actually stole. Rather than depict the less dramatic process by which Power turned herself in to authorities, the program's detectives discover Forrest's secret identity and arrest her. Invented by the program's writers, these details mold Power's case to conform to the conventions of the crime drama in which police and prosecuting attorneys are the program's moral center.

The depiction of Forrest also reinforces the image of the hippie-turned-yuppie who is no more immune to the cult of wealth than more moderate citizens. During the episode, the prosecuting attorneys learn that Forrest recently donated thousands of dollars to the Republican Party. Prosecutors reveal this information to Margaret Pauley to convince her to testify against Forrest. Earlier, Pauley had refused to provide any information that might be used against Forrest, maintaining that "the real criminals killed 50,000 American boys and over a million Vietnamese." Assistant District Attorney Claire Kincaid informs Pauley that "Susan Forrest isn't one of you anymore." Heartbroken to learn that Susan is a fraud, Pauley agrees to testify against her, giving attorneys the evidence they need to secure a conviction.

This conclusion resolves the moral ambiguity surrounding Forrest's actions by contradicting her stated commitments to leftist politics. Her motives appear capricious and self-serving. As the episode aired one year after Power turned herself in to authorities, it invites audiences familiar with the case to speculate that Power might not have acted to promote the cause of justice. Thus, the most prudent response to former militants who emerge from underground is to see them behind bars.

Beyond its domestication of women activists, the episode is an indictment of sixties-era radicalism itself. The episode's conclusion confirms that sixties-era politics was a short-lived trend, not an outcropping of deeper social commitments among citizens opposed to war and political violence against people of color. The dialogue constructs the decade as a historical aberration in which militancy exacerbated criminal activity. Prosecuting attorneys' remarks in the denouement signal the episode's contributions to selective amnesia regarding radical sixties-era dissent. When the younger Detective Logan reflects on the strangeness of the case midway through the episode, Detective Briscoe quips, "It was the sixties, Mike. You had to be there."

In the final scene of the episode, McCoy and Kincaid talk about Forrest's future. Celebrating their success, McCoy remarks, "She'll be in jail until 2003. I think the sixties should be over by then." These remarks defy nostalgic references to the decade by projecting an image of confusion and turbulence that enabled dissidents to get away with murder. This conclusion complements presidential foreign policy rhetoric in the years before the episode aired. Released on the heels of George H. W. Bush's (1991) insistence that America had finally "kicked The Vietnam Syndrome," the episode's focus on the war's most visible and condemnable critics distracts from serious conversations about the legacy of Vietnam and its implications for US foreign policy.[6] The program instructs audiences to look back at the sixties, shake their heads alongside the good detectives and attorneys, and have faith in a future in which US law and order has prevailed over antiwar dissent.

EXAGGERATING MILITANT VIOLENCE AND DEFLECTING POLICE REPRESSION IN *LIFE ON MARS*

The Weather Underground and other clandestine sixties-era radicals continued to function as a powerful and enduring symbol of dangerous, illegitimate citizenship after the nineties. The television episodes most obviously inspired by news media attention to the Weather Underground appeared on ABC's series *Life on Mars* and the FOX Network series *The Chicago Code*. Although they are not the most widely viewed examples, they are the most obvious illustrations of television crime dramas' contributions to the public memory of late sixties militancy. These episodes drew heavily from the controversy surrounding Obama's supposed relationship with Bill Ayers. Thus, they integrated the generic convention of the crime drama established in earlier television police procedurals with contemporary political uses of sixties memory designed to discredit the presidential candidate.

Life on Mars aired from October 2008 to April 2009. A US version of an earlier British series with the same title, the program is set in New York City in 1974 and tells the story of detective Sam Tyler, who struggles to make sense of his life after a present-day car accident mysteriously sends him back to the 1970s. In each episode, Tyler's contemporary values are in conflict with the corrupt police tactics of his 1970s peers. He frequently finds himself at odds with macho fellow detective Ray Carling and his lieutenant Gene Hunt, who uses aggressive and sometimes violent tactics to extract confessions from suspects. While each episode concludes with the closing of a specific case, character relationships develop over the course of the series.

Episode 13, entitled "Revenge of Broken Jaw," explicitly identifies members of the Weather Underground as its primary suspects. Police officers have been murdered in a series of bomb attacks and Detective Tyler suspects that Lieutenant Hunt will be the next target. Through the process of investigation, detectives suspect that Weather Underground sympathizer Pat Olsen is involved. After several interrogations, the police conclude that Olsen has convinced the Weather Underground to avenge the death of charismatic radical Rodney Slavin. Police officer Annie Norris helps detectives realize that Slavin was also Olsen's elicit lover and father to her daughter. The tables are turned on Olsen when detectives uncover the truth; it was her jealous husband who murdered her lover, not the police as she suspects.

Much like the *Law & Order* episode, "White Rabbit," this episode of *Life on Mars* encourages viewers to distrust activists and to view them as a threat to civil society by contributing to the selective amnesia of the devastating consequences of the Vietnam War, of law enforcement's illegal efforts to repress antiwar dissent, and of the FBI's illegal practices during their investigation of Weather Underground members. It also amplified political campaign discourse that condemned any association Barack Obama might have had with Bill Ayers to discredit the presidential candidate from serious consideration.

Given that the episode aired four months after Obama's 2008 election, even audiences who loosely followed the presidential campaign coverage would have likely recognized the program's effort to capitalize on renewed attention to the Weathermen. Although political fact-checking organizations concluded that little other evidence connected Obama to Ayers (Novak 2008; Mikkelson n.d.), conservative politicians and news pundits seized upon the Obama-Ayers "conspiracy," speculating that the two had a close relationship and shared similar ideological perspectives. Sarah Palin (2008) frequently mentioned Obama's relationship with Ayers, famously quipping that Obama "palled around with terrorists," and the McCain campaign circulated Internet and television attack ads highlighting the *New York Times* quote (Novak 2008). FOX News pundits repeatedly expressed concern that Obama had been dishonest about his relationship with "unrepentant terrorist Bill Ayers."[7] The network's programs brought several guests on their programs who asserted that Obama launched his early political career in Ayers's living room.

Efforts to discredit Obama through his relationship to Ayers did not influence the outcome of the election, but the focus on Ayers influenced the tenor of the campaign and perhaps the Obama presidency as well. The spotlight on Ayers during the campaign cast antiwar sentiment outside of the realm of political debate. Obama and McCain both strove to present themselves as foreign policy hawks, willing to go to war if they had to. During his presidency, Obama has portrayed himself as a political moderate, distanced from the political legacy of the sixties. The controversy also impacted Ayers's professional career. Many of his speaking engagements at universities and bookstores across the country were canceled in the years after the election. Although a faculty committee at the University of Chicago agreed to give Ayers emeritus status, the board of trustees refused to approve him because of his earlier activist career.

Released while Ayers was still facing consequences for the publicity surrounding his involvement in the Weather Underground, narrative cues and dialogue within "Revenge of Broken Jaw" signaled the episode's relevance to the political campaign discourse about Ayers, and intimated that Ayers did deserve public approbation. The episode's main suspect Pat Olsen is a Columbia University professor, and the dialogue echoes descriptions of Ayers during the campaign. After the first bomb attack, Lieutenant Hunt describes the Weather Underground as "student radicals, terrorists, good for nothin', taking for granted, spoiled know-it-alls." Convinced of Olsen's guilt, Hunt detains Olsen without a warrant. Detective Carling justifies the detention to Olsen's distraught husband by explaining, "In case you didn't know it, your wife is a terrorist." When evidence of Olsen's involvement in the bombings mounts, she refuses to share information about the location of the remaining bomb that has been hidden in the city. Sneering at the detectives, Olsen declares, "I won't regret anything I've done." These moments portray Olsen as an unrepentant terrorist, overtly affirming the image of Ayers promulgated by McCain's campaign and right-wing pundits. Notably, the program's depiction of Olsen and the Weather Underground are more reflective of the FOX News coverage than the actual circumstances surrounding Ayers's participation in the organization. Ayers never targeted police officers or expressed enthusiasm for police officers' deaths.

The episode integrates its conservative image of radical dissent with a moderately liberal view of the antiwar movement and of police repression of activists. In this way, *Life on Mars* engages in an ideological balancing act that is a staple of the television crime drama. The episode introduces moral ambiguity by noting that Olsen was aggrieved over the enormous death toll to Vietnamese citizens and about the law enforcement's illegal and coercive measures to suppress radical dissent. Midway through the episode, she insists that the targeted police officers were members of the Red Squad, vigilante cops who terrorized the Weathermen. Olsen's reference to the Red Squad highlights police efforts to undermine dissident movements using illegal and coercive measures (Boykoff 2007; Chang 2002).

This program attends to the civil rights violations of law enforcement officers more than any other broadcast television program that has featured sixties militants. Demonstrating the culpability of the police force, Lieutenant Hunt throws Olsen against a set of metal bookshelves and threatens to beat her to force a confession out of her. These scenes problematize the cop-hero crime drama by depicting police violence as the motivation for activist militancy. Echoing a narrative that is told in Green and Siegel's 2003 documentary about the Weather Underground, Olsen reminds Lieutenant Hunt that law enforcement officials "dangled activists by their ankles outside of their windows and threw teargas grenades into their homes." By juxtaposing radical left violence with repressive law enforcement techniques, the first half of the program discourages audiences from clearly demarcating the episode's protagonists from its antagonists. Neither the activists nor the police are above reproach.

Complementing the script for the episode "White Rabbit" in *Law & Order*, *Life on Mars* suggests that incidents of political violence during the late sixties and early seventies are confusing and morally ambiguous. The character with the strongest moral character on *Life on Mars* is Detective Sam Tyler, who is caught between competing claims about the injustices committed by seventies-era police officers. Tyler strives to learn more about the mysterious Red Squad. His conversations with fellow officers indicate that Olsen is paranoid. Detective Carling insists that the Red Squad is a myth, and Lieutenant Hunt tells Olsen that if the Red Squad did exist, its goal was certainly to protect the public. Later, Hunt informs Tyler that the Red Squad was the last of a dying breed of "hard men," but they weren't murderers. Confounded and dislocated, Tyler never seems to draw final conclusions about whether police should be faulted for violating suspects' civil liberties. For audiences born after the seventies, Tyler might stand in for their own indefinite understanding of the decade. The variety of reductive images of conflict between "law and order" conservatives and those sympathetic to the movement in retrospectives of the late sixties and seventies amplifies the image of a period torn asunder by division.

The episode's conclusion resolves the conflict between conservative and liberal interpretations of the late sixties by emphasizing Olsen's criminal behavior and self-serving motives. Potential sympathy for Olsen on the basis of her antiwar stance is cut short when she insists that "anyone who isn't part of the revolution can't be considered important." Ostensibly, her revolutionary fervor has overwhelmed her concern for human life. The program restores moral certainty after detectives realize that Slavin was Olsen's elicit lover and the biological father of her daughter. Realizing her crime, Olsen's husband turns on his wife, condemning her, "I never realized you'd go this far, Patricia, and not over politics, not over some cause, but for love?! You?! Who insisted you couldn't be fully mine while in the middle of a revolution. You're a hypocrite!" This plot twist is another example of the domestication of dissent that routinely imagines women engaged in radical activism through the lens of heterosexual relationships, implying that women could not be purely motivated by political concerns.

As audiences are invited to identify with Tyler, they are encouraged to share his lessons. Tyler's disbelief and concern regarding the Red Squad suggests that the seventies era of law enforcement is far different from the law enforcement techniques post-9/11. One inference that might be made from Tyler's incredulity is that the Red Squad was an aberration and that law enforcement repression against the radical left ended since then. Another implied lesson is that radicals' expressed commitments to revolutionary social change are not to be believed. Ostensibly, Olsen's radicalism was motivated by her attachments to a charismatic male figure, and her appeals for revolutionary change served primarily as cover for her more mundane revenge seeking on behalf of her illicit lover's death. Were other radical figures with more consistent motives presented in the episode, the message could have been that radicalism's social justice cause did not inspire murderous violence, but no character is present to defend the actions and aims of the Weather Underground. Olsen is further discredited because her illicit affair with Slavin betrayed her spouse, and her instigation of bombing attacks against police sacrificed her daughter's well-being. This reiterates the common message that radicals were compelled by self-serving motives that do more harm to the nuclear family than social good.

The episode's vilification of Olsen and the Weather Underground relies upon the blatant forms of selective amnesia of sixties-era militancy that largely forget the context that motivated radical movements. The dialogue offers only trite statements about radicals' antiwar stances as it portrays the Weather Underground's motives tersely in two scenes. In the first, the police station receives an anonymous phone call from a member who credits the organization with the bomb that killed a fourth police officer, "We act on this date in response to continued American tyranny and oppression at home and abroad. These bombings are a strike to the heart of the US Gestapo organization." In the second scene, investigators review film footage of Slavin speaking to a crowd. Slavin tells a campus audience, "Burn the mother down. Bring the war home. We've got to destroy white privilege. We've got to bring down the barriers of class. Start a free society. You feeling me, son?" This dialogue uses the Weather Underground's most provocative phrases that circulated on their promotional posters and print materials. Presented without any context of events including the My Lai Massacre, the invasion of Cambodia, and the police killing of Fred Hampton, this rhetoric is caustic and alienating. Consequently, it positions viewers to empathize with police detectives who find Olsen's politics and demeanor abhorrent.

By depicting Olsen as detestable, the program deflects criticisms of law enforcement repression against nonviolent protest. Indeed, the episode's conclusion suggests that police brutality may be an understandable response to dissent. Early in the episode, Hunt speculates that the Red Squad sought "to protect the public from collegiate communists who were trying to overthrow the government and burn the city down." His speculation that the Red Squad might have been justified is affirmed near the episode's end. It is only after Hunt strong-arms Olsen that detectives are able to track down the Weather Underground's hideout. Apparently, extralegal tactics were required to solve the case and prevent future bombings from killing additional police officers.

The final scenes reiterate the episode's valorization of law and order. In the second to last scene, Hunt introduces his squad to the son of one of the police officers who was murdered by the Weather Underground. The young man is a Vietnam War veteran who was paralyzed in combat. Hunt and the disabled man share a tearful embrace. Appearing in the denouement to a narrative about radical antiwar dissent, this scene invokes the image of activists who spit in the faces of returning soldiers. Thus, it reinforces the message that antiwar radicals deserve our approbation and dismissal. The episode's troubling central lesson is that law enforcement agents must sometimes violate activists' civil liberties in order to protect the public.

ARRESTING THE INFLUENCE OF DANGEROUS COLLEGE RADICALS ON *THE CHICAGO CODE*

Two years after the *Life on Mars* episode aired, the television cop drama series *The Chicago Code* provided another ominous depiction of former sixties-era dissidents. Lasting for only one season in 2011, its story line revolved around the efforts of Superintendent Teresa Colvin to fight city corruption by enlisting talented Detective Jarek Wysocki. Supporting characters, young detective Caleb Evers and police officers Vonda Wysocki and Isaac Joiner, assist their superiors. The program employs both episodic and ongoing narrative structure. While each episode tracks the developments of Colvin's pursuit of city alderman Ronin Gibbons, a different subplot in each episode follows Wysocki and other police officers' investigations of criminal activities in the city. Thus, one case is solved each week. The program's depiction of Chicago as a hotbed of crime and political corruption draws from the city's reputation for corruption by city leaders including Governors Rod Blagojevich and George Ryan and US representatives Dan Rostenkowski and Mel Reynolds. In the program, Chicago police are sympathetic heroes in a struggle to rid Chicago of its criminal influences.

During episode 4, entitled "Cabrini Green," a seemingly random series of bomb attacks terrorizes the city. The detectives suspect members of a former radical political organization, the Chicago Liberation Army; former member David Argyle is their main suspect. Much of the program's history of the fictional Chicago Liberation Army is based on the Weathermen's activism in Chicago in 1969. The Weathermen organized the Days of Rage to protest the Chicago police department's violent suppression of the 1968 Democratic National

Convention protests. The organization led a series of direct actions in the streets of Chicago that led to violent confrontations with police. Before the Days of Rage, the Weathermen bombed the police statue at Haymarket Square to express solidarity with the labor leaders who were executed for throwing a bomb into a crowd of police in 1886. Considering the history of police suppression of nonviolent dissent, the Weathermen concluded that violence was the only language that the city's law enforcement understood. Certainly, the Weathermen's actions deserve criticism. But without this context, the program makes late sixties militancy out to be entirely unsympathetic. Consequently, "Cabrini Green" reinforces the desirability of a world in which radicalism is eliminated from public life.

This unsympathetic portrayal depends upon a fictionalized version of radicalism in Chicago that exaggerates the deadly threat of militancy. In *The Chicago Code*'s fictionalized portrayal of the Chicago Liberation Army, David Argyle was never charged for earlier bombings because he claimed he left the organization before they began using explosives. Argyle maintains his innocence and leads investigators to the real bomber, Trey Stein. In the process of helping the detectives, Argyle inadvertently reveals that he was still a member when the bombings occurred during the seventies. At the end of the episode, police arrest Argyle for his earlier criminal past.

The Chicago Code's use of news coverage about Bill Ayers is even more overt than *Life on Mars*'s references to the Weather Underground. Argyle's character is clearly inspired by Ayers. Argyle is a professor of education and advocate for education reform. His grayish blond disheveled hair bears some semblance to photographs of Ayers's mug shot that circulated in 2008. Several scenes draw upon the history of the Weather Underground and news media descriptions of Ayers. Discussing the case with Superintendent Colvin, Detective Wysocki reminds her that the Chicago Liberation Army grew out of the Days of Rage riots and adds that the group bombed the Haymarket Police Memorial in city hall. Then, he notes that Argyle was the group's leader and was never prosecuted for planning the bombs.

Adding to this ugly portrayal of the organization, *The Chicago Code* detectives mention that the CLA killed civilians. This detail diverges from historical accounts of the Weathermen, but it follows conservative news discourse about Ayers in 2008. In April 2008, Sean Hannity interviewed former New York police detective Paul Ragonese, who witnessed the Weather Underground's 1970 attack on New York City police headquarters. During the interview, Hannity and Ragonese compared the attack with a deadlier and unrelated bomb that killed three police officers in 1982. Ragonese concluded, "I don't understand . . . how anyone could . . . associate with anybody that you know or suspect could damage people" ("A Victim" 2008). This conflation obfuscates the differences between the two attacks. In October, Minnesota congressperson Michele Bachman told MSNBC's Chris Matthews (2008) that Ayers "was happy to be bombing Americans." By inferring that Ayers sought to injure and kill people, these discussions avoided a more nuanced and specific understanding about the Weather Underground's motives and actions. Audiences of FOX News coverage and *The Chicago Code* might presume that the Weathermen murdered civilians. *The Chicago Code* gave fictionalized, dramatic confirmation to this misleading news commentary, providing added drama to the episode.

"Cabrini Green" followed the conventions of television crime drama by creating some uncertainty about Argyle's guilt. Detectives struggle to find any evidence that he was involved in the recent bombings. During an interrogation, Argyle insists that he never made any bombs, and the detectives cannot find physical evidence linking him to the attacks. Although the program revolves around a challenging investigation, it consistently invites audiences to question Argyle's innocence. Detectives presume Argyle's guilt based on his previous involvement with the CLA. During a book signing event for Argyle's latest publication, the son of a police officer killed by a CLA bomb throws blood on Argyle. When he is questioned, the son tells detectives that Argyle "practically brags about" setting bombs "in his damn book." Audiences familiar with the coverage surrounding Ayers would recognize this scene as a reference to the controversy surrounding Ayers's memoir *Fugitive Days* in which he recounts the Weather Underground's history of bomb-making activity.

The episode's conclusion provides televisual confirmation for Sean Hannity's claims that Ayers was an "unrepentant terrorist" and

Michele Bachman's assertion that he was certainly guilty for earlier crimes committed by the Weather Underground. During the interrogation, Wysocki condemns Argyle, "Tell me you don't feel even a little bit sorry for the people that died in those attacks all those years ago." At first, Argyle appears unrepentant; he asks Wysocki to direct his questions to his attorney. Later, he agrees to cooperate with the investigation to help detectives apprehend the current perpetrator. In the process, Argyle inadvertently implicates himself in the previous bomb attacks. When detectives realize this, Wysocki surmises, "I guess he just wanted to do the right thing after all these years." The episode concludes after detectives arrest Argyle in the middle of one of his large public lectures. Shocked, Argyle asks Wysocki why he is being arrested since he cooperated with the investigation. Wysocki replies, "Because I'm a cop and you broke the law and that's how things work."

By depicting Argyle as a murderer who circumvented the law, "Cabrini Green" gives televisual form to conservative discourse about the radical Left's threat to law and order. Since the emergence of the culture wars of the nineties, conservative pundits have condemned the influence of the radical Left on public education and democratic politics (Horowitz 2006; Horowitz and Laskin 2009; Horowitz and Poe 2006; Kimball 2008). These pundits routinely suggest that the Left wields undue social influence because the liberal establishment is unable or unwilling to hold them accountable for their past criminal behavior. In 2008, Bill O'Reilly asserted that "secular progressives" had given Ayers a free pass, and that he ought to be charged for his past crimes ("Defending Bill Ayers" 2008). By giving Argyle the punishment that conservative pundits believe Ayers deserves, *The Chicago Code* provides symbolic wish fulfillment for conservatives who have bemoaned the influence of radical college professors whom they imagine to have influence over the nation's students.

The dangers of radicalism are punctuated by the episode's depiction of Trey Stein and his mother. Detectives learn that Trey was born when his parents were fugitives and that he was thirteen when they were captured. Twenty-one years old now, Trey resents how his own parents had paid for their radicalism while Argyle remained free. Ostensibly, his parents' activism destroyed Trey's life and damaged his moral character. When police attempt to persuade him to give himself up, they allow his mother, Helena, to speak to him from prison. Helena violates their expectations. Rather than talk him out of detonating his last bomb, she encourages him to set it off. As the camera zooms in on her grimacing face, she yells, "Do it! Do it now so I can hear!" Police subdue Trey and wrest the bomb detonator from his hands. The program cuts to the scene of prison guards pulling Helena away from the phone. After officers confirm that everyone is safe, Wysocki comments to a fellow detective, "Mother of the year, huh?" This scene amplifies the lessons of earlier fictionalized depictions of radical women: the belligerence of women radicals threatens the nuclear family life and poisons their children's minds with hate. The depiction of Helena Stein, not unlike the depiction of Pat Olsen, amplifies the idea that committed women radicals are incapable of caring for their own children.

"Cabrini Green" provides an alarming vision about what might happen if radicalism was allowed to flourish. Presumably, attacks on police would proliferate without consequence and civil society would be jeopardized. The caustic image of women radicals amplifies the threat of radicalism to society and to the home. The program's lesson is that we cannot leave the fate of the next generation to the hands of radicals who have influenced higher education and imperiled the nuclear family. Hard-working citizens, those who "play by the rules," must support efforts to prevent their influence in public life.

THE REPRESSIVE POLITICS OF CONFLATING RADICALISM WITH TERRORISM

Episodes of *Law & Order*, *Life on Mars*, and *The Chicago Code* are three examples among several television crime dramas that discourage audiences from sympathizing or identifying with radical late sixties politics. They offer a series of lessons that encourage viewers to distance themselves from the radical Left; presumably, activists' altruistic commitments are hollow; their militancy hurts innocent civilians and impairs law enforcement efforts to protect the public;

and police officers are forced to violate activists' civil liberties on occasion to protect the public. Since there are far fewer positive depictions of radical protest in popular culture, these programs enable a myopic understanding of radicalism that conflates dissent with criminality. Portrayals of women radicals amplify the negative depiction of late sixties militancy by imagining their callous disregard for human life and a willingness to sacrifice their own families for what are ultimately self-serving motives.

The program's limited views of late sixties militancy reaffirm messages conveyed by both political moderates and conservatives that have collapsed all radical challenges to mainstream politics as equally pernicious threats to democracy and civility. Well before the controversy surrounding Barack Obama's supposed relationship with Bill Ayers, politicians had invoked the memory of the Weathermen to score political points with voters. A few weeks after Timothy McVeigh bombed the Oklahoma City federal building, President Clinton delivered a commencement address at Michigan State University that conflated McVeigh's actions with the Weathermen's. "Whenever in our history people have believed that violence is a legitimate extension of politics, they have been wrong," he told the graduates, adding, "[T]he Weathermen of the radical Left who resorted to violence in the 1960s were wrong" (Clinton 1995a). Clinton's comparison between McVeigh and the Weathermen conflated different, albeit problematic forms of political violence. While McVeigh intended to inflict physical injury, the Weather Underground gave advance warning to security officials before bombing buildings late at night. McVeigh's bombing killed 186 people including 19 children whereas the Weather Underground set off twenty-five bombs and accidentally killed three of their own members. Entering into his campaign for reelection, Clinton's reference to the Weathermen articulated a moderate political stance that portrayed both the far Right and Left as misguided and dangerous to national stability. Throughout his presidency, conservatives strove to discredit Bill Clinton by depicting him as a progenitor of sixties-era values (Marcus 2004). By condemning the Weathermen in the aftermath of McVeigh's attack, Clinton could throw off the Right's efforts to depict him as a "radical" without garnering criticism from his Democratic allies.

Toward the end of his address, Clinton extended his condemnation of political violence to chastise anyone who would express radical political beliefs. He insisted that the "obligations of citizenship" call for hard work and government service: "There is nothing patriotic about hating your country or pretending that you can love your country but despise your Government.... The real American heroes today are the citizens who get up every morning and have the courage to work hard and play by the rules." Within the context of McVeigh's attacks, Clinton's references to the Weathermen position the devastation of Oklahoma City within a broader crisis of national division and protest. Anyone who would contest the legitimacy of mainstream politics is suspect.

By reducing the memory of the sixties to its most violent and extreme elements, Clinton summoned audiences to participate in the political project of "getting over the Sixties." Beyond giving Clinton a political advantage, his and other criticisms of late sixties militants have helped to realign the Democratic Party toward the right by distancing it from the memory of the movement. The conflation of radicalism with violent extremism necessarily involves selective amnesia of the thousands of nonviolent dissents who organized against the war and against global exploitation of people of color. By making the sixties concomitant with its violent extremes, these contributions to sixties memory have valorized political quiescence as a civic virtue.

The central problem with the selective amnesia of late sixties militancy is that its suspicion toward dissidents weakens democratic civic life. The image of radicals as self-serving and callous discourages mainstream publics and the press from seriously considering radical arguments for fundamental economic and foreign policy change. Likewise, the depiction of professors as murderous radicals provides symbolic support for public discourse that has expressed disdain for higher education. Derision toward higher education has gone hand in hand with state funding cuts for public universities and growing disregard for academic expertise. The dismissal of academics as out-of-touch radicals contributes to a post-fact society in which evidence-based arguments about issues including the human causes for climate change are dismissed as the machinations of self-interested elites.

Television crime dramas' valorization of law enforcement repression of dissent bolsters political discourse that has denigrated radical beliefs and dissent. While programs such as *Life on Mars* suggest that police repression is a relic of seventies-era political turbulence, it is an ongoing feature of radical organizing in the United States. Large-scale demonstrations against the World Trade Organization in 1999 and the Free Trade Area of America's zone in 2003 were met with indiscriminate, excessive police force including the use of rubber bullets and pepper spray. Furthermore, many unarmed protesters have been subdued by Tasers. The FBI has also ramped up its surveillance of the political Left in recent decades. After 9/11, John Ashcroft issued new regulations that enabled agents and local police to monitor any public event without cause. These policies led to the creation of FBI files on groups including antiwar protesters, the American Civil Liberties Union, and Greenpeace, all of whom were listed as potential terrorist threats (Boykoff 2007). The recurring image of bomb-detonating Weathermen confirms the FBI's equation that activism equals terrorism. Prime-time TV audiences might be hard pressed to understand why civil liberties lawyers and advocates are alarmed by the increasing surveillance of nonviolent dissent over the last fifteen years.

The conflation of activism with terrorism inhibits important conversations about what constitutes a legitimate use of police force in a liberal democracy and why a vibrant democracy must allow for the expression of its most incisive critics. Although the actions of many militant Left organizations deserve strong criticism, the vast majority of radicals from the late sixties and early seventies did not harm civilians or police officers. That television's radicals are so often depicted as deadly, callous criminals has troubling implications because it encourages viewers to disregard all forms of radicalism as dangerous to families, society, and the nation. Certainly, the television viewing public could use more richer, nuanced depictions of dissent that reflect the diversity of radical movements in the United States and the causes they defended. We would also benefit from more images of activists—women and men—who raised well-adjusted successful children, as many children of sixties-era radicals grew up to become successful scholars, artists, and activists themselves. After all, Bill Ayers and his spouse, Bernardine Dohrn, raised Chesa Boudin, the son of convicted radicals David Gilbert and Kathy Boudin. Chesa Boudin who won a Rhodes Scholarship in 2002 and is now a criminal justice lawyer. Images of successful, thriving activists might enable viewers to understand how protest and dissent is part of our national civic identity and is driven by the cause of social justice and participatory democracy.

CONCLUSION

Contestation over Sixties Memory in the New Millennium

Each of the films and television programs discussed in this book illustrates how Hollywood has contributed to derisive attitudes toward dissent. Over the past forty years, viewers have watched a variety of fictionalized characters who have contributed and expanded upon reductive stereotypes of sixties-era protesters. Many of these characters learned to grow out of the sixties. In the eighties, former hippies concluded that dissent is childish and embraced yuppie values. In the nineties, ambivalent activists rejected the machismo of radical militants and pursued nuclear family life with politically moderate good citizens. Film and TV audiences have also seen several fictionalized black militants learn that black rage is the source of inequality and prejudice, not racism.

Viewers have also witnessed the tragic demise of both sympathetic and antagonistic radicals who failed to grow out of the sixties. Committed militants are alienated from friends and family members, harassed and beaten by police officers, and jailed for criminal activity. In proportions that exceed their nonfictional counterparts, many of film and television's fictionalized sixties-era radicals have inadvertently killed themselves, victims of their own violent rage. Hollywood has also reminded us that admirable and charismatic Black Power figures have been tragically assassinated for daring to organize communities in opposition to structural racism and Western imperialism. Over and over again, entertainment media teach viewers that militants are a danger to themselves and civil society; thus, they should warrant our distrust and suspicion.

Considered collectively, these recurring character portrayals and narrative developments highlight the broader processes by which Hollywood has structured selective amnesia of radical sixties-era dissent. Recurring portrayals of ambivalent, caustic, enraged, or criminal dissidents have provided an overarching framework for remembering the sixties that encourages audiences to embrace a shallow understanding of the decade's protest movements. By and large, Hollywood teaches viewers to forget why dissidents took to the streets and obscures the diverse range of groups who sought to radically transform the nation's politics and societal norms.

The nation remains deeply divided over the memory of the sixties. The most recent political election cycle is a case in point. While Senator Bernie Sanders's agenda was hardly radical, his advocacy for democratic socialism was outside of the American political mainstream. His most popular television campaign advertisement framed his candidacy as part of a grassroots movement for social change. The video featured a series of images of young people working together and meeting with Sanders accompanied by Simon and Garfunkel's 1968 song "America." Describing his campaign as a "movement," Bernie resurrected an image of the good sixties.

Conversely, Republican contender Donald Trump grounded his campaign in divisive rhetoric in which he blamed Muslims for terrorist attacks and scapegoated Mexicans for the dearth of well-paying jobs for working-class whites. While Sanders trumpeted his campaign as a return to the good sixties, Trump implicitly evoked conservative ire over the memory of the bad sixties. Borrowing from Nixon's 1968 presidential campaign rhetoric, Trump declared himself the law and order candidate. He also waxed nostalgic about the "old days" when protesters would be "carried out in stretchers" (Deaton 2016). The contrasting uses of sixties memory during these campaigns demonstrate how US leaders still cue the memory of sixties-era dissent as a political tool. With alarming implications, Trump's success suggests that the memory of the bad sixties continues to help candidates win elections. Certainly, Trump's enthusiasm for violent retribution against left-leaning dissent is buttressed by Hollywood's repeated depictions of angry black radicals and dangerous white dissidents.

Public controversy over the role of dissent is ongoing even among liberals. During the Democratic National Convention in Philadelphia, delegates who supported Sanders were understandably irate when a series of leaked e-mails revealed that the Democratic National Committee, chaired by Debbie Wasserman Schultz, actively tried to undermine Sanders's campaign. Sanders and several of his high-profile supporters, including progressive comedian Sarah Silverman, urged the conventioneers to support Hillary Clinton nonetheless. When Sanders's supporters loudly booed Silverman, she pointed her finger toward the crowd and reprimanded them, "You are being ridiculous." Granted, this was a small moment during the first day of the convention in what turned into a large showing of support for Clinton's run in the general election. That the hecklers were less audible for the remaining days of the convention illustrates how quick mainstream political parties are to quell dissent within its ranks in order to cultivate images of unity, order, and civility.

Mainstream news coverage has reinforced dismissive attitudes toward activists in the last decade. When Occupy Wall Street protesters took over Zuccotti Park in 2011, the press offered dismissive commentary about the movement. Kevin DeLuca, Sean Lawson, and Ye Sun (2012, 491) observe that the news coverage's negative framing "represented the protesters as hippies and flakes and the . . . movement as frivolous and aimless." Predictably, Occupy Wall Street's critique of wealth inequality and corporate greed was shadowed by press commentary that the activists had no clear agenda.

While movements led by young white people are often met with ridicule, movements for racial justice receive harsher treatment. The Black Lives Matter movement for the end to police violence against black citizens has prompted reactionary responses by groups suggesting that black protesters themselves put the police officers' safety at risk. When white people protest, they are made to look ridiculous, but when black people do, they are shown to be menacing. As this book has argued, popular culture's image of the bad sixties has primed the public to embrace these attitudes. Consequently, activists' claims for racial justice are often ignored and police violence against black people continues.

THE RECURRING CYCLE OF BAD SIXTIES CARICATURES IN MAINSTREAM TELEVISION

Entertainment television continues to remind viewers of these lessons. NBC's current television series *Aquarius* is the most recent prime-time effort to capitalize on the public's macabre fascination with the bad sixties. The television crime drama revolves around police sergeant Sam Hodiak's efforts to solve a series of heinous murder cases linked to psychotic serial killer Charles Manson. Hodiak's motives are personal and professional, as the adolescent daughter of a close friend has run away to join Manson's hippie commune in the Hollywood hills. The runaway, Emma, quickly immerses herself in a lifestyle of illicit drug use, casual sex, and theft. During his investigation, Hodiak runs into Nation of Islam leader Bunchy Carter. Carter's anger toward the injustice of Los Angeles's law enforcement prompts him to leave the Nation of Islam in order to organize against the police full time. "I am the anger that will burn your truth to the ground," he tells Hodiak at the end of the second episode, "Watch your back."

As my short summary suggests, *Aquarius* recycles many of the same tired caricatures of the counterculture and Black Power movement constructed by previous Hollywood films and television programs. To say the program plays fast and loose with history is an understatement. The runaway hippie, the angry black man, and the macho militant each figure prominently in the program in order to build suspense and sympathy for World War II–generation Sergeant Hodiak. If the program's inspiration was not obvious enough, the lead character's name, Hodiak, is only one letter different from Zodiak, a reference to an infamous serial killer who terrorized northern California during the late sixties. By reinforcing the association between the counterculture and violent criminals, *Aquarius* expands selective amnesia of the decade's dissent.

One of television's most widely acclaimed dramas over the past six years, AMC's *Mad Men*, recalls the turbulence of the decade more obliquely, from the perspective of up-and-coming Madison Avenue advertising agency executives including the dashing creative director Don Draper. Set in the tumultuous year of 1968, season 6 portrays its main characters navigating professional and personal conflicts as news coverage of the year's traumatic national events flicker on television screens in the background. During episode 9, copy editor Peggy Olson ends her romance with radical journalist boyfriend Abe Drexler. Abe condemns the advertising industry for its unapologetic celebration of consumer capitalism, but he and Peggy share their enthusiasm for the civil rights movement. When Abe decides that their relationship is over, he tells Peggy, "You're a scared person who hides behind complacency. I don't know why I thought you'd be braver; you're in advertising." Abe then announces, "Your activities are offensive to my every waking moment. I'm sorry. But you'll always be the enemy." This caustic character does not appear again on the program. Nor does the program provide many cues to contextualize his bitterness.

Although Abe appears in three seasons as Peggy's steady boyfriend, he is not the focus of the program, nor does *Mad Men* spend any particular length of time portraying the burgeoning radical movements after 1967. Like the variety of throwaway radical characters that came before him, Abe's function is to move the plot forward as his hostile remarks persuade Peggy to seek a romantic relationship with her decidedly more conservative boss, Ted. Similar to the female characters who flirted with radicals before her, Peggy grows up. In the program's final season, Peggy continues to excel as an advertising executive, survives a merger that costs other female co-workers their jobs, and confesses her love for Stan, the firm's somewhat edgy but decidedly good workplace citizen. Once again, an ambivalent woman's distance from an alluring macho militant facilitates domestic bliss and stability.

Notably, the counterculture is relatively absent in *Mad Men*'s portrait of the sixties, and the Black Power movement is nowhere in evidence. The program references the counterculture only in its final season. Don's business partner Roger Sterling is dumbfounded after his twenty-something daughter Margaret abandons her son and joins a rural commune. Sterling pretends to support his daughter's new lifestyle until he realizes that its members practice free love. Distraught that Margaret has not only left her son but is sleeping with a variety of hippie men, Roger begs her to return to her husband and child. She refuses. The program does not entirely blame the counterculture for the demise of Margaret's nuclear family. Indeed, the program foregrounds Don and Roger's adultery throughout its seven seasons. Ostensibly, Roger's own illicit affairs created the seedbed for his daughter's dysfunctional life. However, the depiction of the commune suggests that Margaret will find no solace to her inner turmoil so long as she remains there. While Roger Sterling's own story ends happily with a committed monogamous relationship to a woman who clearly loves him, Margaret is never depicted again. Repeating the lessons from nineties films and television programs about young white women's descent into the counterculture, *Mad Men* shows viewers once again that the way of Woodstock is squalid and ruinous.

The counterculture's demise is also suggested in *Mad Men*'s final episode. During the final season, Don is separated from his second wife and disaffected from advertising. He heads out west to connect with his niece Stephanie, a hippie who turned up at his wife's doorstep earlier in the season. Echoing the image of Katie in *The '60s*, Stephanie has no money or means to support herself because her boyfriend's drug habits have landed him in jail, putting the young family in peril. Don is hopeful that he might be able to rebuild his life and help to support her, and the two attend a spiritual retreat on the coast of California. A flaky hippie, Stephanie disappears from his life once Don begins to question the retreat's altruism. The final image of Don shows him meditating atop a bluff overlooking the Pacific coast. Given that the series provided a cynical yet nostalgic depiction of the Manhattan advertising industry, there is some paradox in the program's decision to conclude its narrative at a hippie retreat on the other side of the country. The contrast between the settings might imply that the counterculture offers an antidote to the cynical world of New York advertising, but the program's final moments suggest otherwise. The scene cuts to a famous 1971 Coca-Cola commercial in which a multicultural collection of countercultural teenagers sing, "I'd like to buy the world a Coke." A close look at the teenagers reveals that the entire last episode of *Man Men* was designed to closely mimic the commercial's mise-en-scène, including one singer's long braided hair and red bows. Ostensibly, Don has found his way through his feelings of alienation, and the retreat inadvertently provided inspiration for his next advertising campaign.

Beyond its narrative function, the conclusion provides a broader message about the public memory of the radical sixties. The Coca-Cola commercial itself illustrates how advertisers capitalized on the counterculture by foregrounding resistance to authority and fashion in the decade's soft drink advertisements. In *The Conquest of Cool*, Thomas Frank (1997, 16) explains that America's culture industry transformed countercultural rebellion and dissent into products and brands. The sixties-era image of countercultural resistance was unhinged from its critique of materialism and "translated into harmless consumer commodities, emptied of content, and sold to their very originators as substitutes for the real thing." In *Mad Men*'s final moments, the countercultural retreat has become a new frontier for advertising. Both television culture and *Mad Men*'s portrait of the sixties, which itself is a commentary on the commercialization of social life, is so infused by branding culture that even countercultural spaces of dissent and withdrawal cannot escape its grasp. This message carries additional lessons for this book: the public memory of the late sixties is necessarily imbued with selective amnesia about the decade's most vocal critics of Western imperialism because this memory is primarily a vehicle for promoting the products of neoliberal capitalism.

Aquarius and *Mad Men* illustrate how Hollywood's patterned responses to late sixties dissent has established a template that television networks have continued to draw upon and will likely draw upon in the future. These programs also highlight Hollywood's ongoing investment in attending to the needs and anxieties of white male viewers. Movements for women's liberation, racial justice, and decolonization have challenged white middle-class men to relinquish some of their control over the nation's politics, economy, and civic identity. The construction of the ambivalent female activist who ultimately succumbs to the fantasy of domestic bliss within the nuclear family is a fetish object constructed for the normative male spectator. Her return to the good citizen restores the authority of white, straight middle-class manhood. Likewise, the angry black radical who suffers disastrous consequences for failing to affirm the virtues of the civil rights subject confirms the authority of white power structures that have remained stable throughout modern history.

Hollywood's consistent appeal to white middle-class men contributes, albeit subtly, to the omnipresence of more blatant forms of discrimination against women, people of color, and other marginalized groups in contemporary public life. Thomas Byers (1996, 426) explains in his psychoanalytic reading of *Forrest Gump* that the iconography of the beleaguered, white middle-class father offers compensation for this subject's cultural and political castration anxiety. Writing in 1996, Byers is remarkably prescient when he notes that the New Right ideology that has recently come to dominate American political discourse has relied upon the image of aggrieved and threatened white men. "To 'remember what made America great' is to re-member the great white Father." Indeed, the appeal to "make America great again" has taken on new significance since Trump has made it his campaign slogan. Given Byer's remarks, Donald Trump's political success should perhaps have come as little surprise to political moderates and the left-of-center. Over the past fifty years, popular culture has been nurturing the seeds of resentment toward women, people of color, and other nonnormative identity groups through its appeals to white masculine authority and its fantasy of America's triumphant return to a pre-sixties past.

COUNTERMEMORIES OF THE RADICAL SIXTIES

Although the most widely viewed entertainment fare has discounted late sixties dissent, independent films have provided alternative countermemories about the decade's activism. Over the past fifteen years, several documentaries have offered more nuanced depictions of the radical sixties. As an intervention in the hegemonic practices of sixties memory and forgetting, it is only fitting that I close this book by attending to some of the movies that have resisted Hollywood's selective amnesia of radical dissent.

The 2003 documentary *The Weather Underground* provided a more developed explanation of the organization's motives and actions than other pop culture narratives have. During extended talking-head interviews, several former members discussed their moral outrage regarding a war that had cost the lives of tens of thousands of Vietnamese civilians. They concluded that their duty as citizens obligated them to do whatever they could to end the brutal and unjust war. In 2011, the Swedish film *The Black Power Mixtape, 1967–1971* explored the emergence and demise of radical black activism during the late sixties. The documentary depicted the Black Power movement as a just response to systemic violence against black Americans. Voiceovers from musicians Harry Belafonte and Questlove asserted that the government orchestrated the deaths of Martin Luther King, Malcolm X, and Fred Hampton because they had challenged the stability of liberal capitalism. As Belafonte remarked, King had "tamper[ed] with the playground of the wealthy." Very recently, the documentary *1971* recounted the events surrounding the discovery of the FBI's illegal and covert counterintelligence programs that were designed to undermine a variety of dissident movements including the New Left, Black Power, and the American Indian Movement. The FBI's program was not public knowledge until a group of activists' burglarized FBI offices in Media, Pennsylvania, and leaked its files to the press. *1971* reveals how the FBI's secret activities enabled the government organization to subvert the democratic process and facilitate reprehensible behavior. Each of these documentaries challenged dominant ideological narratives about radical dissent as a threat to civil society. In place of the metanarrative about the bad sixties, they suggest that civil disobedience is a precondition for democratic public life.

Other independent fictionalized portrayals of late sixties dissent including *Chicago 10* and *Cesar Chavez* also challenge conventional

Hollywood portrayals of activists. Premiering at the Sundance Film Festival in 2007 and then released to independent theaters, *Chicago 10* recounts events during the 1968 Democratic National Convention protests in Chicago and the subsequent trial of several of its leaders. The movie provides animated reenactment of the trial based on transcripts and audio recordings, building tension by crosscutting between this animation and archival footage of rallies, marches, and clashes with police. The technique suggests parallels between the brutal police attacks on activists during the convention and Judge Julius Hoffman's disregard for the defendants during the trial. This parallelism invites audiences to conclude that the criminal justice system violated the civil liberties of protesters. Judge Hoffman's callous treatment of the defendants is punctuated during a scene in which he orders that Black Panther member Bobby Seale be bound and gagged in the courtroom. As the film makes clear, Seale was arrested alongside the other white defendants even though he was not one of the protest organizers. Seale insisted that he be allowed to defend himself in court, but Hoffman refused.

Instead of relying on sixties-era rock music, the soundtrack to *Chicago 10* features more contemporary musicians, including Rage Against the Machine, the Beastie Boys, and Eminem, who had been outspoken critics of US foreign policy and Western imperialism in the decade prior to the documentary's release. Three years earlier, Eminem's music video for his song "Mosh" presented an image of multiracial youth marching on the White House to protest the war in Afghanistan. By connecting contemporary protest music with a narrative about the repression of sixties-era dissent, *Chicago 10* signals that public memory about the sixties is implicated in contemporary struggles over US politics and civic engagement. In a reversal of the conventional bad sixties narrative, the criminal justice system poses the threat to democracy and the radical protesters are the good citizens.

The 2014 drama *Cesar Chavez* also presents an image of labor activists as good citizens who fought against the exploitation of fieldworkers during the late sixties. The slow-paced film depicts the United Farm Workers' strike and boycott that led to their contract with growers in 1970. In its intimate portrayal of Chavez, the movie highlights his efforts to recruit hesitant fieldworkers, his hunger strike to protest violent actions of union members, and his personal conflicts with his wife and oldest son. The movie's most arousing moments occur toward the conclusion, when Chavez tells a British reporter that collective dissent is bound to succeed despite trenchant opposition. Crosscut with archival images of fieldworkers marching on a busy street, Chavez explains, "once social change begins, it cannot be reversed . . . You can't oppress someone who's not afraid anymore. We've seen the future and the future is ours."

Of course, neither of these films present historically complete depictions of the events portrayed on screen. In its focus on male leaders of the New Left, *Chicago 10* celebrates a decidedly white and masculine image of radical dissent. Popular movies and television have yet to offer a narrative about radical women in the movement. *Cesar Chavez* also backgrounds women's contributions to the national farmworkers movement, depicting Dolores Huerta more as Chavez's assistant than as the cofounder of the movement. Historian Matt Garcia notes that the film oversimplifies the farmworkers movement by reducing it to the story of Mexican-American protest. In actuality, the movement was multiethnic and involved the leadership of several Filipino activists including Philip Vera Cruz and Pete Velasco (Garcia 2014). The emphasis on the United Farm Workers' fight for recognition during the late sixties also obscures how many fieldworkers still face deplorable working conditions and live in abject poverty. By concluding its narrative with the union's victory, *Cesar Chavez* and other movies about union organizing like it tend to obscure how social justice is won over much longer periods of organizing and dissent.

Despite their shortcomings, these films provide important counternarratives to the depictions of the radical sixties offered by conventional Hollywood films and television. *Cesar Chavez* illustrates how people with little political or economic power organized to resist against their exploitation; likewise, *Chicago 10* shows how both liberal and radical demonstrators collaborated to protest the consequences of a war driven by Western imperialism. These films also respond to the contentious political and social contexts in which they appeared in theaters. Released during the middle of the war in Afghanistan,

Chicago 10 reminded viewers that antiwar demonstration itself is a legitimate form of civic engagement that deserves civil rights protections. *Cesar Chavez* was released to theaters on the heels of activists' efforts to secure residency status for immigrants through Dream Act legislation. The movie offers humanizing images of migrant workers who have been vilified by Dream Act opponents and reminds audiences that collective organizing is a vital tool in the struggle for citizenship and human rights.

The vivid images of police officers beating nonviolent protesters in both of these films also challenged dominant narratives about the inherent justice of law enforcement and the legal system. They remind viewers that rights to free speech and assembly are not guaranteed unless ordinary people vigilantly defend them. These countermemories challenge the prevailing common sense about citizenship and patriotism in the United States. By shining a favorable light on people who have demanded rights and justice for exploited and colonized people at home and abroad, these films highlight the emancipatory potential of memory, capable of resisting a presentist or reified consciousness to recover what has been left out of or excluded from current public debate about government security, civic engagement, and contentious dissent. These are the kinds of film memories we should share and celebrate.

NOTES

INTRODUCTION

1. The key example of what Jameson has referred to as "periodization," the time period during which "the sixties" was supposed to have happened, has been demarcated in a variety of ways by historians, revealing how the era's meaning is a product of interpretation. Periodization is a symbolic practice that situates political, economic, social, and cultural tendencies within a specific historical timeline, giving them a beginning and end point. Such periodization structures contemporary discourse about these trends, in a process that—like the construction of public memory itself—is inevitably rhetorical and ideological. See Frederic Jameson, "Periodizing the '60s," in *The '60s without Apology*, ed. Sohnya Sayres, Anders Stephanson, Stanley Aronowitz, and Fredric Jameson (Minneapolis, MN: Social Text, 1984), 178–209.

2. The interdisciplinary scholarship in memory studies is vast, including contributions across a wide range of disciplines including American studies, history, communication, and media studies. Such scholarship has labeled publicly accessible representations and references to the past as public memory (Kendall Phillips, ed., *Framing Public Memory* [Tuscaloosa: University of Alabama Press, 2004]); collective memory (Jill Edy, *Troubled Pasts: News and the Collective Memory of Social Unrest* [Philadelphia: Temple University Press, 2006], and Michael Schudson, *Watergate in American Memory: How We Remember, Forget, and Construct the Past* [New York: Basic Books, 1992]); and cultural memory (Marita Sturken, *Tangled Memories: The Vietnam War, the AIDS Epidemic, and the Politics of Remembering* [Berkeley: University of California Press, 1997], 24–25). The textual quality of public memory is of particular interest to rhetoric scholars who foreground the symbolic processes that promote a shared sense of the past in a variety of artifacts such as political speeches, museums, memorial structures, films, and other forms of popular culture. Fundamental work within rhetoric includes

Carole Blair, Marsha S. Jeppeson, and Enrico Pucci Jr., "Public Memorializing in Postmodernity: The Vietnam Veterans Memorial as Prototype," *Quarterly Journal of Speech* 77 (1991): 263–88; Stephen H. Browne, "Remembering Crispus Attucks: Race, Rhetoric, and the Politics of Commemoration," *Quarterly Journal of Speech* 85 (1999): 169–87; and Bruce Gronbeck, "The Rhetorics of the Past: History, Argument, and Collective Memory," in *Doing Rhetorical History: Concepts and Cases*, ed. Kathleen J. Turner (Tuscaloosa: University of Alabama Press, 1998), 47–60. My attention to public memories as civics lessons draws from observations in Barbara Biesecker, "Remembering World War II: The Rhetoric and Politics of National Commemoration at the Turn of the 21st Century," *Quarterly Journal of Speech* 88 (2002): 393–409.

3. Peter Ehrenhaus and Susan Owen argue that the 1998 film *Saving Private Ryan* reillusions national identity in the wake of Vietnam. Owen contextualizes the film's construction of white masculine national identity in the context of the variety of films that foregrounded the crisis of this identity in the traumatic aftermath of the Vietnam War. See Peter Ehrenhaus, "Why We Fought: Holocaust Memory in Spielberg's *Saving Private Ryan*," *Critical Studies in Media Communication* 18, no. 3 (September 2001): 321–37; A. Susan Owen, "Memory, War and American Identity: *Saving Private Ryan* as Cinematic Jeremiad," *Critical Studies in Media Communication* 19, no. 3 (September 2002): 249–82.

4. For a discussion of screen images as sources of cultural memory, see Sturken, *Tangled Memories*. Alison Landsberg contends that mass cultural technologies have the radical potential to facilitate the formation of progressive political alliances and solidarities by making "prosthetic memories" available to those who may not have lived or experienced them directly. Alison Landsberg, "Prosthetic Memory: The Ethics and Politics of Memory in an Age of Mass Culture," in *Memory and Popular Film*, ed. Paul Grainge (Manchester: Manchester University Press, 2003), 144–61. I find Landsberg's concept of "prosthetic memory" useful to highlight the role of mass communication technologies as the "grounds upon which social meanings are negotiated, contested, and constructed" (149), but I am less sanguine about the progressive potential of these technologies. I concur with Andrew Paul's assessment that prevailing liberal ideologies reproduced by Hollywood constrain the potential for political alliances to converge around radical Left politics and organizations. See Andrew Paul, "Making the Blacklist White: The Hollywood Red Scare in Popular Memory," *Journal of Popular Film and Television* 41, no. 4 (2013): 208–18.

CHAPTER ONE

1. In 1965, a hundred deputies and state troopers beat and injured over forty peaceful civil rights protesters in Montgomery, Alabama. Also during that year, one thousand activists who gathered for a peace invasion at the Oakland Army

Base near Berkeley, California, were met by three hundred policemen who refused to allow them to continue marching, as well as a number of Hell's Angels who beat them. See Terry H. Anderson, *The Movement and the Sixties: Protest in America from Greensboro to Wounded Knee* (New York: Oxford University Press, 1995), 115 and 144.

2. The organizer of Chaney, Schwerner, and Goodman's murders, Edgar Ray Killen, was not convicted until 2005 because a member of the jury in the first trial refused to convict a preacher. Two years earlier, prosecutors failed to win a conviction against Byron de la Beckwith for the murder of Medgar Evers despite strong physical evidence against him.

3. It is important to distinguish the Black Panther Party that operated during the late sixties and early seventies from the New Black Panther Party (NBPP), a black separatist group that emerged in 1998 and believes black Americans should have their own nation. Previous members of the sixties-era organization have denounced the NBPP, and the Southern Poverty Law Center has identified the more recent group as a white-hate organization. See Southern Poverty Law Center, "New Black Panther Party," https://www.splcenter.org/fighting-hate/extremist-files/group/new-black-panther-party (accessed June 7, 2016), and Southern Poverty Law Center, "The New Black Panther Party Is Unlike Its Namesake of the 1960s," December 6, 2000, https://www.splcenter.org/fighting-hate/intelligence-report/2000/new-black-panther-party-unlike-its-namesake-1960s.

4. Scholarly histories and analyses of the Black Panther Party can be found in Philip S. Foner, ed., *The Black Panthers Speak* (New York: Da Capo Press, 1995); Charles E. Jones, ed., *The Black Panther Party (Reconsidered)* (Baltimore, MD: Black Classic Press, 1998); and Jama Lazerow and Yohuru Williams, eds., *In Search of the Black Panther Party: New Perspectives on a Revolutionary Movement* (Durham, NC: Duke University Press, 2006).

5. Director to All Offices, August 25, 1967, file released by the FBI under the Freedom of Information Act in 1977 and located in microfilm in the collection, *COINTELPRO: The Counterintelligence Program of the FBI*, ed. Athan Theoharis (Wilmington, DE: Scholarly Resources, 1978). For more information on the FBI's counterintelligence activities on civil rights and Black Power activism, see Kenneth O'Reilly, *Racial Matters: The FBI's Secret File on Black America, 1960–1972* (New York: Free Press, 1989).

6. These include the 2000 comedy movie *Road Trip* and an episode of the situation comedy *Everybody Hates Chris* entitled, "Everybody Hates Bomb Threats," which aired on May 1, 2009. A play on the school bomb threat appeared on the situation comedy *30 Rock*. During the episode entitled "Secret Santa," which first aired on December 10, 2009, main character Liz Lemon calls Union Station with a fake bomb threat in order to facilitate a romantic relationship between her employer and his high-school crush who plans to leave New York City for her hometown.

7. After a fan-led campaign, Ben & Jerry's reintroduced Wavy Gravy ice cream in limited scoop shops in 2005. The psychedelic packaging of the grocery-store product is further evidence that the memory of the counterculture has had a long lifespan in commercial culture.

8. For a discussion of the gendered dynamics of the Black Panther Party, see Tracye Matthews, "'No One Ever Asks What a Man's Role in the Revolution Is,' Gender and the Politics of the Black Panther Party, 1966–1971," in *The Black Panther Party (Reconsidered)*, ed. Charles E. Jones (Baltimore, MD: Black Classic Press, 1998), 267–304; and Jane Rhodes, *Framing the Black Panthers: The Spectacular Rise of a Black Power Icon* (New York: New Press, 2007), 107–10.

9. The critique of the New Left's failures for responding to antiracist and feminist activism is elaborated in Barber, *A Hard Rain Fell*.

10. These movies include *Up in Smoke* (1978), *Cheech & Chong's Next Movie* (1980), *Nice Dreams* (1981), *Things Are Tough All Over* (1982) and *Still Smokin* (1983). Subsequent stoner movies that celebrate countercultural drug use include *Dazed and Confused* (1993), *The Stoned Age* (1994), and *Half Baked* (1998). Tommy Chong also appeared regularly in the stoner comedy *That '70s Show* (1998–2006) as the aging hippie owner of a Fotoshop where one of the main characters is employed.

11. These depictions include the characters Duck from a 1990 episode of *Quantum Leap* entitled "Animal Frat"; Kenny, in the ABC miniseries *The '60s* (1999); Jenny's militant boyfriend in *Forrest Gump* (1994); and Paco in *Across the Universe* (2007).

12. Documentaries about radical racial justice activism include the PBS documentaries *Eyes on the Prize II: America at the Racial Crossroads, 1965–1985* (1990), and *Palante, Siempre Palante! The Young Lords* (1996). In 2001, Spike Lee directed the film adaptation of Roger Guenever Smith's one-man performance, *A Huey Newton Story*, which aired on PBS the next year. More recent documentaries *The Black Power Mixtape, 1967–1975* (2011) and *The Black Panthers: Vanguard of the Revolution* (2015) highlight renewed interest in the legacy of Black Power activism. Recent documentaries about the counterculture and antiwar movement include *The Weather Underground* (2002), *William Kunstler: Disturbing the Universe* (2009), *Saint Misbehavin': The Wavy Gravy Movie* (2009), *Phil Ochs: There but for Fortune* (2010), and *1971* (2014).

CHAPTER TWO

1. For instance, Reagan's Working Group on the Family issued a report in 1986 that concluded that Reagan's tax cuts limiting payments to poor mothers and government-supported child care were "major victories for the American family" because they protected the rights of the family from incursions by the state. See Self, *All in the Family*, 383.

2. According to Nielsen data, *Family Ties* was the second top-rated new network TV series that premiered in the 1987–1988 season, earning 19 percent of 88.6 million homes with a TV. (See "List of Season's Top-Rated New Series," *Associated Press*, April 19, 1988. *LexisNexis Academic*, http://www.lexisnexis.com.) Both programs received recognition from the Golden Globes and Primetime Emmy Awards. In addition to Michael J. Fox's Emmy wins, he was nominated for his performance in 1989 and 1985, and the program was nominated for Outstanding Comedy series four years in a row between 1984 and 1987. The Golden Globe Awards also awarded Fox for his acting performance in 1989, and nominated him and the series itself for best comedy television series in 1986, 1987, and 1988. In addition to its 1988 Emmy win, *The Wonder Years* received a Golden Globe for Best Comedy TV series in 1989. It was nominated for an Emmy in 1989 and 1990, and Savage's performance received best actor nominations by the Primetime Emmys in 1989 and 1990 and by the Golden Globes in 1990 and 1991.

3. Internal conflict among baby boomers who have "sold out" to embrace "yuppie" values is perhaps most acutely expressed in the 1983 film *The Big Chill*, which loosely inspired *thirtysomething*.

CHAPTER THREE

1. In return, VH1 agreed to run direct-response spots selling the soundtrack and home video, with revenue split between NBC and VH1. See Jenny Hontz, "The '60s Headed to VH1," *Daily Variety*, February 16, 1999, 5, *LexisNexis Academic*, http://www.lexisnexis.com. NBC also partnered with the Home Shopping Network, selling viewers products connected to the program, including the soundtrack CD featuring a duet with Bob Dylan and Joan Osborne created for the soundtrack. See "Home Shopping Network, NBC Cash in on the '60s," *St. Petersburg Times*, February 9, 1999, 2B. *LexisNexis Academic*, http://www.lexisnexis.com.

2. See chapter 4 for a more extended discussion of *Forrest Gump*'s contribution to selective amnesia surrounding the Black Panther Party.

3. Gitlin is quoting from the Port Huron Statement, the landmark document that announced the emergence of the New Left among a group of students at the University of Michigan in Ann Arbor in 1962. See Gitlin, *The Sixties*, 107.

CHAPTER FOUR

1. The popular music industry is a richer resource for locating public memories of Black Power activism. During its heyday, the movement played a significant role in the music recording industry, influencing established artists such as Marvin Gaye and James Brown, and shaping the lyrics of songwriters such as Sly Stone

and Gil Scott-Heron. Early underground rap groups, the Last Poets and the Watts Prophets, expressed revolutionary consciousness and identified with diverse Black Power movements. These groups created a path for future hip-hop artists such as Public Enemy, who described themselves as "the Black Panthers of rap." Other rap artists, including KRS-One, Digital Underground, Digable Planets, Queen Latifah, Tupac Shakur, Cee-Lo, Paris, and Ded Prez employed images and ideas of Black Power activism in their music. See Pat Thomas, *Listen Whitey! The Sights and Sounds of Black Power, 1965–1975* (Seattle, WA: Fantagraphics Books, 2012); and Jeff Chang, *Can't Stop, Won't Stop: A History of the Hip-Hop Generation* (New York: St. Martin's Press, 2005).

2. For analyses of news coverage of the Black Panther Party, see Amanda Davis Gatchet and Dana L. Cloud, "David, Goliath, and the Black Panthers: The Paradox of the Oppressed Militant in the Rhetoric of Self-Defense," *Journal of Communication Inquiry* 37, no. 1 (2013): 5–25; Edward Morgan, "Media Culture and the Public Memory of the Black Panther Party," in *In Search of the Black Panther Party: New Perspectives on a Revolutionary Movement*, ed. Jama Lazerow and Yohuru Williams (Durham, NC: Duke University Press, 2006), 324–74; and Jane Rhodes, "Fanning the Flames of Racial Discord: The National Press and the Black Panther Party," *International Journal of Press/Politics* 4, no. 4 (1999): 95–118. Details regarding the FBI's campaign to destroy the Black Panther Party can be found in Kristen Hoerl and Erin Ortiz, "Organizational Secrecy and the FBI's COINTELPRO-Black Nationalist Hate Groups Program, 1967–1971," *Management Communication Quarterly* 29, no. 4 (2015): 590–615; and Jeffrey Haas, *The Assassination of Fred Hampton: How the FBI and the Chicago Police Murdered a Black Panther* (Chicago, IL: Lawrence Hill Books, 2010). While Fred Hampton's heinous murder has largely dropped out of public memory, conservatives have continued to sound alarms about the legacy of the Black Power movement. California conservatives made national news when they expressed outrage over Angela Davis's prestigious academic post at the University of California at Davis in 1995. The issue was not about Davis's scholarly credentials; rather it was over her historic support for black radicals during the early 1970s. See Amy Wallace, "Angela Davis again at Center of UC Storm," *Los Angeles Times*, February 20 1995, http://articles.latimes.com/1995-02-20/news/mn-34106_1_uc-santa-cruz.

CHAPTER FIVE

1. These include novels by Jay Cantor, *Great Neck* (New York: Alfred A. Knopf, 2003), and Neil Gordon, *The Company You Keep* (New York: Viking, 2003); the 2011 play *Home/Sick*, created by The Assembly, a Brooklyn theater troupe, and David Mamet's 2012 two-person play *The Anarchist*. Movies featuring former sixties radicals who have evaded law enforcement by living underground in subsequent

decades include *Running on Empty* (1988), *Sneakers* (1992), and *The Company You Keep* (2012).

2. In addition to the crime dramas, militant antiwar radicals are featured in a 1990 episode of *Quantum Leap* entitled "Animal Frat," and a 2004 episode of Lifetime Network medical drama *Strong Medicine* entitled "Identity Crisis."

3. These episodes are ABC, "Revenge of Broken Jaw," *Life on Mars*, March 4, 2009; CBS, "Blood on the Tracks," *Cold Case*, February 18, 2007; FOX, "Soccer Mom in the Mini-Van," *Bones*, October 2, 2007; FOX, "Cabrini Green," *Chicago Code*, February 28, 2011; NBC, "Gung Ho," *Hill Street Blues*, January 20, 1983; NBC, "White Rabbit," *Law & Order*, October 19, 1994; NBC, "Ramparts," *Law & Order*, January 13, 1999; and 20th Century Fox Television, "Save the Mule," *The Practice*, November 15, 1997.

4. Now living in Cuba under political asylum, Shakur has insisted that she is innocent and that the charges against her are part of an effort to repress black radicalism. After President Obama visited Cuba during the spring of 2016, New Jersey governor Chris Christie demanded Shakur's extradition. Christie's concerns about Shakur's freedom in Cuba illustrates how the political right continues to call up the memory of the bad sixties to advance a conservative agenda and to characterize Obama as a radical sympathizer.

5. In a statement released by her lawyer at the time of her surrender, Power took responsibility for Schroeder's death. See Sara Rimer, "60s Radical, Linked to a Killing, Surrenders after Hiding 23 Years," *New York Times*, September 16, 1993, http://www.nytimes.com/1993/09/16/nyregion/60-s-radical-linked-to-a-killing-surrenders-after-hiding-23-years.html. Power later told the judge during her sentencing hearing, "I cannot possibly say in words how sorry I am for the death of Office Schroeder." See Fred Bruning, "The Guilt behind a Tragic Deed," *Maclean's*, November 1, 1993, 31.

6. George Bush, Exchange with Reporters in Kennebunkport, Maine, February 17, 1991. For a discussion of Bush's exchange, see Bernard von Bothmer, *Framing the Sixties: The Use and Abuse of a Decade from Ronald Reagan to George W. Bush* (Boston: University of Massachusetts Press, 2010).

7. The Obama-Ayers connection was an obsession of conservative news media. FOX News mentioned their relationship 691 times, according to my LexisNexis search using the key terms Obama and Ayers between 2007 and 2013. By contrast, the other five major broadcast news sources mentioned Obama and Ayers in the same report 462 times collectively. The majority of those reports came from CNN, which provided 275. FOX News pundit Sean Hannity referred to "Bill Ayers the unrepentant terrorist" 33 times. For example, see "Obama Chronicles: His Relationship with William Ayers," *The O'Reilly Factor*, FOX News, September 22, 2008.

BIBLIOGRAPHY

"A Victim of Weather Underground Speaks Up." 2008. *Hannity's America,* April 27, FOX News. *LexisNexis Academic.* http://www.lexisnexis.com. Lexis-Nexis Database.

Acham, Christine. 2004. *Revolution Televised: Prime Time and the Struggle for Black Power.* Minneapolis: University of Minnesota Press.

Adler, Jerry. 1984. "The Year of the Yuppie." *Newsweek,* December 31, 14.

Alpert, Jane. 1990. *Growing Up Underground.* New York: Citadel.

Alexander, Elizabeth. 1995. "'Can You Be BLACK and Look at This?' Reading the Rodney King Video(s)." In *The Black Public Sphere.* Edited by The Black Public Sphere Collective. Chicago: University of Chicago Press.

Anderson, Terry H. 1995. *The Movement and the Sixties: Protest in America from Greensboro to Wounded Knee.* New York: Oxford University Press.

———. 2007. *The Sixties,* 3rd ed. New York: Pearson Longman.

Appel, Richard. 2005. "Commentary for 'Mother Simpson.'" In *The Simpsons: The Complete Seventh Season.* Los Angeles: 20th Century Fox. DVD.

Ayers, Bill. 2001. *Fugitive Days: A Memoir.* Boston, MA: Beacon.

Barber, David. 2008. *A Hard Rain Fell: SDS and Why It Failed.* Jackson: University Press of Mississippi.

Barnes, Fred. 1995. "Rebel with a Cause." *USA Weekend,* January 20, 4–5.

Barthes, Roland. 1975. *S/Z.* London: Cape.

Berger, Dan. 2006. *Outlaws of America: The Weather Underground and the Politics of Solidarity.* Oakland, CA: AK Press.

Berlant, Lauren. 1997. *The Queen of America Goes to Washington City: Essays on Sex and Citizenship.* Durham, NC: Duke University Press.

Berman, Paul. 1988. "At the Center of the '60s." *New York Times,* June 12. http://www.nytimes.com/1988/06/12/books/at-the-center-of-the-60-s.html?pagewanted=allhttp://ww.nytimes.com/1988/06/12/books/at-the-center-of-the-60s.html.

Biesecker, Barbara. 2002. "Remembering World War II: The Rhetoric and Politics of National Commemoration at the Turn of the 21st Century." *Quarterly Journal of Speech* 88: 393–409.

Blackstock, Nelson. 1988. *COINTELPRO: The FBI's Secret War on Political Freedom*. New York: Pathfinder Press.

Blumenthal, Sidney. 1988. "Reaganism and the Neokitsch Aesthetic." In *The Regan Legacy*. Edited by Sidney Blumenthal and Thomas Byrne Edsall. New York: Pantheon.

Bodroghkozy, Aniko. 2001. *Groove Tube: Sixties Television and the Youth Rebellion*. Durham, NC: Duke University Press.

———. 2002. "Reel Revolutionaries: An Examination of Hollywood's Cycle of 1960s Youth Rebellion Films." *Cinema Journal* 41 (3): 38–58.

Bogle, Donald. 1996. *Toms, Coons, Mulattoes, Mammies, and Blacks: An Interpretive History of Blacks in American Films*, 2nd edition. New York: Continuum.

Bonilla-Silva, Eduardo. 2009. *Racism without Racists: Color-Blind Racism and the Persistence of Racial Inequality in America*. Lanham, MD: Rowman and Littlefield.

Boykoff, Jules. 2007. *Beyond Bullets: The Suppression of Dissent in the United States*. Oakland, CA: AK Press.

Braunstein, Paul, and Michael William Doyle. 2002. "Introduction: Historicizing the American Counterculture of the 1960s and '70s." In *Imagine Nation: The American Counterculture of the 1960s and '70s*. Edited by Paul Breinstein and Michael William Doyle, 5–14. New York: Routledge.

Brown, Wendy. 2003. "Neo-liberalism and the End of Liberal Democracy." *Theory and Event* 7 (1). https://muse.jhu.edu/ (accessed April 29, 2017).

Buchanan, Patrick. 1994. "Hollywood Surprise: Hello, I'm Forrest Gump and I'm a Conservative." *Pittsburgh Post-Gazette*, August 8, sec. B3.

Burgoyne, Robert. 2003. "Memory, History, and Digital Imagery in Contemporary Film." In *Memory and Popular Film*. Edited by Paul Grainge. Manchester: Manchester University Press.

Burke, Kenneth. 1969. *A Rhetoric of Motives*. Berkeley: University of California Press.

Burrough, Bryan. 2015. *Days of Rage: America's Radical Underground, the FBI, and the Forgotten Age of Revolutionary Violence*. New York: Penguin Press.

Bush, George. 1991. Exchange with Reporters in Kennebunkport, Maine, February 17.

Byers, Thomas B. 1996. "History Re-Membered: Forrest Gump, Postfeminist Masculinity, and the Burial of the Counterculture." *MFS: Modern Fiction Studies* 42 (2): 419–44.

Cantor, Jay. 2003. *Great Neck*. New York: Alfred A. Knopf.

Carlson, Margaret, and Joelle Attinger. 1993. "The Return of the Fugitive." *Time*, September 27. Accessed August 1, 2015, on the Academic Search Premier database.

Carson, Allan C. 1980. "Families, Sex, and the Liberal Agenda." *Public Interest* 58 (Winter): 74.

Carter, Bill. 1999. "TV Notes; NBC Basking in '60's Success." *New York Times*, February 10. http://www.nytimes.com/1999/02/10/arts/tv-notes-nbc-basking-in-60-s-success.html.

———. 1999. "NBC Plays On: NBC's Direct-Response Ads Pitched Music from Its Show *The '60s* with Great Success." *National Post*, February 16, C10. *LexisNexis Academic*, http://www.lexisnexis.com.

Cash, Jon David. 2010. "People's Park: Birth and Survival." *California History: The Journal of the California Historical Society* 88: 8–29.

Chang, Jeff. 2005. *Can't Stop, Won't Stop: A History of the Hip-Hop Generation*. New York: St. Martin's Press.

Chang, Nancy. 2002. *Silencing Political Dissent: How Post-September 11 Anti-Terrorism Measures Threaten Our Civil Liberties*. New York: Seven Stories Press.

"Chart Book: TANF at 19." 2016. Center on Budget and Policy Priorities, March 29. http://www.cbpp.org/research/family-income-support/chart-book-tanf-at-19.

Chokshi, Niraj. 2016. "Rudy Giuliani: Beyoncé's Halftime Show Was an 'Outrageous' Affront to Police." *Washington Post*, February 8. https://www.washingtonpost.com/news/arts-and-entertainment/wp/2016/02/08/rudy-giuliani-beyonces-half-time-show-was-an-outrageous-affront-to-police/.

Clinton, William J. 1995a. "Remarks at the Michigan State University Commencement Ceremony in East Lansing, Michigan." Speech, May 5. http://www.presidency.ucsb.edu/ws/?pid=51317.

———. 1995b. "Remarks at Georgetown University, July 6, 1995." In *Public Papers of the Presidents of the United States, William J. Clinton, 1995, Bk. 2, July 1 to December 31, 1995*. National Archives and Records Administration, Office of the Federal Register, 1047.

"Clinton Marks First Year of Welfare to Work Plan at White House Event." 1998. *Jet*, June 12, 6.

Cloud, Dana. 1998a. *Control and Consolation in American Culture and Politics: Rhetorics of Therapy*. Thousand Oaks, CA: SAGE Publications.

———. 1998b. "The Rhetoric of 'Family Values': Scapegoating, Utopia, and the Privatization of Social Responsibility." *Western Journal of Communication* 62 (4): 404.

Colangelo, Lisa. 2016. "Malcolm X's Daughter Praises Beyonce Super Bowl Act." *New York Daily News*, February 19. http://www.nydailynews.com/new-york/malcolm-x-daughter-praises-beyonce-super-bowl-act-article-1.2548175.

Collier, Peter, and David Horowitz. 2006. *Destructive Generation: Second Thoughts about the Sixties*, 2nd edition. San Francisco, CA: Encounter Books.

Condit, Celeste Michelle. 1989. "The Rhetorical Limits of Polysemy." *Critical Studies in Mass Communication* 6: 103–22.

Coppock, Vicki. 1995. *The Illusion of Post-Feminism: New Women, Old Myths*. London: Taylor & Francis.

Corrigan, Lisa. 2016. *Prison Power: How Prison Influenced the Movement for Black Liberation*. Jackson: University Press of Mississippi.

Cullen, Kevin. 2008. "Fox Continues to Go on about Black Panthers." *Irish Times*, November 6. http://www.irishtimes.com/news/fox-continues-to-go-on-about-black-panthers-1.906023.

D'Acci, Julie. 1994. *Defining Women: Television and the Case of Cagney & Lacey*. Chapel Hill: University of North Carolina Press.

Deaton, Chris. 2016. "Protester Would Be 'Carried out on a Stretcher' in the Old Days, Trump Reminisces." *Weekly Standard*, February 23. http://www.weeklystandard.com/protester-would-be-carried-out-on-a-stretcher-in-the-old-days-trump-reminisces/article/2001211.

"Defending Bill Ayers." 2008. *The O'Reilly Factor*, October 14, FOX News. *LexisNexis Academic*, http://www.lexisnexis.com.

DeLuca, Kevin, Sean Lawson, and Ye Sun. 2012. "Occupy Wall Street on the Public Screens of Social Media: The Many Framings of the Birth of a Protest Movement." *Communication, Culture, and Critique* 5 (4): 491.

DeMartini, Joseph. 1983. "Social Movement Participation: Political Socialization, Generational Consciousness, and Lasting Effects." *Youth and Society* 15: 195–223.

Dohrn, Bernardine, Bill Ayers, and Jeff Jones, eds. 2006. *Sing a Battle Song: The Revolutionary Poetry, Statements, and Communiqués of the Weather Underground, 1970–1974*. New York: Seven Stories Press.

Dow, Bonnie J. 1996. *Prime-Time Feminism: Television, Media Culture, and the Women's Movement since 1970*. Philadelphia: University of Pennsylvania Press.

Dowd, Maureen. 1994. "The 1994 Elections: Leaders the G.O.P. Leader; G.O.P.'s Rising Star Pledges to Right Wrongs of the Left." *New York Times*, November 10. http://www.nytimes.com/1994/11/10/us/1994-elections-leaders-gop-leader-gop-s-rising-star-pledges-right-wrongs-left.html.

Dyson, Michael. 1995. *Making Malcolm: The Myth and Meaning of Malcolm X*. New York: Oxford University Press.

———. 1996. *Between God and Gangsta Rap: Bearing Witness to Black Culture*. New York: Oxford University Press.

Echols, Alice. 1989. *Daring to Be BAD: Radical Feminism in America, 1967–1975*. Minneapolis: University of Minnesota Press.

Ehrenfreund, Max. 2016. "Bernie Sanders Is Right: Bill Clinton's Welfare Law Doubled Extreme Poverty." *Washington Post*, February 27. https://www.washingtonpost.com/news/wonk/wp/2016/02/27/bernie-sanders-is-right-bill-clintons-welfare-law-doubled-extreme-poverty/.

Ehrenhaus, Peter. 1989. "Commemorating the Unwon War: On Not Remembering Vietnam." *Journal of Communication* 39 (1): 101.

———. 2001. "Why We Fought: Holocaust Memory in Spielberg's *Saving Private Ryan*." *Critical Studies in Media Communication* 18 (3): 321–37.

Elbaum, Max. 2002. *Revolution in the Air: Sixties Radicals Turn to Lenin, Mao and Che*. London: Verso.
Faludi, Susan. 1991. *Backlash: The Undeclared War against American Women*. New York: Doubleday.
Farber, Stephen. 1970 [1969]. "End of the Road?" *Film Quarterly* 23 (2): 3–15.
Farley, Robert. 2010. "Bill O'Reilly Blames Obama Administration for Not Pursuing Criminal Charges in New Panther Party Case." *Politifact*, July 23. http://www.politifact.com/truth-o-meter/statements/2010/jul/23/bill-oreilly/bill-oreilly-blames-obama-administration-not-pursu.
Ferns, Erin. 2007. "Michigan Voter ID Law Upheld by State Supreme Court." *Daily Kos*, July 20. http://www.dailykos.com/story/2007/7/20/360246/-.
Feuer, Jane. 1995. *Seeing through the Eighties: Television and Reaganism*. Durham, NC: Duke University Press.
Fineman, Howard. 1994. "Clinton's Values Blowout." *Newsweek*, December 19, 24.
"First Night: Clinton Takes to the Stage for the Ultimate Sell." 2004. *The Independent*, June 4. http://www.independent.co.uk/news/world/americas/first-night-clinton-takes-to-the-stage-for-the-ultimate-sell-731119.html.
Fiske, John. 2011. *Television Culture*, 2nd edition. London: Routledge Classics.
Foner, Phillip S., ed. 1995a. *The Black Panthers Speak*. New York: Da Capo Press.
Frank, Thomas. 1997. *The Conquest of Cool: Business Culture, Counterculture, and the Rise of Hip Consumerism*. Chicago: University of Chicago Press.
Garcia, Matt. 2014. "What the New Cesar Chavez Film Gets Wrong about the Labor Activist." Smithsonian.com, April 2. http://www.smithsonianmag.com/ist/?next=/history/what-new-cesar-chavez-film-gets-wrong-about-labor-activist-180950355/.
Gearan, Anne, and Abby Phillip. "Clinton Regrets 1996 Remark on 'Super-Predators' after Encounter with Activist." *Washington Post*, February 25. https://www.washingtonpost.com/news/post-politics/wp/2016/02/25/clinton-heckled-by-black-lives-matter-activist/.
Germain, David. 2004. "Barbershop 2 Cuts into No. 1 Spot." *Gazette* (Montreal, Quebec), February 9. http://www.lexisnexis.com.ezproxy.butler.edu/hottopics/lnacademic/?.
Gilbert, David. 2011. *Love and Struggle: My Life in SDS, the Weather Underground, and Beyond*. Oakland, CA: PM Press.
Gilens, Martin. 2009. *Why Americans Hate Welfare: Race, Media, and the Politics of Antipoverty Policy*. Chicago: University of Chicago Press.
Gingrich, Newt. 1994. *Contract with America: The Bold Plan by Rep. Newt Gingrich, Rep. Dick Armey and the House Republicans to Change the Nation*. New York: Three Rivers Press.
Gitlin, Todd. 1996. *The Sixties: Years of Hope, Days of Rage*. New York: Bantam.
———. 2000. "Prime Time Ideology: The Hegemonic Process in Television Entertainment." In *Television: The Critical View*, 6th edition. Edited by Horace Newcomb. New York: Oxford University Press.

———. 2003. *The Whole World Is Watching: Mass Media in the Making and Unmaking of the New Left*, 2nd ed. Berkeley: University of California Press.

Gordon, Neil. 2003. *The Company You Keep*. New York: Viking.

Gray, Herman. 1997. "Remembering Civil Rights: Television, Memory, and the 1960s." In *The Revolution Wasn't Televised: Sixties Television and Social Conflict*. Edited by Lynn Spigel and Michael Curtin. New York: Routledge.

Greeley, Andrew. 1987. "Today's Morality Play." *New York Times*, May 17, sec. B, 1.

Grossberg, Lawrence. 1997. *Dancing in Spite of Myself*. Durham, NC: Duke University Press.

Hall, Simon. 2011. *American Patriotism, American Protest: Social Movements since the Sixties*. Philadelphia: University of Pennsylvania Press.

Hall, Stuart. 1986. "Gramsci's Relevance for the Study of Race and Ethnicity." *Journal of Communication Inquiry* 10: 5–27.

Heffernan, Nick. 2015. "No Parents, No Church, No Authorities in Our Films: Exploitation Movies, the Youth Audience, and Roger Corman's Counterculture Trilogy." *Journal of Film and Video* 67 (2): 3–20.

Herring, Henry. 1983. "Out of the Dream and into the Nightmare: Dennis Hopper's Apocalyptic Vision of America." *Journal of Popular Film & TV* 10 (4): 144–54.

Hoerl, Kristen. 2007. "Mario Van Peebles's *Panther* and Popular Memories of the Black Panther Party." *Critical Studies in Media Communication* 24 (3): 206–27.

———. 2008. "Cinematic Jujitsu: Resisting White Hegemony through the American Dream in Spike Lee's *Malcolm X*." *Communication Studies* 59 (4): 355–70.

———. 2012. "Selective Amnesia and Racial Transcendence in News Coverage of President Obama's Inauguration." *Quarterly Journal of Speech* 98 (2): 178–202.

———. 2014. "Remembering Radical Black Dissent: Traumatic Counter-Memories in Contemporary Documentaries about the Black Power Movement." In *Race and Hegemonic Struggle in the United States: Pop Culture, Politics, and Protest*. Edited by Michael G. Lacy and Mary E. Triece. Madison, NJ: Farleigh Dickinson Press.

Hontz, Jenny. 1999. "The '60s Headed to VH1." *Daily Variety*, February 16. LexisNexis Academic, http://www.lexisnexis.com.

Horowitz, David. 2006. *The Professors: The 101 Most Dangerous Academics in America*. Washington, DC: Regnery Publishing.

Horowitz, David, and Jacob Laskin. 2009. *One-Party Classroom: How Radical Professors at America's Top Colleges Indoctrinate Students and Undermine Our Democracy*. New York: Crown Forum.

Horowitz, David, and Richard Poe. 2006. *The Shadow Party: How George Soros, Hillary Clinton, and Sixties Radicals Seized Control of the Democratic Party*. Nashville, TN: Nelson Current.

Hunt, Andrew. 1999. "'When Did the Sixties Happen?' Searching for New Directions." *Journal of Social History* 33: 147–61.

Infiltrating Hollywood: The Rise and Fall of "The Spook Who Sat by the Door." 2011. Directed by Christine Acham and Clifford Ward. Los Angeles: University of Southern California. DVD.

Jacobs, Harold, ed. 1970. *Weatherman*. Ramparts Press.

Jacobs, Ron. 1997. *The Way the Wind Blew: A History of the Weather Underground*. London: Verso.

Jennings, M. Kent, and Richard G. Neimi. 1981. *Generations and Politics: A Panel Study of Young Adults and Their Parents*. Princeton, NJ: Princeton University Press.

Jones, Charles E., ed. 1998. *The Black Panther Party (Reconsidered)*. Baltimore, MD: Black Classic Press.

Joseph, Peniel. 2006. "Introduction." In *The Black Power Movement: Rethinking the Civil Rights–Black Power Era*. Edited by Peniel E. Joseph. New York: Routledge.

Kimball, Roger. 2008. *Tenured Radicals: How Politics Has Corrupted Our Higher Education*, 3rd edition. Chicago, IL: Ivan R. Dee.

King, Claire Sisco. 2012. *Washed in Blood: Male Sacrifice, Trauma, and the Cinema*. New Brunswick, NJ: Rutgers University Press.

King Jr., Martin Luther. 1967. "Beyond Vietnam—A Time to Break Silence." Speech, Riverside Church, New York City, NY, April 4, 1967. *American Rhetoric Online Speech Bank*. http://www.americanrhetoric.com/speeches/mlkatimetobreaksilence.htm.

Kitts, Thomas M. 2009. "Documenting, Creating, and Interpreting Moments of Definition: Monterey Pop, Woodstock, and Gimme Shelter." *Journal of Popular Culture* 42 (4): 715–32.

Lassiter, M. D. 2007. *The Silent Majority: Suburban Politics in the Sunbelt South*. Princeton, NJ: Princeton University Press.

———. 2011. "Who Speaks for the Silent Majority?" *New York Times*, November 2. http://www.nytimes.com/2011/11/03/opinion/populism-and-the-silent-majority.html?_r=0.

Lazerow, Jama, and Yohuru Williams, eds. 2006. *In Search of the Black Panther Party: New Perspectives on a Revolutionary Movement*. Durham, NC: Duke University Press.

Lev, Peter. 2000. *American Films of the 70s: Competing Visions*. Austin: University of Texas Press.

Levin, Gary. 1991. "Sweeping Miniseries: To Be Continued . . ." *USA Today*, March 1, sec. D3. *LexisNexis Academic*, http://www.lexisnexis.com.

Lipsitz, George. 1990. *Time Passages: Collective Memory and American Popular Culture*. Minneapolis: University of Minnesota Press.

———. 2012. "Interview with George Lipsitz." *European Journal of Cultural Studies* 15: 380–98.

Lyne, William. 2000. "No Accident: From Black Power to Black Box Office." *African American Review* 34: 39–59.

Marable, Manning. 1995. *Beyond Black and White: Rethinking Race in American Politics*. New York: Verso.

Marcus, Daniel. 2004. *Happy Days and Wonder Years: The Fifties and the Sixties in Contemporary Cultural Politics*. New Brunswick, NJ: Rutgers University Press.

Matthews, Chris. 2008. *Hardball*, October 17, MSNBC. *LexisNexis Academic*. http://www.lexisnexis.com. Lexis-Nexis Database.

Matthews, Tracye. 1998. "'No One Ever Asks What a Man's Place in the Revolution Is': Gender and the Politics of the Black Panther Party, 1967–1971." In *The Black Panther Party (Reconsidered)*. Edited by Charles E. Jones. Baltimore, MD: Black Classic Press.

McCann, Bryan J. 2010. "Genocide as Representative Anecdote: Crack Cocaine, the CIA, and the Nation of Islam in Gary Webb's 'Dark Alliance.'" *Western Journal of Communication* 74 (4): 400.

McMillian, John. 2003. "'You Didn't Have to Be There': Revisiting the New Left Consensus." In *The New Left Revisited: Critical Perspectives on the Past*. Edited by John McMillan and Paul Buhle. Philadelphia, PA: Temple University Press.

Mendel-Reyes, Meta. 1995. *Reclaiming Democracy: The Sixties in Politics and Memory*. New York: Routledge.

Metcalf, Greg. 1996. "Discounting the '60s: Hollywood Revisits the Counterculture." In *Beyond the Stars 5: Themes and Ideologies in American Popular Film*. Edited by Paul Loukides and Linda K. Fuller. Bowling Green, OH: Bowling Green State University Popular Press.

Mikkelson, David. n.d. "Putting on Ayers: Barack Obama's Education and House Were Paid for with Money from Questionable Sources." *Snopes.com*. http://www.snopes.com/politics/obama/ayers.asp.

Miller, Jim. 1987. "Tears and Riots, Love and Regrets." *New York Times*, November 8. http://www.nytimes.com/1987/11/08/books/tears-and-riots-love-and-regrets.html.

Morgan, Edward. 2010. *What Really Happened to the 1960s: How Mass Media Culture Failed American Democracy*. Lawrence: University Press of Kansas.

Morris, Richard, and Peter Ehrenhaus, eds. 1990. *Cultural Legacies of Vietnam: Uses of the Past in the Present*. Norwood, NJ: Ablex Publishing Corporation.

Mukhergee, Roopali. 2006. "The Ghetto Fabulous Aesthetics in Contemporary Black Culture." *Cultural Studies* 20 (6): 599–629.

Murch, Donna. 2016. "The Clintons' War on Drugs: When Black Lives Didn't Matter." *New Republic*, February 9. https://newrepublic.com/article/129433/clintons-war-drugs-black-lives-didnt-matter.

Noah, Timothy. 1984. "The Big Massage: How the Idea of the Sixties Takes the Politics out of the Eighties." *Washington Monthly*, February, 39–44.

Novak, Viveca. 2008. "'He Lied' about Bill Ayers? McCain Cranks Out Some False and Misleading Attacks on Obama's Connection to a 1960s Radical." *FactCheck.org*, October 10. http://www.factcheck.org/2008/10/he-lied-about-bill-ayers.

O'Reilly, Kenneth. 1989. *Racial Matters: The FBI's Secret File on Black America, 1960–1972*. New York: Free Press.

Oakley, Bill. 2005. Commentary for "Mother Simpson." In *The Simpsons: The Complete Seventh Season*. Los Angeles: 20th Century Fox. DVD.

"Obama and Clinton Debate." 2008. Transcript. *ABC News*, April 16. http://abcnews.go.com/Politics/DemocraticDebate/story?id=4670271&page=1&singlePage=true.

Omi, Michael, and Howard Winant. 1994. *Racial Formation in the United States from the 1960s to the 1990s*, 2nd edition. New York: Routledge.

Ono, Kent. 2009. *Contemporary Media Culture and the Remnants of a Colonial Past*. New York: Peter Lang Press.

"Oscar and Box Office Winner." 1995. *USA Today*, March 29, 1A.

Owen, A. Susan. 2002. "Memory, War and American Identity: *Saving Private Ryan* as Cinematic Jeremiad." *Critical Studies in Media Communication* 19 (3): 249–82.

Paglia, Camille. 1992. *Sex, Art and American Culture: Essays*. New York: Vintage Books.

Palin, Sarah. 2008. "Palin Criticizes Obama's 'Terrorist' Connection." YouTube, Uploaded October 5. https://www.youtube.com/watch?v=ezkJ3zUJ_RI;%20https://www.youtube.com/watch?v=ONfJ7YSXE5w.

Phillips, Kendall. 2010. "The Failure of Memory: Reflections on Rhetoric and Public Remembrance." *Western Journal of Communication* 74 (2): 220.

Probyn, Elspeth. 1990. "New Traditionalism and Post-Feminism: TV Does the Home." *Screen* 31: 147–59.

Quayle, Dan. 1992. "Address to the Commonwealth Club of California." Dan Quayle: 44th Vice President of the United States, 1989–1993. May 19. http://www.vicepresidentdanquayle.com/speeches_StandingFirm_CCC_2.htm.

Rapping, Elayne. 2003. *Law and Justice as Seen on TV*. New York: New York University Press.

Reagan, Ronald. 1989. "Transcript of Reagan's Farewell Address." *New York Times*, January 12. http://www.nytimes.com/1989/01/12/news/transcript-of-reagan-s-farewell-address-to-american-people.html.

Reed, T. V. 2005. *The Art of Protest: Culture and Activism from the Civil Rights Movement to the Streets of Seattle*. Minneapolis: University of Minnesota Press.

Reeves, Jimmie L., and Richard Campbell. 1994. *Cracked Coverage: Television News, The Anti-Cocaine Crusade, and the Reagan Legacy*. Durham, NC: Duke University Press.

Rhodes, Jane. 2007. *Framing the Black Panthers: The Spectacular Rise of a Black Power Icon*. New York: New Press.

Rimer, Sara. 1993. "'60s Radical, Linked to a Killing, Surrenders after Hiding 23 Years." *New York Times*, September 16. http://www.nytimes.com/1993/09/16/nyregion/60-s-radical-linked-to-a-killing-surrenders-after-hiding-23-years.html.

Roszak, Theodore. 1969. *The Making of a Counter Culture: Reflections on the Technocratic Society and Its Youthful Opposition.* Garden City, NY: Doubleday.
Rubin, Jerry. 1980. "Guess Who's Coming to Wall Street." *New York Times*, July 30, A21.
Rudd, Mark. 2009. *Underground: My Life with SDS and the Weathermen.* New York: HarperCollins.
Ryan, Michael, and Douglas Kellner. 1988. *Camera Politica: The Politics and Ideology of Contemporary Hollywood Film.* Bloomington: Indiana University Press.
Sayres, Sohnya, Anders Stephanson, Stanley Aronowitz, and Frederic Jameson. 1984. "Introduction." In *The '60s without Apology.* Edited by Sohnya Sayres, Anders Stephanson, Stanley Aronowitz, and Fredric Jameson. Minneapolis, MN: Social Text.
Schneider, Matt. 1999. "Business Is Booming for Nostalgia Projects." *Electronic Media*, February 15. C1.
Self, Robert O. 2006. "The Black Panther Party and the Long Civil Rights Era." In *In Search of the Black Panther Party: New Perspectives on a Revolutionary Movement.* Edited by Jama Lazerow and Yohuru Williams, 15–55. Durham, NC: Duke University Press.
———. 2012. *All in the Family: The Realignment of American Democracy since the 1960s.* New York: Hill and Wang.
Sirota, David. 2011. *Back to Our Future: How the 1980s Explain the World We Live in Now—Our Culture, Our Politics, Our Everything.* New York: Ballantine Books.
Spigel, Lynn. 1992. *Make Room for TV: Television and the Family Ideal in Postwar America.* Chicago: University of Chicago Press.
Spigel, Lynn, and Michael Curtin, eds. 1997. *The Revolution Wasn't Televised: Sixties Television and Social Conflict.* New York: Routledge.
Stein, Marc. 2012. *Rethinking the Gay and Lesbian Movement.* New York: Routledge.
Stern, Susan Ellen. 2007. *With the Weathermen: The Personal Journal of a Revolutionary Woman*, 2nd edition. New Brunswick, NJ: Rutgers University Press.
Sturken, Marita. 1997. *Tangled Memories: The Vietnam War, the AIDS Epidemic, and the Politics of Remembering.* Berkeley: University of California Press.
Tasker, Yvonne, and Diane Negra, eds. 2007. *Interrogating Post-Feminism: Gender and the Politics of Popular Culture.* Durham, NC: Duke University Press.
Taylor, Ella. 1991. *Prime Time Families: Television Culture in Postwar America.* Berkeley: University of California Press.
The Weather Underground. 2003. Directed by Sam Green and Bill Siegel. 2002. Los Angeles: Docurama. DVD.
Theoharis, Athan, ed. 1978. *COINTELPRO: The Counterintelligence Program of the FBI.* Wilmington, DE: Scholarly Resources.
Thomas, Pat. 2012. *Listen Whitey! The Sights and Sounds of Black Power, 1965–1975.* Seattle, WA: Fantagraphics Books.
Triece, Mary E. 2013. *Tell It Like It Is: Women in the National Welfare Rights Movement.* Columbia: University of South Carolina Press.

Troy, Gil. 2007. *Morning in America: How Reagan Invented the 1980s*. Princeton, NJ: Princeton University Press.
Turner, M. 1995. "Father, Son Make Film Their Own Way." *Omaha World-Herald*, May 14.
Varon, Jeremy. 2004. *Bringing the War Home: The Weather Underground, the Red Army Faction, and Revolutionary Violence in the Sixties and Seventies*. Berkeley: University of California Press.
Vavrus, Mary Douglas. 2007. "Opting Out Moms in the News: Selling New Traditionalism in the New Millennium." *Feminist Media Studies* 7: 47–63.
Vivian, Bradford. 2010. *Public Forgetting: The Rhetoric and Politics of Beginning Again*. University Park: Pennsylvania State University Press.
von Bothmer, Bernard. 2010. *Framing the Sixties: The Use and Abuse of a Decade from Ronald Reagan to George W. Bush*. Boston: University of Massachusetts Press.
Wang, Jennifer Hyland. 2000. "'A Struggle of Contenting Stories': Race, Gender, and Political Memory in *Forrest Gump*." *Cinema Journal* 39 (3): 92–115.
Ward, Stephen. 2006. "The Third World Women's Alliance: Black Feminist Radicalism and Black Power Politics." In *The Black Power Movement: Rethinking the Civil Rights–Black Power Era*. Edited by Peniel E. Joseph, 119–44. London: Routledge.
Whalen, Jack, and Richard Flacks. 1989. *Beyond the Barricades: The Sixties Generation Grows Up*. Philadelphia: Temple University Press.
Wilkerson, Cathy. 2007. *Flying Close to the Sun: My Life and Times as a Weatherman*. New York: Seven Stories Press.
Will, George. 1991. "Slamming Doors." *Newsweek*, March 31, 66.
Winn, J. Emmett. 2001. "Challenges and Compromises in Spike Lee's *Malcolm X*." *Critical Studies in Media Communication* 18 (4): 452–65.
Woodard, Kozomi. 2006. "Amiri Baraka, the Congress of African People, and Black Power Politics from the 1961 United Nations Protest to the 1972 Gary Convention." In *The Black Power Movement: Rethinking the Civil Rights–Black Power Era*. Edited by Peniel E. Joseph, 55–78. London: Routledge.
X, Malcolm. 1964. "The Ballot or the Bullet." Speech at Cory Methodist Church, Cleveland, Ohio, April 3.
———. 1992. *By Any Means Necessary: Malcolm X Speeches and Writings*. 1970; repr., New York: Betty Shabazz and Pathfinder Press.
Young, Cynthia A. 2006. *Soul Power: Culture, Radicalism, and the Making of a U.S. Third World Left*. Durham, NC: Duke University Press.
Zaroulis, N. L., and Gerald Sullivan. 1985. *Who Spoke Up? American Protest against the War in Vietnam, 1963–1975*. New York: Owl Book.

INDEX

30 Rock (television program), 201n6
'60s, The (television miniseries), 18, 24–25, 55, 95–97, 202n11; and Black Power, 143–46; and the counterculture and antiwar movement, 108–20; hippie drifters, 45; soundtrack for, 95
'68 (motion picture), 50
1969 (motion picture), 50
1971 (documentary), 195

Abyss, The (motion picture), 52
Across the Universe (motion picture), 55, 120–21, 202n11
Activist, The (motion picture, 1970), 41–42
Activist, The (motion picture, 2014), 57
African Liberation Support Committee, 31
AIDS, 107
Alexander, Elizabeth, 139
Alice's Restaurant (motion picture), 43
All in the Family (television program), 46, 51, 65
All the President's Men (motion picture), 48
Altamont music concert, 37, 44
ambivalent activist, 22–23, 58, 96–97, 187; in *Across the Universe*, 120; in *Forrest Gump*, 102, 107; political implications of, 122; in *Quantum Leap*, 120; in *The '60s*, 114–16; and women radicals, 119
American Dream, 8, 132, 138, 153
American Indian Movement, 57
American International Pictures, 41
Anarchist, The (theatrical performance), 204n1
Anderson, Terry, 34, 201n1
Angel Unchained (motion picture), 42
Anti-Drug Abuse Act of 1986, 137
Aquarius (television program), 190
Arrested Development (music group), 128
Attica State Prison police massacre, 48
Ayers, Bill, 119, 157–58, 165, 172–74, 179–85, 205n7

bad sixties, 11–18, 26; in *Aquarius*, 190; Assata Shakur, 205n4; challenges to, 195–96; in *Dharma and Greg*, 91; and Donald Trump's campaign rhetoric, 188–90; in *Forrest Gump*, 97, 99–100; in Newt Gingrich's rhetoric, 94; in *Quantum Leap*, 120; in *The '60s*, 108–10, 116–17, 146
Bachman, Michele, 180–81
Baraka, Amiri, 31

Barber, David, 13
Barbershop 2: Back in Business (motion picture), 25, 56, 143, 149–53
Barthes, Roland, 19
Beastie Boys (music group), 196
Belafonte, Harry, 195
Berlant, Lauren, 68, 99
Beyoncé (performer), 123
Bias, Leonard, 137
Biesecker, Barbara, 16, 200n2
Big Brother (television program), 56
Big Cube, The (motion picture), 41
Big Chill, The (motion picture), 3–5, 52–54, 80, 203n3
Big Fix, The (motion picture), 52
Big Lebowski, The (motion picture), 52
Billy Jack (motion picture), 42–43
Bird on a Wire (motion picture), 53
Black Liberation Army (BLA), 25, 35, 158, 159
Black Lives Matter, 6, 123, 163, 189
Black Nationalism, 29, 125, 138
Black Panther Party (BPP), 30, 35, 38, 40, 201n4; in *Barbershop 2*, 25, 150–52; and Beyoncé, 123; Brinks truck robbery, 159; in *The Butler*, 25, 56, 109, 154–55; in *Chicago 10*, 196; and civil rights backlash, 153; FBI repression of, 30–31, 129, 134–35; in *Forrest Gump*, 18, 25, 56, 103–4, 106, 142–43; FOX News coverage, 155; gender dynamics of, 202n8; in hip-hop, 204n1; in *Law & Order*, 25, 147–49, 168; and Marxism, 138; and New Black Panther Party (NBPP), 201n3; in *Night Catches Us*, 56; print news coverage of, 129, 142, 204n2; and public memory, 124–25, 128; in *The '60s*, 25, 119, 143–45; and white radicalism, 163. See also *Panther* (motion picture)

Black Panthers: Vanguard of the Revolution, The (documentary), 202n12
Black Power, 14, 15; in *The Big Chill*, 4–5; in conservative discourse, 12; influences on, 27–29; in Hollywood film and television, 25, 45–48, 55–56, 96; organizations influenced by, 31, 39. See also Black Panther Party
Black Power Mixtape 1967-1974 (documentary), 140, 195, 202n12
Black Women's Alliance, 39
Bodroghkozy, Aniko, 42, 43
Bold Ones, The (television program), 45
Bonanza (television program), 44
Bond, Stanley, 168
Bones (television program), 58, 159–61, 169, 205n3
Bonnie and Clyde (motion picture), 43
Born on the Fourth of July (motion picture), 50, 54
Boudin, Chesa, 186
Boudin, Kathy, 165, 186
Bracken's World (television program), 45, 50
Brothers (motion picture), 47
Brown, Elaine, 38
Brown, H. Rap, 147
Brown, James (singer), 109, 203n1
Brown, Murphy (television character), 93, 102
Brown, Wendy, 68
Brown Berets, 31–32, 119
Buchanan, Patrick, 95, 102, 106
Buck, Marilyn, 165
Burgoyne, Robert, 98
Burke, Kenneth, 22
Bush, George H. W., 11, 63, 66, 90–91, 171, 205n6

Bush, George W., 11
Butler, The (motion picture), 25, 56, 143, 154
Byers, Thomas, 98, 105, 194
Byrds, The (musical group), 19

Cantor, Jay, 204n1
Carmichael, Stokely, 29
Carson, Allan, 65
Car Wash (motion picture), 47
Cee-Lo (musician), 204n1 (chap. 4)
Cesar Chavez (motion picture), 56, 195–98
Chaney, James, 28, 201n2
Chavez, Cesar, 32, 196–98
Cheech & Chong's Next Movie (motion picture), 202n10
Chicago Code, The (television program), 25, 58, 159–60, 172, 178–82
Chicago 10 (motion picture), 58, 195–98
Chicano Moratorium, 32
Chicanx movement, 6, 18, 23, 31–32, 57
Chong, Tommy, 51, 202n10
Civil Rights Act of 1965, 28, 155
civil rights movement: in *The Butler*, 154–55; and *The Cosby Show*, 126–27; Democratic Party, 28; influence on the New Left, 32–33; and *Mad Men*, 191; and *Malcolm X*, 127; and *Panther*, 127; political backlash, 6, 25, 56, 125, 153; protest strategies, 9; repression of, 28, 30, 133, 175, 200n1, 201n5; vis-à-vis Black Power, 27–32, 124, 145; in *The '60s*, 109, 110, 112, 143, 145; and *The Wonder Years*, 69
civil rights subject, 25, 55, 91, 126, 194; alternatives to, 128–33, 141; and *Barbershop 2*, 149–52; in *The Butler*, 154–55; in *The Cosby Show*, 126–27; and *Forrest Gump*, 142; in *The '60s*, 145

Clark, Judith, 165
Clark, Mark, 31, 129
Cleaver, Eldridge, 30
Cleaver, Kathleen, 38
Clinton, Bill, 7, 12, 66, 94, 101, 108, 118–19; and the Personal Responsibility and Work Opportunity Act, 152; and postracism, 125; and the Violent Crime Control and Law Enforcement Act, 137; on the Weathermen, 183–84
Clinton, Hillary, 137, 157, 189
Cloud, Dana, 101, 169
Cold Case (television program), 58, 159–61, 169, 205n3
collective memory, 199n1
Columbia University, 33, 42, 112, 113–14, 162, 174
Company You Keep, The (motion picture), 57, 158, 205n1 (chap. 5)
Congress of African People, 31
Congress on Racial Equality (CORE), 28, 143, 147
consumer protection, 6, 88
Contract with America, 94
Corman, Roger, 41, 80
Corrigan, Lisa, 28
Cosby Show, The (television program), 66, 90–91, 126–27
counterculture, 6–7, 13, 27, 36–38, 65; in *Across the Universe*, 120; and *Aquarius*, 190; and *The Big Chill*, 4–5; and *Chicago 10*, 58; and conservativism, 12, 62, 94–95, 106; in documentary film, 202n12; in eighties era film and television, 50–54; in *Family Ties*, 19–20, 24, 62–64, 70–71, 76–80, 90; fashion of, 6, 19–21, 36; in *Forrest Gump*, 96, 100, 105; and the GLBTQ activism, 39; and *Mad Men*, 192–93; and New

Hollywood, 43–44, 49; in public memory, 17, 202n7; in sixties era Hollywood and television, 41–43, 44–46, 48; and *The '60s*, 110, 116; in *thirtysomething*, 81–83, 88; in *The Wonder Years*, 62, 72–73, 76, 85–88
countermemory, 17, 25, 58, 127–29, 138–41, 194–98
Cream (music band), 109
Crow Dog, Mary, 57
cultural memory, 199n2, 200n4
Curtin, Michael, 44

Daniel (motion picture), 50, 53
Daniels, Lee, 154
Davis, Angela, 128, 204n2
Days of Rage protests, 35, 178–79
Dazed and Confused (motion picture), 202n10
Death Wish (motion picture), 49
Debray, Régis, 28
Ded Prez (musician), 204n1 (chap. 4)
DeLuca, Kevin, 189
Democratic National Convention of 1968, 33, 35, 110, 113–14, 178–79, 196
Democrats, 7, 12, 28, 91, 183–84
Dharma and Greg (television program), 51, 52, 91
Diallo, Amadou, 147
Dick Cavett Show (television program), 98
Digable Planets (music group), 204n1 (chap. 4)
Digital Underground (music group), 204n1 (chap. 4)
Dirty Harry (motion picture), 49
Dog Day Afternoon (motion picture), 48
Dohrn, Bernardine, 57, 158, 186
Doors, The (music band), 93, 109
Dow, Bonnie, 10, 66, 86

Dragnet '67 (television program), 44
Dream Act, 198
Drunk History (television program), 158
Dukakis, Kitty, 11
Dukakis, Michael, 11
Dylan, Bob, 42, 109, 110, 203n1
Dyson, Michael, 135

Easy Rider (motion picture), 42, 43, 45, 49–50
Ehrenhaus, Peter, 14, 200n3
Eminem (performer), 196
Enforcer, The (motion picture), 49
environmentalism, 6, 14. *See also* environmental conservation
environmental conservation, 36
Equal Rights Amendment, 4, 39, 120
Evans, Linda Sue, 165
Everybody Hates Chris (television program), 201n6
Eyes on the Prize II: America at the Racial Crossroads, 1965–Mid-1980s (documentary), 140, 202n12

Falwell, Jerry, 107
Faludi, Susan, 89
Family Ties (television program), 18; Alex Keaton (character), 53, 67–68; and the generation gap 51, 76–77; halting nostalgia for dissent, 70–72; the hippie-turned-yuppie, 83; and memory cues, 19–21, 24; and political centrism, 77–79, 90; ratings and awards, 203n2; and the Reagan Revolution, 61–62, 66, 70–72
Fanon, Franz, 28–29, 113
Fargo (motion picture), 5
Farrakhan, Louis, 123
Father Knows Best (television program), 65

feminism, 11, 15, 62, 64, 90; backlash, 25, 120; black women, 39; conservative response to, 66, 94; lesbian feminism, 40; liberal feminism, 39, 165; New Left response to, 202; selective amnesia of, 38, 119; in *The Wonder Years*, 72, 83–88. *See also* postfeminism; second-wave feminism.
Feuer, Jane, 80, 82
Field of Dreams (motion picture), 54
Fiske, John, 18–19, 22
Flashback (motion picture), 53, 54
Fonda, Peter, 80
Ford, Gerald, 14
Forrest Gump (motion picture), 5, 18, 97–107; Black Panthers, 56, 95, 124, 142–43, 203n2 (chap. 2); macho militant, 202n11; masculine national identity, 24–25, 97, 116–21, 194; Patrick Buchanan, 95; soundtrack, 55
Four Friends (motion picture), 53
FOX News (television network), 123, 155, 173–74, 180, 205n7
Frank, Thomas, 193
free love, 36; and authenticity, 65; conservative response to, 107; in *Forrest Gump*, 98, 101, 103; in *Mad Men*, 192; in *The '60s*, 117; in *The Wonder Years*, 84, 87
Full Metal Jacket (motion picture), 54

Garcia, Matt, 197
Gas-s-s-s (motion picture), 41
gay liberation, 6, 15, 23, 36, 94, 97
Gay Liberation Front, 39–40
Getting Straight (motion picture), 41
Gilbert, David, 186
Gilday, William, 168
Gimme Shelter (motion picture), 44

Gingrich, Newt, 94–95, 107
Gitlin, Todd, 9, 13, 42–43, 111–12, 115, 162, 203n3
GLBTQ activism, 23, 39–40, 96, 119
Gold, Ted, 35, 113
Gordon, Neil, 158, 204n1
good citizen, 22, 24, 96, 187, 194; in *Across the Universe*, 121, 187; alternatives to, 196; in *Forrest Gump*, 107; in *Quantum Leap*, 120; in *The '60s*, 110, 114–15, 119
Goodman, Andrew, 28, 201n1
Good Times (television program), 48
Gordon, Neil, 158
Graduate, The (motion picture), 43
Gray, Herman, 55, 91, 126–27
Great Society Program: the bad sixties, 11, 12; civil rights, 25, 56, 126, 153; Newt Gingrich, 94, 107; the Reagan Revolution, 62, 66
Greene, Ralph "Petey," 55
Giuliani, Rudy, 123

Hair (motion picture), 48
Haley, Alex, 124, 128
Half Baked (motion picture), 202n10
Hall, Simon, 9
Hallucination Generation (motion picture), 41
Hampton, Fred, 31; assassination, 129; in *The Black Power Mixtape*, 195; selective amnesia, 106, 163, 177, 205n2; in *The '60s*, 144–46
Hannity, Sean, 180–81, 205n7
Hawaii Five-O (television program), 44
Hayden, Tom, 111–12
Hearst, Patty, 158, 160, 165
Hefferman, Nick, 81
Hell's Angels, 37, 44, 201n1
Helms, Jesse, 107

Hendrix, Jimi, 42
Hill Street Blues (television program), 58, 159, 160, 205n3
hippie drifter, 117
hippies. *See* counterculture
hippie-turned-yuppie, 22, 24, 52, 54, 58, 81–83, 170
Hoffman, Abbie, 33, 58, 97, 100, 103
Hog Farm, 37, 108, 110
Home/Sick (theatrical performance), 204n1
Huerta, Dolores, 197
Huey Newton Story, A (motion picture), 202n12
Hutton, Bobby, 30, 134

Incident at Oglala (motion picture), 57
Indians of All Tribes, 31
infantile citizen, 68, 74, 99–100
Informer, The (motion picture), 46
Inherent Vice (motion picture), 52
intertextuality, 19, 21, 162
Ironside (television program), 44
I Wor Kuen, 31

Jackson, George, 47
Jameson, Frederic, 199n1
Jefferson Airplane (music band), 109
Johnson, Lyndon, 11–12, 28–29, 62, 66, 94, 97, 125

Kellner, Douglas, 10, 47
Kennedy, John, 97, 108, 110
Kennedy, Robert F., 20, 133
Kent State University, 34–35
Kerry, John F., 11, 34
King, Claire, 117
King, Martin Luther, Jr.: assassination, 33, 106, 150; in *The Black Power Mixtape*, 195; in *Malcolm X*, 131; in *Panther*, 133; public memory of, 128; radical views of, 29, 155; and the SCLC, 143; on the Vietnam War, 27; in *The Wonder Years*, 20
King, Rodney, 125, 132, 139
Kovic, Ron, 50
KRS-One (music group), 204n1 (chap. 4)
Kunstler, William, 162, 167

labor activism, 6, 8, 15
Lakota Woman: Siege at Wounded Knee (motion picture), 57
Landsberg, Alison, 200
La Raza Unida, 32, 56
Last Poets (music group), 204n1 (chap. 4)
Laugh-In (television program), 44
Law & Order (television program), 18; depictions of black radicalism, 25, 56, 124, 143, 146–49; depictions of radical fugitives, 58, 159–71, 182
Lawson, Sean, 189
League of Revolutionary Black Workers, 31
Leary, Timothy, 36
Leave It to Beaver (television program), 65
Lee, Spike, 55, 124, 128, 130, 132, 140, 202n12
Lennon, John, 97–98, 106
Lev, Peter, 43
Life on Mars (US television program), 25, 58, 159–60, 170, 171–79, 182, 185, 205n3
Lipsitz, George, 7, 50, 54, 129

macho militant, 22, 24, 55, 58, 96; in *Across the Universe*, 121; in *Aquarius*, 190; in *Forrest Gump*, 106–7; historical resonances, 119; in *Law & Order*, 169; in *Mad Men*,

191; in *Quantum Leap*, 120; in *The '60s*, 112, 115
Mad Men (television program), 5, 45, 191–93
Malcolm X (motion picture), 25, 55, 124, 127–33, 138–41
Mandela, Nelson, 140
Manson, Charles, 37, 49, 190
March Against Fear, 29
March on the Pentagon, 110–11
Marcus, Daniel, 10–12, 62
Marcus Welby, M.D. (television program), 45
Marin, Richard "Cheech," 51
McCain, John, 173–74
McCann, Bryan, 138
McCarthy, Eugene, 33, 110
McMillian, John, 13
McVeigh, Timothy, 183
Medium Cool (motion picture), 41–42
Mendel-Reyes, Meta, 9
Meredith, James, 29
Miss America Pageant Protest of 1968, 38
Mississippi Freedom Democratic Party, 28
Mississippi Freedom Summer, 110
Mobilization Against the War (MOBE), 34
Mod Squad, The (television program), 45, 48
Monkees, The (television program), 44
Monterey Pop (motion picture), 44
Moral Majority, 10, 107
More American Graffiti (motion picture), 50
Morgan, Edward, 70, 107
Movimiento Estudiantil Chicano de Azlán, 31
Mukherjee, Roopali, 150
Murch, Donna, 137

Murtagh, John, 35
Music Never Stopped, The (motion picture), 55

Name of the Game (television program), 44
National Organization for Women, 39
National Teach-In Against the War, 109
National Women's Rights Welfare Organization, 39
Nation of Islam, 29, 47, 123, 130, 131–32, 190
Native American activism, 6, 31, 57
neoliberalism: acceptance of, 79–81; and citizenship, 101; civil rights subject, 55; and family television, 66; the neoliberal subject, 67–68; and Reaganism, 24, 62, 66, 80; and trade policy, 152
Network (motion picture), 49
New Black Panther Party, 155, 201n3
New Left, 6, 7, 14–15, 32–36, 38, 39, 111, 202n9 (chap. 1); FBI repression of, 163, 195; gender divisions, 38, 114; Hollywood depictions of, 42–43, 101, 106, 197; television depictions of, 62–64, 70–83, 110, 113, 115
New Left consensus, 13
news routines, 163
Newsweek (magazine), 8, 81, 93, 129
Newton, Huey, 4, 30, 38, 134, 136, 144
new traditionalism, 86, 88–89
New Year's Gang, 35
New York Radical Women, 38
New York Times (newspaper), 66, 81, 112, 129, 157, 168, 173
Nice Dreams (motion picture), 202n10
Night Catches Us (motion picture), 56
Nixon, Richard, 11, 13, 20, 34, 69, 97, 188
Noah, Timothy, 5

nuclear family: and ambivalent activists, 4, 24, 45, 83–86, 96, 101, 116–22, 187, 194; in conservative thought, 11; and the counterculture, 192; in fifties nostalgia, 62; in *Forrest Gump*, 105–7; and national identity, 97; as a neoliberal value, 80; radicals as threat to, 14, 161, 166, 176, 182; and Reaganism, 62; and second-wave feminism, 39, 88, 105; in situation comedies, 64–66, 76, 90–91
nuclear freeze movement, 14, 53

Obama, Barack, 154–55, 157–58, 172–73, 183, 205n4, 205n7
Occupy Wall Street, 6, 189
Olsen, Sara Jane, 165
Omi, Michael, 153
One Day at a Time (television program), 65
One Flew Over the Cuckoo's Nest (motion picture), 48
Ono, Kent, 15
Operation Dewey Canyon III, 34
O'Reilly, Bill, 155, 181
Oughton, Diana, 35, 45
Owen, Susan, 200

Paglia, Camille, 107
Palante, Siempre Palante! The Young Lords (documentary), 202n12
Palin, Sarah, 173
Panther (motion picture), 18, 25, 55, 124, 127, 128, 133–41
Paul, Andrew, 200n4
Pence, Mike, 122
People's Park, 37
Personal Responsibility and Work Opportunities Act of 1996, 152
Phillips, Kendall, 16
Phil Ochs: There but for Fortune (documentary), 202n12

Pittsburgh Post-Gazette, 102
polysemy, 22
Poor People's Campaign, 29
Port Huron Statement, 52, 203n3
postfeminism, 24, 62, 86–88
Power, Katherine Ann, 162, 165–66, 168–71, 205n5
Practice, The (television program), 58, 159, 205n3
Presley, Elvis (musician), 97
Probyn, Elspeth, 86, 89
Public Enemy (music group), 128, 204n1 (chap. 4)
public memory, 7, 15–19, 199n1 (intro.), 199n2 (intro.); in *Barbershop 2*, 150; of Black Power, 147, 150, 155; in *Chicago 10*, 196; and family television, 61, 67; in *Forrest Gump*, 98–99, 119; in *Law & Order*, 147; in *Mad Men*, 193; in television crime dramas, 172

Quantum Leap (television program), 120, 202n11
Quayle, Dan, 93–94, 102
Queen Latifah (performer), 204n1 (chap. 4)
Questlove (musician), 195

Radicalesbians, 40
Rage Against the Machine (music band), 196
Rainbow Coalition, 31
Rapping, Elayne, 164
Reagan, Ronald: bad sixties rhetoric, 11–12; dismantling of the New Deal, 61; drug policy, 136; and *Family Ties*, 63, 77, 80; and family values, 65–66; and People's Park, 38; on welfare, 125, 152, 202n1
Redford, Robert, 158
Redstockings, 38

Republicans, 10–11, 91, 170, 188
Republic of New Africa, 31
Resistance (antidraft organization), 34
Return of the Secaucus 7 (motion picture), 54
Rhodes, Jane, 123
Riot on the Sunset Strip (motion picture), 41
Road Trip (motion picture), 201n6
Robbins, Terry, 35, 113
Robertson, Pat, 107
Rosenberg, Susan, 165
Roszak, Theodore, 51, 76, 84
RPM (motion picture), 41
Rubin, Jerry, 33, 81, 103, 113, 119
Rudd, Mark, 113, 119, 158, 162, 165
Rude Awakenings (motion picture), 52
Running on Empty (motion picture), 53, 57, 205n1 (chap. 5)
Ryan, Michael, 10, 47

Saint Misbehavin': The Wavy Gravy Movie (documentary), 202n12
Sanders, Bernie, 188–89
Sanford and Son (television program), 48
Saxe, Susan, 168
Schwerner, Michael, 28, 201n2
Scott-Heron, Gil, 204n1
Seale, Bobby, 144, 196
Seattle Seven, 52
second-wave feminism, 38, 40, 84–86, 88–90, 97, 105. *See also* feminism
selective amnesia: of black activism, 91, 109, 126, 144–46, 154; definition of, 14–16; in *Forrest Gump*, 98, 106; implications of, 184; intertextual construction of, 21–22, 188; in news coverage of dissent, 163; of nonviolent dissent, 184; of political repression, 173; and postfeminism, 87; of radicals' motives, 171, 177; relationship to public memory, 16; resistance to in film, 195; in television, 67, 81, 91, 97, 190–93; and traumatic memory, 141
Self, Robert, 66, 107
sexual liberation, 36, 117. *See also* sexual revolution
sexual revolution, 11, 62, 110. *See also* sexual liberation
Shabazz, Ilyasah, 123
Shaft (motion picture), 46–47
Shakur, Assata, 160, 205n4
Shakur, Tupac, 204n1 (chap. 4)
silent majority, 11, 69
Simon and Garfunkel (musical group), 109, 188
Simpsons, The (television program), 57, 158
Sirota, David, 12
Smothers Brothers Comedy Hour, The (television program), 44–45
Sneakers (motion picture), 57, 205n1 (chap. 5)
Soul Train (television program), 48
Southern Christian Leadership Council (SCLC), 143
Spigel, Lynn, 44, 61
Spook Who Sat by the Door, The (motion picture), 47
Star Trek (television program), 44
Steal This Movie (motion picture), 58
Steffenwolf (music group), 42
Still Smokin (motion picture), 202n10
Stone, Oliver, 50, 93
Stone, Sly (songwriter), 203n1
Stoned Age, The (motion picture), 202n10
Stop the Draft Week, 32
Strawberry Statement, The (motion picture), 41–42
Student Nonviolent Coordinating Committee (SNCC), 28, 29, 143

Students for a Democratic Society (SDS), 13, 32, 40, 52, 110–11, 113, 121, 162
Sturken, Marita, 15, 200n4
Sweet Sweetback's Baadasssss Song (motion picture), 46
Sun, Ye, 189
Super Fly (motion picture), 47
Swift Boat Veterans for Truth, 11
Symbionese Liberation Army (SLA), 25, 35, 49, 57, 158, 160, 161

Taking Woodstock (motion picture), 55
Talk to Me (motion picture), 55
Taylor, Ella, 65
That '70s Show (television program), 202n10
They Shoot Horses, Don't They (motion picture), 43
Things Are Tough All Over (motion picture), 202n10
Third World Women's Alliance, 39
thirtysomething (television program), 24, 52–53, 61–62, 64, 67, 76, 90. *See also* new traditionalism; yuppies
Three's Company (television program), 65
Thunderheart (motion picture), 57
Trip, The (motion picture), 41, 80
Troy, Gil, 14
Trump, Donald, 188–89, 194

United Farm Workers, 32, 40, 196–97
University of California at Berkeley, 201n1 (chap. 1); in *Family Ties*, 71, 78–79; Hollywood portrayals of, 54, 101–3; Patrick Buchanan on, 106; and Todd Gitlin, 112. *See also* People's Park
Up in Smoke (motion picture), 202n10
Uptight (motion picture), 46

Valeri, Robert, 168
Van Peebles, Mario, 18, 55, 124, 128–29, 133–34
Van Peebles, Melvin, 46
Velasco, Pete, 197
Vera Cruz, Philip, 197
Vietnam Veterans Against the War (VVAW), 34
Vietnam War: conservative discourse about, 11, 171; end of, 14; My Lai Massacre, 106, 163, 177; Tet Offensive, 33, 106
Vietnam War protest, 6, 8–9, 11, 27, 32–35; and the black freedom movement, 27, 32; gendered meanings, 24, 160; Hollywood portrayals, 5, 43, 51, 54, 98, 100, 103, 121; and the New Left, 13, 40; press coverage of, 162; television portrayals, 20, 24, 69, 71–76, 109, 163–182. *See also* Weathermen
Violent Crime Control and Law Enforcement Act, 137
Vivian, Bradford, 15
von Bothmer, Bernard, 10–12, 108, 205n6

Walkout (motion picture), 18, 56
Wang, Jennifer, 102–3
War on Poverty, 12
Watermelon Man (motion picture), 46
Watts Prophets (music group), 204n1 (chap. 4)
Wavy Gravy, 37, 108, 202n7
Weathermen: Ayers-Obama conspiracy, 157–58, 173; Bill Clinton on, 183; Greenwich townhouse explosion, 45, 115, 159; history of, 35; television portrayals of, 45, 57, 113, 115, 158, 165, 171, 178–82; Todd Gitlin on, 112. *See also* Ayers, Bill;

Boudin, Kathy; Dohrn, Bernardine; Weather Underground
Weather Underground: conservative media attention to, 158, 180–81; film depictions, 158; history of, 35, 159; television portrayals of, 25, 57, 158, 161, 171–77, 179. *See also* Ayers, Bill; Rudd, Mark; *Weather Underground (documentary)*
Weather Underground (documentary), 158, 175, 195, 202n12
Wild Angels (motion picture), 41
Wild in the Streets (motion picture), 41
Will, George, 93, 96
William Kunstler: Disturbing the Universe (documentary), 202n12
Wilson, Brian (singer), 108
Wilson, Carnie (singer), 108
Winant, Howard, 153
Winn, Emmett, 138
Women's International Terrorist Conspiracy from Hell, 38
women's liberation movement, 4, 6, 14, 23, 38–40, 101, 114, 146, 194
women's rights, 6, 8, 86, 100, 114, 120, 122. *See also* second-wave feminism; women's liberation movement
Wonder Years (television program), 18, 24, 51, 63; awards, 203n2 (chap. 2); and feminist backlash, 84–88, 90; halting nostalgia for protest, 72–76; and neoliberalism, 62, 64, 66, 68–70; opening credits for, 19–20; as public memory, 61; ratings for, 67
World According to Garp, The (motion picture), 50
World Trade Organization protest, 185
Woodstock (motion picture), 44
Woodstock music festival, 37, 102, 192
Wounded Knee occupation, 57

X, Malcolm: as activist symbol, 125; assassination of, 139, 195; in *Panther*, 133; speeches of, 29, 132–33, 138, 140, 153; in traumatic memory, 140–41. *See also Malcolm X* (motion picture)

Yippies, 33, 81, 103
yuppies, 80–83, 89, 170, 187, 203n3. *See also* hippie-turned-yuppie
Young Lords, 31, 40, 56, 119
Young Patriots, 31, 119

Zabriskie Point (motion picture), 41–42
Zedong, Mao, 28
Zemeckis, Robert, 95, 104
Zwick, Edward, 89

www.ingramcontent.com/pod-product-compliance
Lightning Source LLC
Chambersburg PA
CBHW030620230426
43661CB00053B/2082